THE CONTAGION OF JESUS

5

THE CONTAGION OF
JESUS
Doing Theology as if it Mattered

Sebastian Moore

Edited by Stephen McCarthy

ORBIS BOOKS

Maryknoll, New York 10545

Founded in 1970, Orbis Books endeavors to publish works that enlighten the mind, nourish the spirit, and challenge the conscience. The publishing arm of the Maryknoll Fathers and Brothers, Orbis seeks to explore the global dimensions of the Christian faith and mission, to invite dialogue with diverse cultures and religious traditions, and to serve the cause of reconciliation and peace. The books published reflect the views of their authors and do not represent the official position of the Maryknoll Society. To learn more about Maryknoll and Orbis Books, please visit our website at www.maryknoll.org

First published in Great Britain in 2007 by
Darton, Longman and Todd Ltd
1 Spencer Court 140-142
Wandsworth High Street
London SW18 4JJ

First published in the USA in 2008 by
Orbis Books
P.O.Box 308
Maryknoll, New York 10545-0308

Printed and bound in Great Britain by
Athenaeum Press Ltd., Gateshead, Tyne & Wear

Library of Congress Cataloging-in-Publication Data

Moore, Sebastian, 1917-
The contagion of Jesus : doing theology as if it mattered / Sebastian Moore.
p. cm.
Includes bibliographical references.
ISBN-13: 978-1-57075-781-5
1. Jesus Christ--Person and offices. 2. Catholic Church--Doctrines. I. Title.
BT203.M665 2008
230'.2--dc22
2007036167

CONTENTS

EDITORIAL NOTE

Sebastian Moore is a family friend of many years. But it was only when Elisabeth Chasteau, who at the time was directing me in a retreat, pointed me towards his writing that I began to discover the originality and freshness of his understanding of the Christian story and of our place in it. Around the same time my father handed me a file of some of Sebastian's unpublished essays saying that they might interest me. I thought them worth publishing, so that others might share in the excitement of discovering his ideas and of following his own personal faith journey. When I contacted Sebastian about putting together a book he responded with enthusiasm and produced from the depths of his computer hard drive a whole treasure trove of additional material. This book, in the end rather longer than I had originally envisaged, is thus a selection and compilation of just a fraction of the available material: I estimate about a quarter of the prose and about a tenth of the verse. Fortunately in Brendan Walsh at Darton, Longman and Todd we found someone who shared our enthusiasm.

Not being theologically trained, my selection criteria were very largely those that served to deepen my own faith. At times this was a heavy responsibility. I knew that what I set aside, just because it didn't 'work' for me, might well appeal to someone else – but would now likely disappear for ever. Fortunately, in Sebastian's writing everything is connected, as indeed it is in life. Thoughts and ideas that are not chosen in one place are very likely to reappear in a slightly different form in another. So although some thematic structure had to be imposed on the book as a whole, what emerges, to me at least, is a single 'elephant' of which each essay offers a different view. The reader should feel free to choose the 'views' he wishes rather than be obliged to start at the beginning and work through to the end. And some of the 'views' are brilliantly exhilarating. To cite just one example: the hugely important connection between the doctrine of the Holy Trinity and human sexuality is not often made from the Sunday pulpit – indeed never in my experience!

Sebastian himself was very willing to accept my selection and arrangement of the material. In due course we were drawn into a type of conversation. He produced the ideas and the texts; I summed them up in the short italicised sections at the beginning of each piece. In summarising, while trying to avoid making my own judgements, I inevitably draw attention to whatever it is that interests me. Nevertheless I hope that these summaries are not too eccentric and will serve the reader as useful guides to what lies ahead.

Stephen McCarthy
Luxembourg
March 2007

INTRODUCTION

Looking back over my life I increasingly see it as a journey of discovery – a discovery of God through Jesus and of my own bodily self
as part of Jesus' 'bodiliness'. And as I get older it keeps coming –
pouring out in greater abundance. So this book is a selection and
collection of my thoughts and discoveries, mostly from recent years.
For I am utterly convinced that theology matters – more so than ever
in our lost, confused world – and doing theology as if it matters is
what I like to think I am about.

Yet to so many people of our time the Christian story, half-
understood, seems all too familiar, even boring. How would it be for
the newly arrived man from Mars, or woman from Venus, to discover
this amazing radical story for the first time – a story so incredible that
it can only be believed 'in the Spirit'? What would it be like to
experience the contagion of Jesus for the very first time?

First comes humanity's growing awareness some few thousand
years ago that a panoply of powerful mini-gods should be replaced by
the idea of one all-powerful over-god. And in due course one particular middle-eastern tribe discovers that their one god was interested
in and involved with them in a special, faithful way.

Some few hundred years later a man with an overwhelming sense
of destiny appears out of obscurity. Convinced of his special relationship with the Hebrew God, whom he refers to as his Abba
(Father), he wanders through the territory of the Israelites, driven by
his mission, proclaiming the good news that this Abba wants nothing
other than to love humanity, all of humanity, and that, if only we were
to relax into this love, we would learn to love in return and live in
freedom and without fear. Anything that gets in the way of this love,
not least the rules and customs of organised religion, should be
discarded.

Unsurprisingly this driven iconoclast seems threatening to the
religious and civil authorities of his day. And, since he will not turn
away from his purpose, he is duly apprehended and executed in a
horrible way. Yet three days later his tomb is empty and Jesus, for that
is his name, appears again for a period to his immediate followers and

friends – not least, and rather unusually for his time and culture, to his women friends. The 'risen' Jesus is real, bodily real, yet somehow different, has a different allure. He now seems beyond anything that can touch him in the world, especially death itself. His presence causes their hearts to burn within them. And far from condemning his followers for running away after his arrest and death, the risen Jesus embraces them and instils in them the same Spirit of purpose and destiny that is in him.

So his followers come to believe that this man, Jesus, had such a close relationship with his God-Abba as could only be described as equality – in the way that a son is equal with a father. And that the Spirit of God, of whom Jesus had frequently spoken, has opened their eyes to a new understanding of these events – the most important events in the whole history of humanity. Thus the original story of one God becomes refined and formalised into a story of a God with three personal manifestations – Father, Son and Spirit – existing in loving relationship.

Thus the Church came into being – initially a small frenetic group of followers of Jesus who were inspired to maintain the story of this man, in due course to write about him and most importantly to preserve his memory, this dangerous memory, through the form of a ritual meal which Jesus had instituted shortly before he died and in which they believed that they participated in a real way in his continuing bodily presence.

The young Church, although persecuted by authority, grew like wildfire throughout the Roman Empire, until it was co-opted by the empire as its official religion, whereupon it began to absorb the ways and culture of the world. Yet the Church preserved intact, if often imperfectly and frequently controversially, the dangerous memory on which it continued to reflect and contemplate.

Moreover, the Church has always proclaimed the equality of all people, male and female, though uncomfortably, as it were through gritted teeth, since, for historical and cultural reasons, its teaching has largely been articulated by celibate males. So its teaching is somewhat ambivalent, embracing the feminine but rejecting the female. The beautifully erotic poem, the Song of Songs, was incorporated in the canon of the Bible, but theologians then pretended it meant something else. And the Church, in its stumbling way, came as close as it possibly could to divinising the status of Jesus' mother, without actually proclaiming her divine.

So now, in our time, those in authority in the Church are in uncomfortable *travail* as they discover that the 'signs of the time' are pointing to a deeper understanding of human gender and to realising and celebrating the feminine in us all.

All of these themes I explore in Part I of the book. This might be described as the theoretical part, with Part II the practical side – except of course that life, and certainly life in Christ, does not divide so neatly into such categories.

Part II opens with a chapter on 'focusing', which in recent years has been for me a way of discovering my bodily self, almost for the first time. In learning to live more comfortably in my own body, I find I have come to live more comfortably in the body of Christ.

Focusing deepens our realisation that what God wants for us is that which at the deepest level of our being we desire for ourselves. So we should embrace not shun our real desires, for desire is love trying to happen – a favourite aphorism of mine. And sin is the frustration of our real desire.

Since relationship is at the heart of our trinitarian God, so also is it at the heart of being human in God's image. We are wired for love and relationship. And where is relationship experienced most intensely, other than through human sexuality – whether towards the opposite sex or, for a significant minority, towards the same sex? In our bodily sexuality is God to be truly encountered. This surely is God's gift to us all, the most powerful way that we are enabled to move from desire towards another in delightful love.

There is a truth here that needs to be more deeply explored which I attempt to do in Chapters 8 and 9 particularly. Unfortunately, the teaching Church, perhaps because it consists entirely of celibate males, has some difficulty in proclaiming this truth. Concerning sexual relations it frequently expresses very black and white opinions that do not seem to be sensitive to the huge range and experience of the human condition and of human relations. Moreover, particularly concerning same-sex relations, the teaching Church is still in the grip of a cultural taboo. As a result its views are no longer widely shared by the laity and hence are not 'received' by the Church as a whole. Fortunately, as I believe, the pastoral Church has in many situations already moved on. So these two chapters, which should be seen as passionate rather than rigorous theology, represent a *cri de coeur* on my part to the teaching Church to 'think again'. One day I am sure that it will do so and will throw off the influence of St Augustine and its own taboos and rediscover its own deep wisdom, concerning sexuality and relationship. All will be well in the end.

All this is part of my own life journey, as I slowly learn to abandon myself to the unknown, but so utterly present, reality of God – in what can only be called prayer. At the same time I am beginning, perhaps still only beginning, to confront my own demons, my acceptance and celebration of my own imperfect bodily self, my own weaknesses and sensitivities, knowing that Jesus has been there before me and encourages and challenges me to become continually who I really am.

How to convey to you, the reader, some of the excitement of this journey, its ups and downs even today and my own continuing wonder at this amazing Christian story? Perhaps the verse that has been included in the collection will help to reveal a little of my personal discovery and growth in allowing the mystery to work in me. For this is theology speaking through the head, but emanating from the heart – or, better, the gut.

Finally, I should like to acknowledge and thank some of those who have accompanied me on different stages of this journey. My first acknowledgement is for this book's existence *as* a book. For it started not as a book but as handouts over the years, written in different moods – wonder, joy, excitement, anger, disappointment. They were not primarily intended to form a book but were assiduously collected by a friend, Stephen McCarthy, and, with enormous labour, built into a book. Thank you, Steve, before I start, and for the many lunches over which we worked!

Then there is James Alison, to whom I owe so much of my present mind inspired by the genius of René Girard. James is in the process of creating a whole new catechesis, in which our minds grow together, he always ahead. He is making this catechesis available, as it grows, to any group in the world that calls on him to come and talk. This operation is really amazing and exciting to be part of. When I get depressed about the Church, I have only to think of James. Then there is Robert Wiggs, who said something I shall never forget, for it made my own mind visible to me: 'I know that the ultimate is benign, for otherwise I would not care.' Thank you, Robert, for caring, shown by your work with the Corrymeela community for peace in Northern Ireland. I owe so much to Adrian Johnson, who has made available to me his insight and experience as director, for many years, of the old Third Programme. I owe much to Michael Ware, in the way of poetry shared, and countless meals over many years, the bill not far short of four figures I'm sure. We tease each other about God and climate change. Then there is Patrick Early, whose deep friendship overflows into suggestions and support down the years, and there's the inspiration of time with him in my beloved Languedoc. I may be a reincarnate and reorthodoxised Cathar. And there are my many friends in the States, especially Fred and Sue Lawrence. My roots in the thought of Bernard Lonergan were watered for countless years at the annual Lonergan Workshop, at which I got to know Glenn Hughes, 'Chip', who has connected me with the best that is thought today, especially Erik Voegelin. Chip gave me a taste of the America I love, that still remembers Whitman, especially the Northwest with its impregnable Bishop Hunthausen, assailed for peace and justice, over a decade or so, by the powers that be.

Finally, there are my brethren at Downside, living and dead, who are more patient with me than I ever notice. I am most grateful to Fr David, for reading my manuscript with much attention to detail and for encouragement. And I really feel backed up by Abbot Aidan Bellenger. Finally there is Father Dominic, an inestimable friend and now an eminent magician, who is introducing me to the magic of God.

In conclusion, I don't make much sense to myself other than as a Downside monk, and this I want to acknowledge.

Sebastian Moore
Downside Abbey
March 2007

PART ONE

Jesus offers a seemingly impossible example: that of the willing victim, who lets us kill him and returns to us, unaccusing, inviting us into his Body that we have entered violently to murder. God says to a violent world:

'Do it to me, and I'll show you who I am. Welcome!'

CHAPTER 1

Our God of Love

The biblical story starts when a small tribe in the Middle East came to believe in one single god, and rejected all their former gods and the gods of neighbouring tribes. Theirs was a god who 'in the beginning' had created the world – everything; a god who represented a reality trying to get our attention, an answer to the question: 'Why do I exist?'; a god who simply is in the void that opens up when we dump all our false gods of power and projections of our own ego; yet, a god who was not just powerful and distant but was also near and intimately involved with his chosen people.

This god progressively revealed himself as the God of freedom from fear, of life and of love for the whole world, and who ultimately sends his only Son, Jesus, into the world to identify not with the powerful but with the weak and the vulnerable.

In the Beginning?
Written in the millennial year 2000, this essay on the beginning is a good place to start!

Somebody said to me last night: 'I don't share your belief in God. I think it all started by chance.' I started to think about this.

First of all, there was nothing and then, by chance, it started. Now what am I describing when I say this is a void, an emptiness, just space, and then a 'beginning'? But that is not nothing, it's an empty space, it's something I'm imagining. And when I go on to say 'and then ...', I show that this original nothing is already *in time*. It's *before* anything came to be. But 'before' is already in time, and time is not nothing.

So that notion of the whole thing just starting by chance cannot be thought. It cannot be said, so it cannot be thought. When I try to think it, I find myself thinking something else. When I try to think of nothing at the beginning, I'm already thinking of something, as the Book of Genesis does. It begins with 'waste and void, and darkness upon the face of the deep' before God gets to work, and that's certainly not nothing. So we can't think of the world as just happening by chance, out of nothing.

But the believer in God is strapped in exactly the same way. For he, too, says: 'In the beginning there was nothing, *and then* God started the world.' That's nonsense too. The believer is in exactly the same fix as the non-believer.

Where does this lead us? It means that 'the beginning' is not the place to start! Neither belief nor unbelief can make sense if we're trying to think in terms of a beginning – Big Bang and all that.

So the question: 'Is there God?' has to be phrased in some other way, like: 'Is there a purpose? Am I here for a reason? Is there a meaning to existence?'

And the only way to pursue this question is somehow to ask myself, or the universe, or my feelings, 'Is there a "You" at the heart of everything?' It is to ask, 'Are you there?' And that is to pray. God cannot be any sort of a maker or starter that we can conceive, but something more like 'happiness trying to make us happy, to spread itself among us' or 'meaning trying to make sense in us', above all, I think, *a reality trying to get our attention!*

> Time has a history, is not absolute
> While space is buried at the heart of things
> And consciousness attains beyond its brute
> Existence, to converse with spirit's kings.
>
> The origin of time is understood
> And likewise that of space, that is time's pair,
> Science's absolutes thus gone for good
> In the Big Bang that happened everywhere.
>
> There is no time before, or space outside
> The happening where science turns to God
> From being God itself to whom it lied:
> In the only beginning is the word.

At last our thinking, used to being right,
Is blinded by the words: let there be light!

The Revelatory Breakthrough of God

We need fully to understand the importance of the biblical change which occurred in the Hebrew Scriptures from a big god, more powerful than all the others, to the one good God who is the source and explanation for our whole existence. This was a big breakthrough for the Israelites. Likewise for our author, writing this essay was a big breakthrough.

The crucial shift registered in the Hebrew Scriptures was from henotheism[1] to monotheism and the prophetic voice. This was a change of God that we are still short of getting the measure of, from the Big Imagined Being – our big being as opposed to the beings of our neighbours, the best God – the shift from this to, why we are at all, in whom we live and move and have our being, as Paul says. This big shift had the most beautiful and wonderful implication, that this 'God' was trustworthy, and eventually, through the Jesus affair, revealed himself as a passionate lover who makes us lovers also. How lovely is this conjunction of the mystery of 'God' with this God's trustworthiness, lovingness, loving-kindness as the Scripture calls it. I can't get over this. That which simply *is*, is to be trusted, relaxed into. St John of the Cross talks of our need to grow in God.

As a result of this big shift, and under the inspiration and goading of the prophets, this tribe among other tribes, this people with their god as the other tribes had theirs (only ours is the best god!) becomes that new thing – the people of the only God, the non-discriminating cause of all out of nothing. And this God was not identified, as the national gods were, with the interests of a ruling group. In consequence the tribe became exposed to terrible persecution, so that the Hebrew Scriptures count four huge horrors of this kind: Egypt, Babylon, Rome, and of course the *shoah* or holocaust.

Am I putting too much weight on the shift from henotheism to monotheism? After all, the monotheistic phase had its sacrifices galore borrowed from pagan neighbours; the image of human sacrifice still lurked in these. But what we are talking about is not a philosophical

---

[1] Henotheism can be described as belief in, and worship of, one god without denying the existence of others.

discovery. No, it's a huge implied shift, a religious landslide, the coming to be of an implied space where before there were holy places with gods – our life aggrandised. The shift from that to the sheer 'why' of our existence at all, a creation story with everything good to a God beyond all that we can imagine, with no clean and unclean – this is enormous.

Above all, the mental space this creates is never adequately appreciated or responded to, because the response involves a sense of ourselves that is bottomless, so that really to understand this is to understand myself for the first time – my only question now is not about the array of the heavens, but 'What am I here for?' What am I here for, I who contemplate the heavens and now am learning to think of these as millions of light years apart? Who, what, why am I in all this that comes to consciousness in me? What it means to be brought into being out of nothing does not send the mind back to a past event, my conception and birth; it exposes me to myself as next to nothing with a 'God' who is all.

The notion of creation out of nothing is the most sophisticated philosophical notion there is. But it is prepared for, it is implied, in that first huge step when the gods became 'nought' and I/we are creation happening. And we owe this notion not so much to Greek philosophy (which was already feeding on the Christian idea anyway) as to the earlier seismic shift in consciousness that requires it.

This shift is for a people, as the Greek philosophic shift is not. This is of crucial importance. This shift into a God beyond the world is a shift that throws people together. It creates the consciousness of a people that, with our God-representing victim slain and risen, is *ecclesia*, the called-together, the new human polity – not of power and the force of rivalry and its uneasy resultants – but of love. The withdrawal of God into all-enclosing mystery and the throwing of people together is a single process, so that John, the most visionary of the evangelists, sees 'love one another' as the sufficient statement of the creation process brought to term.

It is with this vision in mind that we know that our radical ill is the absence of the love that the vision sees. And if it is now being brought home to us that we are rendering our planet uninhabitable for future generations by the way we live, then the big shift has its enormous implication. For it asks us 'why we exist at all', to which the only answer is that we are in the process of being created and that we are refusing to co-operate and thus setting up the friction of the spirit with all anti-life movements. So let God be God and us God's creation – next to nothing with God as all.

The seeming impossibility of getting agreement on what to do or abstain from for the continuance of our life on the planet, and the seeming impossibility of securing international order, forces Christian belief to declare itself as the certainty that we are created to love one another and live together. As Auden saw and said: 'We must love one another or die.'

I knew a man who asked, 'why am I here?'
And lived inside this question which became
His flesh and blood, it was good to be near,
Once I knew him, nothing was quite the same.

It was the question turned our race around
Of prophets of a people with a mission
Which became clear when Moses heard the sound
Of words beside a bush ablaze with fission.

Exodus put the question to the test
Of forty desert years and intermingling
With peoples, searching for a place of rest
And disappointment with the heart still tingling,

Until they killed the God who'd brought them out
Of slavery, and ended all my doubt.

Do Not Be Afraid. I Have Overcome the World

This piece was given as a homily. Sebastian refers to Eckhart Tolle and his Book The Power of Now, *which he has found hugely influential over recent years.*

Hosea, the lovable minor prophet, hears the words: 'I am God not man'. This echoes a revolution in religious consciousness with which we are still trying to catch up. Technically it is called the transition from henotheism to monotheism, from the top god to the only god, but this is no scholar's shift. It means losing all the gods that we rely on, that are simply the projections of our fears and needs, the many faces of nature, and plunging into a void where the only God asks of us the risk and the trust of life itself. This plunge into the void is documented for us by Eckhart Tolle who, I am convinced, is only one of a growing number who are pulled into the void and return to love life and spread it. They can make Church pronouncements look wearisome, if not dishonest.

The big shift has its prophets, who are trying to refashion a small amphictyony[2] of tribes into a people at risk and nurturing an extra-ordinary hope for the world and, perforce, of the world. This destiny exposes Israel to the terror of history, and her *memory* records four major near-triumphs of the world against hope: Egypt, Babylon, Rome, and the Nazi abomination. Four times when the world asked contemptuously, 'Where is your god now?'

I wonder whether this gives us a way to read the Psalms that *can* be read as an orgy of paranoia. Grimly they list the forces that assail the chooser of life: wild beasts, bulls of Bashan, scavenging dogs, nets, snares, traps, pits, deep mud to sink in, mighty waters to be swal-lowed in – you name it, and the Psalms do! Perhaps we are invited to revel, even to gloat, over the hazards from which a simple dive into the void of prayer would set us free, although we spend most of our time somewhere between the fear and the dive. The God of Abraham, of Isaac, of Jacob, the God of risk and trust, is inside each of us whispering: 'Choose life!' The relapse from this voice is into fear, the paranoia that can seize a whole nation, and you and me. I have tasted this recently, very lightly, and I have got just a hint that there is in me and in every one a self-enjoyment that dissolves paranoia, though it is scary to live in. This is the stirring, in each of us, of the only God, displacing all the gods of security in which we invest. It stirred cru-cially in Jesus, and dictated the enormous risk of heading for Jer-usalem and certain death.

Will we follow him, will we take the cross – not as crusaders that are two a penny – but as disciples? This means, do we believe in the resurrection? To believe in the resurrection is to know that the ques-tion posed by the world in us to the only God is answered, that life chosen by Jesus has come through death into a diffusion of the Spirit whose brooding makes light of the darkest of futures. In the world,

---

[2] Amphictyony is a Greek concept for a type of religious organisation that gathers people together around the worship of a common God, or, in ancient Greece, at a common temple.

says Jesus, you will have lots of trouble. 'But do not be afraid. I have
overcome the world.'

Tolle

I want it now not in the power of now
In panic filling of a coming void
To fill with half of me and not allow
Me whole unable to be unalloyed.

The power of now makes one the two of me
If I will let this be, the opposite
Of scheming time, the tyrant memory
Forbidding me to be and still to sit,

Yet always ready to assemble all
There is of me to sink into the deep
Where I can always hear you when you call
Me out of me as once again I leap.

But when I read him in full consequence
I tremble and retreat to the felt sense.

A passionate involvement with a stranger
Undertaken by the Samaritan
Who was in trade and likely a free-ranger
Shows what it is to be truly a man.

Eckhart prepares you to be in the way
For this to happen, heart free of the mind
To be attuned to every fresh today
And taste the fruit of it and not the rind.

How shall they meet, the heart and the occasion
Is the whole question: Jesus is the answer
The other who is God by heart's persuasion
For the next person of the schooled God-chancer.

We need the mystery of Incarnation
For training of a spiritual elation.

Two Kinds of Conversion

Too easily we see God as a sort of projection of our own images of power, a power which controls us all. We need to be converted to the true God, who is prepared through Jesus to be humiliated out of love for us.

There are two kinds of conversion. There is the conversion of the godless to God, and there is the conversion of the godly to the realisation that he has been radically wrong about God, and about what God is asking of us. As a little girl was once heard to pray, 'God, make all bad people good, and make all good people nice!' This second kind happened to Saul, an exceedingly godly man, on the way to Damascus about his God's business. He had got God wrong. All-powerful over us, his God had become the image of our lust for power; God had what we wanted. And we have all remade God in our own image of being the power over us, reflecting a long history of violence and war.

To be converted from this God is devastating. And the image of this conversion is of a God not over us but under us, spat upon by priests and a barrack-square joke for soldiers, finally nailed to two bits of wood. Saul the Pharisee, trained in the God of law and rigour, knew of and abominated that image which a new sect was promulgating; it was against everything he'd stood for as a religious man, and so he had got God wrong. He was thrown, and fell helplessly in love with the humiliated one whom the real God had raised up, the God who comes to us from below, the oppressed among us and, in us, the tender self we have oppressed in order to dominate each other, the God who – his arms stretched out to all the world by being nailed to our cross – is behind us so we don't see him but sink into him and let him feed us with his flesh and blood – a horrendous idea for the then religion – and turn us slowly into himself, his body given to others in a new and all-enduring love.

The Christian God is Different

We have to dump all our gods that are merely projections of ourselves, and instead open ourselves to the mystery of the authentic God who reveals himself not in power but in vulnerability and powerlessness. The great world religions may be inclined to think they acknowledge the same one 'god', like seeing the same elephant from a different angle; but the suffering, loving God revealed by Jesus is quite different; it is not the same elephant at all.

What is called the discovery that God is one is really, we see in ret-
rospect, the discovery that the beings we have taken for gods do not
exist and are simply the projections of our sense of identity as tribe or
nation or 'humanity' perhaps.

The crucial question, however, is: What follows from this realisation? Does it follow that it is up to us to forge our destiny, that we are
'all there is', we're 'on our own' and we must get on with it? It's up to
us who or what we become.

Surely this does not follow! All that 'follows' or is implied in this
disenchantment is that where we have made gods there is a void. The
blank left by the discovery that our gods are our projections is not the
blank of a neutral empty space. It engenders awe.

And at this point a new distinction occurs, of a psychological nature, in consciousness itself, between the ego and a centre of consciousness explored, for instance, by Jung, but discovered by people
we call mystics or whatever name we choose for them. From the
standpoint of this discovery of a distinction within ourselves between
'ego' and a deeper centre of consciousness, those who draw the conclusion, 'since there are no gods, it's up to us to forge our destiny' are
speaking in the ego, thus not giving full expression to the breathtaking
discovery that we live in the unknown, a discovery to which Erich
Voegelin devoted a lifetime of exploration.

In an attempted history of consciousness, Voegelin seeks in every
society or polity what he calls a 'tension toward the ground of being'.
Obstinately he insisted that the translation preserve the awkward
phrase 'tension toward', because he had to keep together the unrest,
the tension within ourselves, entailed in the discovery of 'no God'
following on the earlier 'no gods', between this tension and the
unknown that is giving rise to it. This state of tension Voegelin calls
the 'metaxy', the sense of our existence in-between the relative and the
absolute, the state of the elusive absolute.

This void engendering awe that arises from the dumping of all our
gods requires only that we open to it. That is what I pray in, what
Tolle helps us to centre in, what I think Merton and the Dalai Lama –
the Trappist monk and the leader of worldwide Buddhism – shared
in. Abbot Chapman, who taught us Downside monks to pray, said to
E. I. Watkin in a letter, 'My friends call me a Buddhist'. For me this
void becomes 'articulate' – though I hesitate for a word here – in three
interrelating realities called Father (beyond), Son (among us) and
Spirit (their 'go-between' – another word I hesitate over). Then there is

the Hindu triad of *sat-cit-ananda*, being-energy-bliss. Tolle embraces Buddhism for its enormous relief from 'suffering', that is suffering clung-to, the pain body, and he quotes Jesus the most of all his authorities, and introduces his work as dependent on *A Course in Miracles*, which is a monumental work of Christian revisionism.

All this is converging on something quite different from a democracy of world religions with Christianity, Judaism and Islam (constituting an awkward and troublesome member) because these believe in 'a God' who has to be defined to be denied and is, at least for the more conscious members of these three groups, not definable or needing to be defined!

Finally, another thing has to be said about the 'one God' whose self-revelation exposes all our gods as the projections of rulers and the powerful, and leaves us in the draught of this sweeping-away. Not only does this God dis-identify with worldly power: he is, over and over again through the fulminations of poets and prophets, on the side of the powerless, the widow and the orphan, the victims of worldly power that you hear crying all over the Psalms. Now, put together this dis-identifying with the powers that be, and the identifying with their victims, and the ground is prepared for Christianity's revealing moment, the abandoned crucified Son of this transcendent Other, nailed to a cross by worldly power subsequently revealed to his scared and scattered followers as the new human being, the Body of Christ.

Of this astonishing revelatory moment of the God that is love, who 'disarmed the rulers and authorities and made a public example of them, triumphing over them in it' (Col. 2:15), Christian doctrine as we receive it with all its imperial baggage is a travesty, recognisable as such. Once one has a taste of this inversion of our normal way of seeing things, any notion of a democracy of world religions becomes boring by contrast.

CHAPTER 2

The Trinity and Human Relationship

It is natural to move from Our God of Love to Jesus as Love Incarnate, God's Son. But how can we understand this? Only by being 'in the Spirit'. So, in pondering the incredible mystery of the incarnation, we are inevitably drawn into the unfathomable mystery of the Trinity. Yet the conventional way in which the Trinity is 'understood', as three co-equal persons, although appealing to the western mind, fails to capture its essence. Persons live in relationship and Trinity is 'relationship at infinity'. Thus, as human persons, we are relationships in the making, who experience God, the Trinity, in our 'interdividual' relationships.

Now human relationship is never more intensely experienced than through sexuality. The Church rightly makes the link between relationship and sexuality (a link which our culture increasingly ignores), but it still needs to learn to celebrate human sexuality as an, albeit imperfect, image of the Trinity. We come back to this theme in later chapters.

Incarnation – Living in the Spirit

This piece, written in 1992, was one of Sebastian's first attempts at pondering the mystery of the incarnation. That he came back to it with two afterthoughts just shows how difficult the mystery is to put into words, rather than just to live in it.

Let us start with the central Christian belief: that Jesus Christ is God.

Now before we tackle this seemingly outlandish statement, here is a rule for outlandish statements generally. The more ambitious a statement, that is, the more wide-ranging its sweep and the more it tries to catch, in language which is so limiting, the very depths of reality, then the more necessary it is to know and to understand the question to which it is being given as the answer. Take for instance the statement of Einstein that space is curved. To someone like me who is a moron in the world of mathematical physics, the statement is almost meaningless. I do not know, I am not versed in, the kind of questions that people come up with when they get into the world of physics and astrophysics. But once you begin to understand that world and to ask its questions, the statement of Einstein is seen as the product of breathtaking genius.

Now the statement, 'A man who lived two thousand years ago and has left us nothing but the memoirs of his disciples is God' is so revolutionary and far-reaching that here my principle applies to the maximum extent. If we are not clear as to the question in those disciples' minds, to which their experience compelled them to give this amazing answer, the statement either has no meaning or the wrong meaning.

So what was their question? Was it: 'Is this man God?', meaning: 'Does he deserve divine honours in the way, for instance, that emperors – once they're dead – do?' Or is the question: 'Is this person so outstanding that we feel he must be more than human, some sort of an incarnation of divinity? Is he divine in the way that we sometimes call a great composer divine?'

Now neither of these two sorts of questions was in the minds of Jesus' promoters. Being Jews, they were not into divinising emperors, and for them no human excellence could take a person across the infinite gulf between the human and the divine.

They had a different question, namely this: Jesus is the Son of God, as is the people of Israel, and as are all good people. This is an accepted metaphor. The question is: 'Is this metaphor in the case of Jesus carrying an exceptional weight? Is the equality that exists between a father and a son, an equality that only the son's minority holds in suspension, found in the case of Jesus as Son of God?'

What pushed them to ask this extraordinary question was this. Shortly after Jesus' atrocious death, that had reduced them psychologically to pulp, they had an experience of him as alive, in a way that neither the living nor the dead are thought of as alive: neither in the body as we know it, nor in the soul as we are taught to think about it. Rather he was a presence that changed everything. He was, as St Paul says, a life-giving spirit. And that this new life-giving presence was really he, was made known in the most amazing way: his tomb was empty!

This new all-changing presence of Jesus after his death put enormous pressure on the metaphor of divine sonship. This 'Son' had dissolved the barrier that separates the dead from the living, for he was now unclassifiable as either. This meant that God, who alone is Lord of living and dead, had 'raised him from the dead' to be with himself as his co-equal Son.

So the Christian statement that Christ is God is the answer to the question: 'In what way is he God's son?' The answer is: 'In the way that is the essence of sonship, namely equality.'

But the moment we say this, we run into a problem. It is *the* Christian problem, failure to deal with which accounts for all Christianity's serious failures – as I hope to show. The problem is, how can the infinite, the incomprehensible, the ground of being, the ultimate mystery behind everything, have a son – in the serious literal way we are now claiming? What conceivable sense can this make?

They got off this hook to some extent by equating the divine Son with 'the Word of God' or *Logos*, an idea which had a lot going for it from both Jewish and Greek thought. But still the problem remains. How are we to think of the infinite producing its equal – especially when this divine product is someone we have known, very much a person? How can God 'generate' a 'second person'? How do we think of Jesus not only as related *to* God but as manifesting a relationship *in* God? Remember that we are driven to this kind of thinking by the resurrection-presence of Jesus as life-giving Spirit, but how, once thereto driven, do we do it? How do we actually think this way?

The answer is surprisingly simple. The people who experienced this new presence of Jesus were enabled to think of God in this new way, as having a co-equal Son, by the very force that drove them to it, namely the Spirit of Jesus risen. The Spirit enlarges the mind, draws us together, breaks down the citadel of our ego, and in this new mind we know Jesus as the Son, ourselves as his extension, and God as our intimate Father. So what you have is three realities: God as Father, the co-equal Son, and 'thinking-about-God-differently because we are being changed into God', that is, the Holy Spirit. All three.

For the first Christians, the 'third' was the most real of all. Read the New Testament again. Look up a biblical concordance and see how many columns the word 'spirit' occupies for New Testament authors.

You could almost call the Christian Scriptures the spirit section of the Bible. It is the record of a consciousness revolution, people dancing around 'in the Spirit' crying out: 'Jesus is Lord'. According to that weird scholar Allegro, they'd been eating a very potent mushroom! But at least he got the main point, which everyone seems to have missed: that Christianity started on a high. Paul says very clearly: 'No one can say "Jesus is Lord" save in the Holy Spirit.' Translation: 'If you are not tuned in to thinking quite differently about God, you can't make any sense of God having a co-equal Son.' Unless it's changing you, unless you are becoming more than you thought you were, the incarnation makes no sense.

So what started as the question, 'How is Jesus God's Son?' leads to thinking quite differently about God. Now we must spell this out.

How did we think about God? As a super-powerful person. The image was of power and we get our images of power from powerful people, people who 'make others do what they want'. God is the all-powerful, the Almighty, the omnipotent. The new thinking subverts our way of enthroning God. God is not solitary power. God is relationship. And God is all relationship. For when the brightest of the Greek theologians thought about this, they found that the divine persons must be the relationships they are in. The Father only is Father in respect of the Son and vice versa, and they depend, for their reality in our minds, on the Spirit. This bit is awfully tricky, the Spirit as, at one and the same time, transforming us into the Son and completing the Trinity. The Spirit completes the Trinity in transforming us.

Rather as scientists are now discovering that nature is not something we observe but something we can only understand as participating in it, so the relationship of God-the-Father with God-the-Son is only understood in and through our spiritual participation in it. The Latin Fathers never really got this one. They were trying to think of the Father producing the Son and them together producing the Spirit, without realising that the Spirit is what we have to be *in* to be thinking of the Father and the Son at all. Outside the Spirit, the mind expander, there is no answer to the laconic Islamic question: 'How can God have a Son, since he hasn't got a wife?' It's all very well to reply to this: 'Oh, that's very materialistic. You've got to understand these things spiritually!' Indeed you have. Do we? I suspect not. The 'third person' is the most difficult to understand only because it *is* our understanding, *is* the Son spreading in us and so taking us to the Father.

I don't really understand this. But I do know why I don't

understand it: it is because I am not enough 'in the Spirit'. And neither is the Church. Hence the mess the Church makes of things.

Are you with me still? We are at the heart of the matter. It is where I try to think of the eternal as having a Son, and find I can't – except in the Spirit that makes *me* a son. For most of my life as a Christian thinker, I have failed to grasp this. With the whole mental habit of the western Church behind me, I have thought I understood about the Father and the Son and that it was the Spirit I didn't quite get. Whereas in fact I did *not* understand about the Father and the Son *because* I did not get the Spirit. And the whole western Church has been in this bind. Augustine, our main source for Trinitarian theology, was a towering genius. But he didn't know Greek, and so didn't have the feel of the Greek Fathers, for whom Spirit was everything.

All this sounds quite irrelevant to the world we're living in, but it's not.

At crucial moments in history like the present, the original flaws in our thinking tend to reveal themselves. It was because the western Church had ceased to understand itself in the Spirit, had thought of its unity as 'produced by organisation rather than by the Spirit', that it was unable to cope with the scientific revolution when it came, dithered when Darwin discovered evolution and Freud the unconscious, and now resists the feminist movement and the rethinking of sexuality. It all goes back to a Church that understood God and his Son in legal terms – God authorising the Son and the Son authorising the Church – rather than in the Spirit, that got relegated to the role of someone you pray to before taking an exam.

So the risen Jesus makes us think of God differently. God is all relationship, and this is the antithesis of solitary power. And when we begin to think of God in this different way, we begin to see why it is that the real God, the surprising God, shows up in our power-crazy world naked on a cross, tortured to death by the ruling power as a disturber of what it calls the peace. The disturbing, subversive nature of Christianity begins to appear. Borrowing the fine phrase – indeed stealing it! – from Nietzsche, the theologian Johann Baptist Metz has said that Christianity is the perpetuation of a 'dangerous memory'. What Nietzsche meant by a dangerous memory is some moment in the past when a highly conscious person 'pushed it', took a huge risk and showed that life could be quite different, turned the world upside down – for example Socrates, and supremely, Christ.

Christianity is always being pulled back into the old way of thinking about God that Jesus in the Spirit subverts. The first big test was the Council of Nicaea in 325. The Arian heresy put Jesus under God, and that's what the emperor wanted: God on top, the solitary absolute monarch; under him, the Son; under the Son, the Emperor; under him, the nobility; under the lot, Joe Soap. Miraculously the Council said no, the Son is the equal of the Father in a relationship that only makes sense when we become part of it in the Spirit. So instead of an oppressive hierarchy, you have three persons in each other in a manner of which sexual ecstasy is the image. Nietzsche said: 'I can only believe in a dancing God'. No one told him about the Trinity, in which the persons only are in each other, so that all is movement, recalling that line of Eliot, 'and there is only the dance'. In Nietzsche's time, Christianity was sunk in the old-time religion of the lonely absolute monarch, who of course brings out the lonely absolute monarch in all of us. As I've said already, everything that is wrong with the Church, the obsession with its authority, the legalism, the fear of women, homophobia – which is the fear of women, in disguise – the fear of sex, the distrust of feeling, all stem from falling out of the Spirit, out of the dance, out of the equality-God.

And falling out of the Spirit means ceasing to be the incarnation, not letting the incarnation happen in us to liberate our humanity, our sexuality, our yearning to be in love. We need a new Pentecost. If the Church came alive again in the Spirit, the New Age would begin to look very old hat. Indeed the New Age, and all the other spiritual movements of our time, show people trying to get into the Spirit, the larger consciousness – to which the Church holds the key, and is sitting on it. 'Come Holy Spirit!' we piously pray. I wonder what would happen if she did!

Now let me try again with some afterthoughts.

First, what I am saying, in essence, is that, while all will agree that the Holy Spirit is both the completion of the Trinity and the transforming principle in our lives, these two roles of the Spirit may be thought of as identical. The Eastern Church has no difficulty with this, I think, but the Western Church is uneasy with it. It is to be noted, however, that there is a hallowed theological phrase that means both these roles of the Spirit at once, the term 'uncreated grace'. Uncreated grace is the Holy Spirit, and it is grace, transformation.

What follows is a bit more technical, but I think it is important. I seem to be saying that the Holy Spirit is, identically and in one formality, the completion of the Trinity and the transformation of us.

No, what I am saying is that it is only in our transformation that we get a sense of how the Spirit completes the Trinity. That completion in itself is a mystery, and by saying that we only know it in our transformation we keep it so. It is the mystery of the Father in the Son, the Son in the Father, drawing us in so that we 'become one as they are one' as John's gospel puts it. We can be quite clear that the Spirit, as fullness of the Godhead, is not simply identical with the Spirit as our transformation, without saying something quite definite about the Spirit as completion of the Godhead, such as, that the Spirit is the love between the Father and the Son. In fact the latter description, while it does show the Trinitarian completion as distinct from our transformation, hardly suggests the mystery of the Spirit, what we sense when we try, with word after word, to fill in the blank in 'The Spirit is the ———— of the Father and the Son.' We soon find that there just is no word.

The point is, I think, that we come closer to the mystery when we sense it in our transformation than we do when we call it 'the love between the Father and the Son', though with the latter formula we are talking about the Trinity in itself and not in its action in us. Transcendence is one thing, and it resonates within the transcended. Marking the transcendent off by itself is another, and it is in danger of cutting the lifeline whereby transcendence is known.

When we turn away from our transformation in the Spirit and thus confine ourselves to other sources for thinking about the Spirit as Trinitarian completion, going through the endless process of trying to see how we can get a third out of the first two persons, we produce a closed-circuit Trinity, living its own 'inner life' and, just because we thus find ourselves able to say so much more about it, quite dependent on our speculation. The attempt to secure transcendence in this way lands us in anthropomorphism.

Finally on this point there is a beautiful text of Paul's which suggests the affinity between the mystery that each person is to him- or herself and the mystery that God is. It suggests, in other words, that our own transformation experience is the medium in which we are to understand God's mystery. 'For what human being knows what is truly human except the human spirit that is within? So also no one comprehends what is truly God's except the Spirit of God' (1 Cor. 2: 11).

Second, of course this is oversimplified. For history happened. The Roman Empire collapsed, and in the chaos that ensued the Church found itself the only civilising force. So what was designed to be a higher education in the spirit found itself running a kindergarten. This is not new. Paul wrote to the Corinthians: 'And so, brothers and sisters, I could not speak to you as spiritual people, but rather as people of the flesh, as infants in Christ. I fed you with milk, not solid food, for you were not ready for solid food. Even now you are still not ready.' (1 Cor. 3: 1-2.) But that phase is long gone, and in this new bewildering time when, as Jaspers put it, scores of centuries are coming to a close, Christian belief has to discover its mystical, deep-self dimension, or it will perish. Of course it won't, Jesus won't let it, but we shall pay dearly if we don't wake up now.

> Jesus made obsolete the monarchy
> And with his Father and the Holy Spirit
> Revealed the absolute as Trinity
> A model that his church could then inherit.

> This model, though, ran into Constantine
> And his successors to the name of Rome
> And so there was confusion of the sign
> And monarchy would give the church a home

> Whose liturgy was of the court, addressed
> To an Almighty Monarch of the sky
> Who 'deigned', no longer from the heart confessed
> And liturgy forgot the ecstasy

> With Trinity left to the expertise
> Of experts with another God to please.

Holy Trinity and Human Sexuality

Sebastian wrote this piece some eleven years later, in 2003. By this time he had discovered the enormous contribution of René Girard to understanding human nature and what Christ was about. More on this in Chapter 3. The important point being made here is that human love and desire, not least sexual desire, is essential to human nature and echoes the unfathomable Trinity in whose image we are all created.

What is the alternative to individualism? Better, what is the mistake of individualism? René Girard offers 'interdividualism', not as the answer to this question but as the anthropology implied in his account of the human animal as mimetic. According to this account, I first meet my desire in the other – as with a pair of two-year-olds in a playpen, each excited by the toy the other has noticed.

Desire is not to be thought of as mine or yours, what I want or what you want, but as the force that, working in us, puts us in each other's way as models in which to recognise our desire, whether as rival or as encouragement. In other words, we are mutually involved in the coming-alive of desire, thrown into each other's way by desire, a force beyond our control, subject only to that control of which Paul speaks as one of the gifts of the Holy Spirit.

It is the primacy of desire over us as individuals that makes us, as individuals, inescapably involved in each other. When Marshal Rosenberg,[1] whose life is devoted to conflict resolution in the most unpromising conditions, says that our supreme joy is found in being a source of joy in another, he is describing our interdividual existence in its full flourishing, the sheer joy of seeing our own happiness in another. Now if we ask what is the most striking and universal instance of desire as involving us in each other in the pursuit of security and happiness, the obvious answer is sex. Sex is the most dramatic way in which people become interested in each other long before they have had time to develop interests that they share. It is the drama of our interdividual existence. In this drama, I see myself in the other and, thus enticed, I come to see the other as fascinating. By what other means than sex do human existences worm their way into each other so relentlessly and thus so revealingly of our humanity?

Now it has been said that it was in the attempt to show that the three divine persons are one God that we first thought seriously of our own reality and interdependence as persons. This makes a lot of sense. The flowering of religion into that very different reality called 'reve-lation', as it sprang upon us with the resurrection of our 'scapegoat' victim, sinks a plumb line into our experience of ourselves in our mutual involvement. Thus when the problem of how to show the three 'Persons' of the revelation as one found its solution in the idea of relationship 'carried to infinity' at which each of the Persons is its relationship to the others, what we had was our own interdividual

---

[1] Founder of the Center for Non-Violent Communication. See: www.cnvc.org

existence presented with its divine model, an infinite intersubjectivity. The 'subsistent relations' of the Trinity are not a recondite formula for a divine life beyond our comprehension: they are our own obscure interconnectedness brought infinitely into the light.

The driving energy here, to fail to understand which is to be left with a purely verbal notion of our connection with the Trinity, is desire, raw desire; and, of this, sex is the rawest and the most to do with bringing people together, so that Dorothy Day could write, in a notebook: 'I am more and more convinced that every sexual encounter, however depraved, is an attempt at relationship'. Better, perhaps, would have been 'a reaction to loneliness'. In Harlem, she knew whereof she spoke.

Now, imagine this drama of revelation in three persons deprived of the principal image of human interconnectedness that will find in this drama its elucidation, and you have a great deal of Christian teaching, even official teaching, on sexuality. This systematically de-emphasises sexuality as mutual attraction and sees it as much as it can as the means of procreation. Anything less *procreative*, in the sense of representative of an infinitely resourceful creator, cannot be imagined, than the way such teaching uses that word.

But the teaching Church still has marriage before it as the divinely revealed image of 'the great mystery' to which Paul refers. Now marriage gives the Church an example of sexual desire as imitative of the divine. But it gives the Church this example in a form that allows her to ignore the element of desire in favour of mutual comfort and procreation. Mutual desire need not figure in the presentation, so that the great connection, between our constitutive erotic interdividuality and the Trinity is not made. The result is an account of the divine persons that resembles a nice family, or a boardroom.

In conclusion, I remember a Roman classroom in the late forties, in which the name of one author was singled out for special reprobation, especially as he was, alas, a Benedictine. The moral theologian Herbert Doms was subjected to all the power of the Holy Office, being forbidden to teach and to publish, because he had emphasised the role of sexual desire in marriage. I have lived long enough to have real problems with the Church. For the Church has still to look at our sexual hunger not under the long phallic shadow cast by Augustine.

The Human Person

A homily that makes much the same point as the previous essay, but rather more succinctly.

St Augustine wrote that if you stop someone in the street and ask him: 'Are you a friend?', this will make no sense to him, although he is a friend, to Peter, Mary and a few others. What Augustine is doing here is telling us the kind of thing a person is, namely a 'someone' to other persons. A person is a walking relationship.

Now the first Christians to think the thing out found themselves faced with: Jesus (God) and his Father (God), and this seemed to make two Gods, which is clearly wrong. Then someone had the same insight Augustine had: these two only are, each, not the other because they are persons to each other in the relationship of bearing and borne. Push this to infinity, and they seem to disappear into each other, and this disappearing into each other is explosive, sheer energy, Holy Spirit.

Now there was a spin-off to this. In tackling the problem of understanding Father and Son as one, they had come up, almost accidentally, with a definition of what a person is. He is the man you went up to in the street with that silly question. A person is a relationship in the making.

But then occurred perhaps the biggest bloomer theology has ever made. People asked 'What is a person?' and came up with the obvious, unsubtle answer formulated by Boethius. A person is rational nature exemplified in Peter or John. Forget how Peter meets John!

Then when they went back to the God question, having forgotten that a person is a being in relation, they again asked: 'How are Father and Son not two Gods?' and of course they remembered the answer reached by those early thinkers: Father and Son are two relations. But, forgetting that we are relations in the making, they saw the divine persons-as-relations as something outlandish to fascinate the theologians, instead of seeing the Trinity as the dynamic originating of ourselves.

Modern culture makes the same mistake, of forgetting the person as to-others and seeing him as the individual, his or her 'needs' met by a more and more lavish technology that has to starve the poorer half of humankind.

Now take this pattern of ideas as a transparency to place over the

Church's attitude to sex, and we see sex as the main casualty of a failure to think of ourselves as relationships in the making. Sex is how this works, and this, through the transparency, shows us what we are missing.

Trinity

A sermon for Trinity Sunday in 2005. The Church urgently needs to speak again to 'people in relationship' from within the heart of the Trinity – which is relationship. At the start of the pontificate of Benedict XVI, let us dare to hope that this might happen.

On Sunday the liturgy of the Church celebrated the Trinity. This celebration has something strange about it. On the one hand, it recaps the whole story. On the other, its language is a complex of abstractions, absolutely fascinating for those who like that sort of thing, but inexplicable to ordinary people. Rahner once said that were it given out from the pulpit that this doctrine had been abrogated, it would make no difference to that now fictitious character the man in the pew.

And yet the doctrine ravishes the heart. It is the shape God takes as Jesus in his cross and rising draws us into unity in the Spirit.

How does this gap open up between the doctrine of the Trinity and us? The answer stares us in the face. The heart of the doctrine is *relationship at infinity*, of persons who are into each other because *relationship* is all they are. (In a flash one might see this as the heart of sacrifice and the shedding of Christ's blood to the last drop.) If it were speaking out of the Trinity, the Church would address us as people in relationships; but it really doesn't, and that's where the gap yawns. There is a nice person inside each of us that wants to make friends. A false spirituality taught us to bully this nice self. 'It is easier than one thinks to hate oneself', as Bernanos said.[2] And when the friendly self got excited at someone else in 'that' way, this spirituality rang alarm bells and was ready with the fire brigade. The whole task of maturing is to bring our emotional side into harmony with the befriending self.

The Church, too, has to undergo this maturing. It has to grow up to the full stature of Christ. This involves coming to the seminal insight that, as sexual beings, we are relationships in the making, and thus reflect a relational Godhead. Our culture, at its best, is coming to know

[2] Georges Bernanos (1888 – 1948) was a French novelist and political writer.

us as relational, and the Church has to catch up with the culture, as we have had to do with slavery and intolerance and war and the death penalty. As Lonergan said, eventually the Church does catch up, breathless and a little late.[3] He thought Vatican II was such a catching-up. 'We woke up', he said, 'to a world we didn't know existed.' Before that seismic shift in Catholic awareness, we were telling ourselves a private story about the universal mystery.

And make no mistake: of course our culture at its commonest and meanest finds the Church irrelevant on sex, because the culture trivialises and commercialises it. The Church alone takes sex seriously but is still learning how to do so, by making the big connection, between sex and relationship.

For many years now, I have found over and over again that discussion of sensitive moral issues ends with people saying: 'But no one pays any attention to what the Church says, so that's OK, no harm done!'

It is not OK at all! The Church is our only contact with the uncreated energy that alone can save us from the triviality of life today with its endless media hype. She is the oldest institution in the world because she holds the only reliable memory of people who underwent the big change and found all our meaning and the meaning of life itself in a man nailed to a cross. That dangerous memory creates the conviction that man matters to God, which arguably has motivated the passionate urge of science to understand our universe. What the Church has to say was, as Paul tells us, a joke for the cultured and an unpleasantness for the pious, but for those who get it, the wisdom that creates and contains all things. Jesus put to death by the sin of the world – 'disappeared', in the horrible sense – by our sin that must try to destroy truth, then reappeared to his scattered followers, his reappearing their coming alive as never before, coming alive as before sin, in the mind of God conceived immaculate. His deathless body, which is now ours, tells the world over and over again of a life larger than death. When that collapses into a bemoaning moralism, then we have a power cut, the relational God cut off from a relational people by a Church too eager for control.

---

[3] Bernard Lonergan (1904 – 1984), a Canadian Jesuit, was one of the finest theologians of the twentieth century, whose work is still being explored and deepened. See: www.lonergan.on.ca/index.htm. I had the privilege of studying and working under him for a while.

Yes, it matters a great deal that people take notice of the Church in matters close to life. The other day I asked a dear friend, an esteemed Catholic professor of literature, how the Church has managed to be thought irrelevant to life's pains and problems. His answer was 'gutlessness'. I know what he meant, because he's a close and valued friend; his speciality: language as the art of telling it like it is.

Perhaps we may speak of sacrifice as the origin of creation, the mutual gift of the non-manifest and the manifest issuing in the creator spirit. Of the original sacrifice, the cross is the manifestation in time. And so we are to see in our time a development of doctrine of a most radical kind in respect of the Trinity, from an arcane abstraction to a sublime concreteness: the relational and sacrificial nature of the Godhead and the consequent relational and sacrificial nature of the human being.

At the start of a new pontificate, at a critical time in the world's history, we must pray for the Spirit to go through the Church with a shiver of truth, so that she can once again show the world to the world.

CHAPTER 3

Jesus – Our Scapegoat

An idea that needs to be exorcised from the Catholic mind is that God, Jesus' Abba, wanted Jesus as a human sacrifice in order to atone for our sins. Such a mistaken notion is so contrary to the Christian understanding of a God who is only love, and indeed to the words of the prophet Hosea, that it is difficult to understand how it has infiltrated the Christian psyche for so long.

But if not as a sacrificial offering, how are we to understand Jesus' passion and death? René Girard's understanding, which is both psychological and theological, of this mystery is perhaps the best explanation available. Human societies are held together by what he calls the 'scapegoat mechanism', whereby the collective fear of a society is taken out on a scapegoat victim who is sacrificed, the ritual sacrifice thereby serving to hold the society together. Now we can see Jesus as the supreme voluntary scapegoat, who by his passion, and importantly his resurrection, destroys the whole scapegoat mechanism and takes away our human fear – in particular the ultimate fear of death – and unites the community of his followers into his body. What he leaves us with is a ritual meal, initiated at his last supper, by which this overcoming of death and corporal reuniting of us all is enacted in the Eucharist.

We struggle really to understand this, and this chapter includes repeated attempts to do so – each one perhaps revealing a little chink of light on the mystery. Of course there is, at the same time, another more straightforwardly human way of looking at the mystery of the passion. That is that Jesus was so driven by his mission, by what his Abba wanted him to do, that there was no possibility of turning aside even though it inevitably was going to lead him to clash fatally with the religious and civil authorities of his time. Such an explanation, so far as it goes, is not incompatible with a more theological interpretation. But it does leave out the resurrection, and it is that which changes everything – his first followers, us and the whole history of the world.

The Big Religious Mistake about God

We have so often heard Christ's passion spoken of as a 'sacrifice' to God that it comes as a shock suddenly to realise that God did not want sacrifice. Rather Christ's passion was precisely to end such bloody rituals and to change humanity for ever.

'I desire steadfast love and not sacrifice, the knowledge of God rather than burnt-offerings' (Hos. 6: 6). These words from the incisive prophet Hosea are a crucial example of what has been called a text 'in travail' or 'in transition', meaning that they are saying more than they can say at the time they are written.

Now we have an unusually vivid example of God's mind outstripping ours in the way we have been taught to understand how Christ saved us by his death. By that death, we were told, he paid a debt incurred by the sin of Adam. This explanation, called 'vicarious satisfaction', once preferred by theologians, has God implementing our miserable ideas, of offence, debt and payment, the rules of the game under the reign of death. Whereas at Calvary God's Son exposes these ideas, by becoming their victim and then, once dead, coming to us as our true self free of death that makes us enemies, in order to love each other as members of his body.

These things have a way of hitting me suddenly – generally when I am preoccupied with some worry as we process in to Vespers. This one went like this: Good heavens, God's attempt to *subvert* our deadly custom, of having one die in place of all, was taken to be the *implementation* of it, and the heavy irony of John, who has the High Priest, no less, define the event, was missed.

Actually, it is very easy to see how the total mistake about the sacrifice of the cross arose. It comes from John's description of Jesus as the *sacrificial lamb*. Thus the believer who contemplates the crucifix tends to see double. On the one hand, a man done to death 'by wicked men', on the other a human sacrifice that, by reason of the theological status of the victim, is acceptable to God. Now what has to be said is that the assumption of the role of sacrificial lamb by Jesus is *strictly and exclusively his own*, embodying his deliberate assumption of the role of scapegoat-victim which is the basis of human sacrifice, for which animal sacrifice is the substitute or dramatic euphemism. The moment the role of lamb is *imposed* on Jesus, the primitive attachment to sacrifice as violent, as bloodletting, takes over, and then we get the ghastly notion of the unbloody sacrifice, as the real bloody sacrifice drained of blood for liturgical purposes.

How could we get it so wrong? God must see us as missing the point of his best story ever. No wonder the resurrection did not figure in the classic account of our redemption that we all learned in theology school. Of course it didn't! It couldn't, for the resurrection makes the theory of vicarious payment impossible. What Jesus showed to his chosen ones was life free of our world, a world that death rules by fear and takes one victim to do for all, the world of Caiaphas. Those who saw him burned inwardly with this new life, larger than death, as the Emmaus story makes clear.

Of course, to say that Jesus was paying the price of Adam's sin is a heavily coded way of saying he was, in the power of the Spirit, pioneering a new humanity not having the fear of death as its hard currency. But this kind of understanding was way beyond the men who taught me in Rome, and warned us about the new theology that was to fashion *Gaudium et Spes*.

The witnesses of Jesus risen became the Church – whose nature we tend to forget. It is Christ in us, our life free of death and its fears and its calculations. And do we not see at this crucial time two rival accounts of what the Church is: one forward-looking to a humanity in love, the other nostalgic and full of suspicion and fear? The nostalgic account takes a low view of the Vatican II document *Gaudium et Spes*, as representing the shallow optimism of the nineteen sixties. The other, dynamic, account celebrates that document and sees in it the mind of him who prayed 'that they, all humans, be one, Father, as you and I are one'.

To be a Catholic Christian is to dare to foresee in a humanity that is still murderous the humanity born of our great murder, in which the neighbour is the beloved. And God desires merciful forgiveness and not sacrifice – the knowledge of God not burnt offerings. And so we come back to our text in travail. I want mercy not sacrifice, knowledge of God not burnt offerings. Let up and know me. Be still and know the loving silence. You missed the point when I gave you back your victim as yourself. You miss it still as you fill the air with your religious noise in my name, starting in Rome and echoing in an angry reacting Church.

Nothing so deafens us to the word of God as religious noise. And this is no big deal. The suspension of thinking to hear the heart of creativity has been taught to children, and creative scientists have always known it. E. M. Forster wrote of 'poor talkative Christianity', powerless against the 'ou-boom' of the Malabar caves. As the world begins to hear the sound of silence, the Church cannot continue to associate God with religious noise. The Church's task is the huge one, to get the triumph of life over death into non-mythic language, into the triumph of life in you and me over the fear in you and me that is also fear *between* you and me.

Saving Passion
A sermon on the same topic.

As we again inch up to the crucial event of all history, I feel the need further to exorcise a notion that has absolutely bedevilled our thinking about the sacrifice of Calvary. This is the pestilential notion, never spelt out because it can't be without blasphemy, that Calvary is a human sacrifice in the primitive sense that, because of the theological status of the victim, is acceptable to God. This never-spelt-out idea tries to preserve itself like a neurosis, for it suits precisely the cruelty in the psyche that God is working to cure us of. Thus when I try to smoke out the idea, it says: 'No, you've got it wrong, you have to think of the love with which Jesus offered himself to his Father on the cross.'

But this love had no truck with the monster God of human sacrifice. This love led Jesus to walk deliberately into the role of scapegoat on which our fallen world depends for its ordering, in order to set us free forever of this horror and make us lovers not cannibals. He took the place of the paschal lamb, thus going to the human root of animal sacrifice in order to pull it up by the root. This involved a psychological suffering that hardly bears thinking about. The only other place in Scripture where a prophet is tragically candid with the God who is exposing him to mob violence is Jeremiah. The contrast between that man's outspoken bitterness at God and the attitude of Jesus is astonishing. With Jesus there is an absorption of his coming annihilation in a huge incomprehensible tenderness, expressed in the angel of the agony. We are in another dimension, getting a psychological insight into the birth of the new man in groans and cries, and it was this opening of the heart that broke the body's language code into a sweat of blood. And this God does not 'accept' him as a 'sacrifice'. He says: 'Folks, let's call things by their names. It's murder. You did my boy in, and it's by forgiving you this most deeply rooted sin that I change you forever. So let's have a party to celebrate till the end of the world your emancipation from hating me and killing one another to disguise this ugly secret!'

The first Christians were known as atheists because they didn't have a sacrifice. The only cultic sacrifice we know is the ritual meal shared by the victim with his friends on the eve of the horror they were all to go through. I understand now why I was fascinated by the theory of Maurice de la Taille SJ, the only theologian who understood the ritual meal as the substance of Christ's sacrifice. One of his fans, incidentally, was Paul Cézanne. Beauty recognises itself across any gap.

The Mass is a ritual meal that takes a long time over grace – a grace heavy with a dangerous and transforming memory. And here is a vital conclusion. God did not accept the bleeding body of his Son as a sacrifice in any intelligible and decent sense of those words.

> A meal that takes a long time over grace
> We have to know him by whose blood we spilled
> That genius inspired him to embrace
> Within the rite he with his Father willed.

> This fix of flesh and blood in bread and wine
> Imprints their owner on us for all time.
> No one else figures in this way to mine
> Our treasury of memory and crime.

> All our attempts at peace will founder on
> Partial foundations, we are split in two,
> Body and mind divide, we are alone,
> The rite that makes them one is human true.

> Festal and murderous, we must succumb
> To him who lays this table and says 'Come!'

The One Coming

Written in December 1995, this was an early, but rather clear, attempt to articulate the mystery of Jesus on the cross as our scapegoat.

Last week, everyone, even non-cricket people like myself, was stunned by the achievement of Michael Atherton, the batsman who held out for over ten hours under blazing sun and saved our side. Now an article in the *Independent* tells me that not so long ago Atherton was very unpopular over a decision he made as captain. We should not be surprised at this. There is only a hair's breadth between lionising someone and crucifying him. Palm Sunday and Good Friday are two sides of the same coin.

The coin is called scapegoating. Man the intelligent animal is, because of intelligence, by far the most violent animal on earth. Rivalry is woven into the way we become aware of ourselves. Again I recall the example of two two-year-olds on the rug surrounded with toys. John picks up one toy, and immediately Peter wants that one and no other. The reason is that Peter is seeing, in John's grabbing of the toy, his own desire, which therefore has to be for that toy that John is interested in. If I only know I want something when I see someone else wanting it, rivalry is woven right into wanting.

Now scapegoating is the worldwide and world-old way whereby we contain this violence in us. The whole tribe focuses on one person to take it out on, and this brings them together. In the ancient world, the king was the scapegoat, and had to be slaughtered to hold the tribe together. Slowly people learned to cool this, and the time interval between crowning and sacrifice became longer and longer. But there are so many other forms for scapegoating to take. We in this country have lived for a record number of years without war, without an official Enemy. But the process is everywhere. Politics are full of it, and never more than now. Families are seldom without it – the one member everyone tends to take it out on.

It seems that we cannot live as a society without scapegoating. Yet Jesus challenges it. The parable of the Good Samaritan is so well known that we forget what Jesus was saying in choosing as his hero the most despised figure there then was. He was challenging the whole way of thinking that needs scapegoats.

So powerful and all-pervasive is the system of scapegoating that it makes a scapegoat of the one who challenges it. This is an irony that any good novelist would give a fortune to have invented. Jesus says: 'You don't need to marginalise anyone, to victimise anyone', and for saying this he is himself victimised. He is lifted up on the very cross that he says we don't have to put people on out of fear. God's story is the best novel in the world. God's plan is the best plot. God, in the person of his Son, lets himself be caught in the trap we're all in, and then he does the most outrageous thing of all. He becomes, on his cross, attractive to us, and this breaks the fundamental rule on which the whole system of scapegoating rests: the victim is supposed to stay victim, stay on the other side, stay excluded – that's what victimising is for. Perhaps you can remember a moment in a long-standing family row when suddenly you found yourself in sympathy with the person you had all united in disapproving of. Well, Jesus is that person drawing you to himself. In John's account he says: 'Lift me up on your cross, and I'll draw everyone to myself!'

This scapegoat becomes the person we want to be. He comes to us with all his allure out of his death, meets us by the lake. There is Jesus, on the side of the excluded, inviting us across to that side! And so he shines before us as God's alluring alternative to the way we live. (If you want to get the feel of who the risen Jesus was for his disciples, read that last chapter of John's gospel, substituting 'we' for 'they'.)

To join him, though, we must be ready to listen to what he says, particularly about loving our enemies. The main thing he is teaching me is that being unforgiving and taking myself too seriously are one and the same thing. I have to let go of this, to let myself experience the strange excitement in thinking differently about someone I have always regarded as my enemy, as on the other side of the gap. 'Love your enemies, pray for those who persecute you!' says this amazing new man who is offering you new life in place of the half-life we've all become contented with.

Now here comes the point. This new life free of the old way of living is continuously coming to be in us, continually hatching. We're still stuck in the old, and so he is continually coming for us. The new life beyond scapegoating, the new politics of love, is always erupting. It has happened. It is happening. It is still to come. It's all one coming. Anyone who has tasted Jesus knows this: he or she knows something so new and wonderful that it is always just coming, always at the doors. There's only one coming, and that is Jesus becoming himself in you and me and all the world. Tidy little minds have divided this up into three comings: two thousand years ago, now, and in heaven. Tidy little minds always win. It's part of the conspiracy to stop the real Jesus getting through to us as something wildly exciting. So we carve him up: into a Jesus in the remote past, wandering around in Palestine, a Jesus said to be in the present, just how never explained, a Jesus waiting for us in heaven, of which we have no idea whatsoever. No, give me the real Jesus whom I crucify in the person I am rejecting, who recovers that person to me as I let Jesus draw me across that gap.

The Triumph of the Holy Cross
This sermon was preached at Downside ten years later in 2005.

To know the triumph of the holy cross, don't listen to Constantine's 'In this sign you will conquer!' Listen to the most stunning dialogue in the Scripture, in any Scripture:

> 'Saul, Saul, why do you persecute me?'
> 'Who are you, Sir?'
> 'I am Jesus, whom you are persecuting.'

For us moderns, this dialogue is made even more luminous by René Girard who is telling us why we crucified Jesus.

While theologians down the centuries have been looking, piously and pie-eyed, at the figure on the cross and coming up with all sorts of pious reflections, here comes René Girard, the Poirot of theology, and asks: 'Who did it, does it, and why?' And, cunning Frenchman that he is, he looks not only at Christianity but at all the big religions, and finds them all channelling violence into human sacrifice. And then the blinding truth comes upon him that will estrange him from all his colleagues in the academic world. In Christianity alone, the innocence of the victim which, once it comes out, exposes the killing as nothing but a social stabiliser, not only comes out but shines forth: he is the word of God in the flesh who embraces his repentant killers who become his body, crying out in the mind of the Pharisee: 'Saul, Saul why are you persecuting me, your rejected humanity?'

In one of Paul's accounts, the voice goes on to say: 'It is hard for you to kick against the goad!' No one hates truth until it contradicts a bias you are living in, then you hate it because it hurts. That's the goad, and when Paul gave way, the glory of truth burst in on him and blinded him and threw him to the ground leaving him helpless, to take instruction from others who too had seen the risen victim, and then piece it all together in the covenantal language he knew. The biased mind of a provincial religious man, disarranged by truth and reassembled, became the mind of Paul, to which come the certainties we live by: that we are the body of the man we killed in ignorance, that we have the mind of Christ, that we are a new humanity, *ecclesia*, a polity of love not power, that loving one another as we love ourselves is the fulfilment not of a command but of our radical desire.

It is a wonderful contemplative exercise to set side by side in the mind, '*l'horreur humaine de la crucifixion*', as Girard calls it, and the new man described in the incandescent words of Paul, and to say: this comes out of that in the mind of a man disarranged and reassembled by 'the power that raised Jesus from the dead', not thought of as a celestial crane but as the power to make all things new.

This is the triumph of the holy cross. We enjoy it articulated in his ritual of bread and wine: the victim, till then muzzled and silenced by the world, speaking for himself and for all of us: 'My body for you!'

After the Above Sermon!

If they had all said to me 'that was great!'
There would not be the feel that there is now
Happy bewilderment, a lifted weight,
Something in me I can at last allow.

Allow me, God said to the raging Saul:
It threw him to the ground and made him blind,
The violence in his religious soul
Confronted with its victim, him to find.

Allow, allow, aloud his word at last
The victim in us risen to embrace
In a new body, all our cares cast
Away into the silence that is grace

That rises in me in the aftermath
Of failed communication under wrath.

A Fuller Account of our Salvation by the Cross
Sebastian keeps straining for a deeper understanding of salvation by the cross. In this very recent piece there is a bit more progress. It draws, as so often in his writing, on the thought of James Alison.

According to the ideas of Girard, scapegoating is a social mechanism that puts an end to 'violence as the price of order'. And Jesus, in the most religiously focused event in the most explicitly monotheistic faith – that of Israel – is the universal scapegoat. But why *have* a universal scapegoat at all if not to put an end to all 'violence as the price of order', and how does this work?

First, let me spell out the way in which 'violence is the price of order'. It is the way of intimidation; its weapon is fear. So the purpose of the universal scapegoat, that is the scapegoat for everybody, that is the willing scapegoat, is to set people free of the horrible need to kill people in order to survive, which means to introduce them into a world no longer ruled by death as intimidation.

But how is this done? How does the willing scapegoat set people free of the need to survive at the expense of others as victims – a survival that is shameful, cowardly, and without human dignity; a survival that is most manifest in the traitor who *sells* the victim. (This, by the way, is not Judas-bashing. Judas has a key role in the drama.) So let me repeat my present question: How does the willing scapegoat set people free of the need to survive at each others' expense, the shameful need horribly manifest in Orwell's *1984* when Winston, under the threat of 'the worst thing in the world', cries out: 'Do it to Julia!'? How does the willing scapegoat set people free of this awful need?

Here, I suggest, is the answer to this question. He does it by going to his death in a way that makes his own *followers* its most immediate and shameful beneficiaries – siding with the enemy to save their own skins, by deserting him, betraying him, denying him. It is these men who, shamefully spared the tortured death of Rome's victims by deserting their leader, are later shown him risen and all-forgiving, unaccusing, all-embracing, the nearest there can be to a realistic understanding of us being part of his body. Caiaphas, prophetically and correctly, said that one man must die to save the people. The people that man most poignantly saved by dying alone were his *followers* to whom, totally demoralised through betraying him, he showed himself the new man for all of us.

Once we have seen this, the text shouts it at us. Arrested, Jesus says: 'Let these go!' and good old Matthew finds a prophetic verification here. Peter says: 'I'll die with you!' and Jesus says: 'No you won't, you'll deny me!' John, who spells it all out (spills the beans if you like) has Jesus say to Peter: 'Where I am going you cannot come now, but you will come hereafter, converted, confirming the brethren, dying in imitation of *my* new world-saving death'.

This is how *that* man's death puts death behind *me* his disciple. I've had to go through the route of fear and betrayal and denial into the freedom of the Kingdom of God that ends the reign of death.

Certainly it is by a sacrament, baptism, that I die his death. But the sacrament expresses the transformative human event of being delivered from the fear that besets and rules us all. Otherwise, baptism into his death is a game of 'let's pretend!' For the vast majority of us, the allowing him to take the fear out of us takes place years after our baptism, and acts it out.

Having fear taken out of you is, come to think of it, a frightening experience. You wouldn't think so, perhaps, but really reflect on how useful fear has been to you since your life began, from the first burn. To have that safety device removed would certainly be scary; that's why Tolle, as he felt himself detached from his life with all its cares, scars and fears, and sucked down into a void, heard the words: 'Resist nothing!' Fear is the ego's constant companion, and he was to be deprived of it! Fear keeps the show going the way we know it and prefer it. That's why the unwise politicians of our time love and foster fear as 'security'. Fear is the torturer's litany to be recited as the treatment is administered: 'You're on your own; your wife's taken a lover; you're worthless!' Fear was awakened with the arrest of Jesus, and extracted when he came to them and said: 'Peace be to you, do not be afraid!' 'Do not be afraid!' is the leitmotif of the revealer; it is all over the gospel story.

> Our native hunger for an unknown God
> Points straight to Jesus its own naked witness
> Who says be children, never take the sword
> And turns the question thus to my own fitness
>
> Asking what do I fear, with my defence
> Touching the dread of nothing underneath
> A passionate requirement to make sense
> In spite of Hardy and his Egdon Heath.
>
> This fear of nothing is God in reverse,
> I've got to go there, and there Jesus goes
> And lifts from those who see a primal curse
> To wake a tingle fingers feel and toes,

For there is meeting we have yet to find:
Jesus and Buddha in a fuller mind.

Jesus – the Nakedness of God

Before He revealed himself in Jesus, it seemed as if God were behind many of the violent and fearful things that happened to us. But, through the vulnerability of Jesus we now see that this is not so. God is on our side and, in this passage from Romans, Paul strains to express this amazing revolution.

> What then are we to say about these things? If God is for us, who is against us? He who did not withhold his own Son, but gave him up for all of us, will he not with him also give us everything else? Who will bring any charge against God's elect? It is God who justifies. Who is to condemn? It is Christ Jesus, who died, yes, who was raised, who is at the right hand of God, who indeed intercedes for us. Who will separate us from the love of Christ? Will hardship, or distress, or persecution, or famine, or nakedness, or peril, or sword? As it is written, 'For your sake we are being killed all the day long; we are accounted as sheep to be slaughtered.' No, in all these things we are more than conquerors through him who loved us. For I am convinced that neither death, nor life, nor angels, nor rulers, nor things present, nor things to come, nor powers, nor height, nor depth, nor anything else in all creation, will be able to separate us from the love of God in Christ Jesus our Lord. (Rom. 8: 31-39.)

To understand how totally revolutionary this passage is, we have to remember, what Paul does not say, that until Jesus, and still for us in our normal spiritual torpor, all the violent things in the world that we live in fear of seemed to have God behind them, were parts of God's control over us, were giving God a bad name. With the execution of his Son by us, God has let us use the violence of the world against him, and he doesn't mind, he comes through to us as who he really is – God for us in love. The power, the force which we took to be his armour, he lets us use against him – and here I use a double, and I hope not mixed metaphor, in which this armour, used against him with his permission, vanishes to leave him naked to us as our lover. Paul never knew Jesus, yet, ecstatic with what Jesus had shown him, he makes a list of all the fearful things he can think of in the world and makes them zero in face of 'the love of God in Christ Jesus our Lord'. Don't make a vague pious package of that phrase; understand it as Calvary bursting on Saul on his way to Damascus. With Jesus killed by us and raised to show God, God has changed sides. He is now with us against all the terrible things in the world that we feared he would use against us. Zbigniew Herbert, the modern Jewish poet, understood this, and he thought God cheated and should have left things as they were, with death 'God's baton' to keep us in order. He understood, as Christian authors tend not to understand, as they consign those amazing words of Paul to the funeral parlour. With Jesus crucified and raised up before us, death peals away from God as the skin from a ripe fruit.

> Jesus stripper for God
> Whose armour, death, we use
> Against him and, how odd,
> He doesn't mind, this ruse
>
> Divests him of the threat
> We saw as his at us:
> This is his biggest bet
> The jackpot all and plus.
>
> Us killing him he lets
> Divest him of the armour
> Of all our guilty debts
> To find him naked, amor.
>
> And now lazy old Rome
> May copy his strip-tease
> And be at last our home
> Put us in love at ease.

After a Good Friday Sermon

How easy it is to be seduced into seeing Christ as 'God in disguise' – if only they had known! And the passion story becomes like a well-known movie, that all comes right in the end, three days later. But Christ was actually God, not in disguise but revealed, and through the passion we all took it out on him –

all our fear, frustration and anger at God's ways. (This was in 2005 soon after the Asian tsunami.) Yet through the resurrection, God takes us out of fear into love.

The best book on the Eucharist ever written has long been out of print. It is called *On Breaking Bread* by Fr P. Fitzpatrick, whom some have known as the most brilliant lecturer in philosophy. One of his key ideas is that there are two notions of how sacraments work, one right, the other wrong. In the right one, sacraments are *signs*. In the wrong one, they are *disguises*.

The 'disguises' view he characterises by the 'imagined Galilean'. There he was, pacing the countryside, God in human disguise. It's 'little did they realise' language. When it comes to the sacraments, and supremely with the Eucharist, it's the *Adoro te devote, latens deitas*. 'Sight taste and touch in thee are each deceived.' But deception through the senses is what a sacrament does *not* do. The bread and wine reveal Jesus as our *real* food and drink. The Mass is a ritual meal that takes a long time over grace because there's so much to be thankful for, including ourselves, and also that there is anything at all.

Now this Good Friday I have come to see that Christ is not 'God in disguise' but God made visible. He is not God in disguise and crucified because they didn't know who he was, but God made visible and thus able to have taken out on him all our real feelings about the hidden face behind all that afflicts us. The sayings of Jesus are freedom-sayings straight from God as he provokes all our fear of each other into freedom with each other. Outrageous sayings like 'Oh leave the dead to bury their dead!' They are sayings of the eminently crucifiable. That's why he never answers questions the way they are put to him: he's putting off his crucifixion until his 'time has come'. And always there is Paul's use of a verse in Psalm 69: 'The insults of those who insult you (God) have fallen on me (your Son)'.

What triggered this new realisation was the recognition that the God-intimacy of Jesus – the theme of the beautiful ending discourses in John – is the cause of the trouble they are in. Outside is the night ready to arrest him in the small hours and destroy him in the daylight. We have been seduced by the beauty of these discourses into the 'imagined Galilean' whose mystery wasn't allowed to interfere, in our minds, with the politics of the occasion. Thinking about the beautiful Good Friday sermon, I was (mistakenly) hearing it in 'imagined Galilean' terms: the horrible deed done by people who should have known better, being God's people, but never mind, it all comes right on Sunday.

Heard this way, the passion story is a too-well-known movie, with a paid projectionist to show it. Replay it now, with us the projectionist, put our agency into the crucifixion, and the whole scene changes. For then the resurrection comes not as a happy ending to a worn-out story but as the self-revelation of the God we crucify in fear of each other (he put us together so it's his fault!). He relaxes us out of this fear into love – the *ecclesia* of the drawn-together by him raised up. All that the passion sermon needs is for the hearer to be recalling the inspired words in a new Mass canon: 'He gave himself into our hands and was nailed to a cross'. And just to reiterate: God gave himself into our hands to act out our *real* feelings on him, to kill him who only in death was able to relax us out of fear into love.

The divinity of Jesus was not the hidden reality that *we* know – and crucifying Jews should have known but didn't – but what was *actually getting him crucified*. Jesus is our God-given chance of taking it out on God – Jesus as sign of God, not as God in disguise. So the resurrection is God getting through to us at last as the victim of our fear who returns to us, relaxing us into love. 'Those hands that once blessed and healed now mutilated, but cheer up, tomorrow they will bless again' – actually we didn't need cheering up, we were too bored. No, what I should hear is: 'Those hands we transfixed to keep our fear, now hold us and relax us into peace in love'.

> Those hands we crucified to keep our fear
> Relax us now into our peace in love.
> We never understood how God came near
> Or why a victim must be from above.
>
> Sublime discourses in the Upper Room
> Tell of the rage now gathering outside
> So that the diners feed only on doom
> Words off his tongue who will be crucified.
>
> Not for our entertainment liturgy
> Recalls the death whose sequel we well know
> And yawn at, for we miss God's making-free
> With us who keep our fear at endless No.

> I wish I could persuade all those who preached
> To us the place in me so nearly reached.

(A Holy Week liturgy that is not about our transformation by the God
we crucify becomes a movie too well known and boring.)

> Liturgy not about our transformation
> By God we crucify relaxes us
> Is played before us with all the vexation
> Of a bad movie, we incurious.

> We know the end, it is the church tomorrow
> All flowers and white as now it is all bare
> And nothing that will touch effective sorrow
> Totally lost to us the Jesus dare.

> Do this, he said, and not to tame me with
> But to wake so into a deeper sleep
> Beyond all the resources of our myth
> The true complacency of pastured sheep.

> Don't run it by me again and leave me dry
> But wake in me the voice says 'crucify!'

Progress Report – 2005

*This is the text of a short address given to Downside 'old boys' during their
annual Eastertide Retreat in 2005. It is a kind of summing up of what the
preceding pieces have been straining towards. Why did Jesus become a
'willing scapegoat'? In some sense or another we have to see him as 'taking a
big risk'.*

Every Good Friday I'm allowed to make a progress report on my
lifelong attempt to understand Jesus and what he does for us. This
time, I remember Lynn Marie, a little girl friend of mine (she's married
now) in Columbia, Maryland. She was being prepared by her father
for her first communion, which she was to have from me at the
Christmas family mass. Her reaction to the story of Jesus when it came
to the passion was: 'Why didn't he run away?' Eric her father replied:

'I suppose he thought he wasn't supposed to', and her reaction was: 'But that's dumb!'

Her remark exposed the inability of preachers to describe in non-theological language the action that changed the world for ever. Experts in anything get trapped in their language. Some time ago, a questionnaire was sent out to science graduate students in the States, asking them to say what went on in the mind of Archimedes as he lowered himself in his bath and saw the water rising. None of them was able to do so without using technical terms like specific gravity. If even experts in physics are trapped in their language, how much more so are experts in the salvation of the world!

What, in his gut thinking, told Jesus he had to go up to Jerusalem and the horror that was crucifixion? What was it that he accepted into himself at Gethsemani causing him to sweat blood? Just once I heard a preacher say: 'Jesus took a big risk' – but he didn't go on to say what the risk was. He left that to Jesus. The boldest attempt I ever heard was in the form of a question asked by that rugged Scottish theologian Donald McKinnon, who stopped in his tracks as he walked up and down thinking out loud, and asked: 'Was there that which Jesus alone could do, in the way in which it had to be done, which was of such moment for humanity that the risk was justified, the cost well spent?'

Now look at those sublime discourses of Jesus at the end of John's gospel, where he talks about him and his Father. It is only this year, at the age of eighty-seven, that I have noticed that this unique oneness of Jesus with God is what's got them all into the trouble they're in tonight at supper, their hearts full of fear. For this relationship, lived out of and taught out of and contagious for his disciples, challenged religion to crucify him. And it caused in his followers a complete psychological breakdown, precipitated by being brutally deprived of that presence after all those years, making it possible for the real God, who is all peace and love, to get through to them with the sight of him risen.

Thus God relaxes us out of our deep fear of each other and creates, out of our murderous species, an *ecclesia* united, not by power, but by love, the extension of Jesus the intimate of God, a community that is 'one, Father, as you and I are one'.

I think that's an improvement.

CHAPTER 4

Resurrection and Eucharist

To understand the resurrection we have first to understand the 'reign of death'. Man, out of communion with God, however much he may create his own lesser gods or deny his need for God, is faced with that ultimate darkness – fear of death and of the unknown beyond. Now Jesus was a real man who lived in a real historical time and place and who died, and in his resurrection swept away this ultimate fear of death – conquered the 'reign of death'. The most visible sign of death is the corpse; the most visible sign of Jesus' resurrection was the empty tomb – there was no corpse.

The resurrection itself remains mysterious. It was neither some 'conjuring trick with bones', nor some 'spiritualist' manifestation from the 'other side'. Its most important evidence comes from the small band of Jesus' followers. Their life was completely renewed, shaken with delirious joy as their 'hearts burned within them'. This was far more important to them, and to us, than any kind of attempted rational explanation of what actually 'happened'. In some real sense they were taken up into Jesus' new corporal body.

And this touches on our understanding of the Eucharist. Theology has debated over the formula: 'bread becomes the body of Jesus', leading to the awkward neologism of 'transubstantiation'. But it is much more important to contemplate Jesus' own formulation: 'my body for you' – his body becomes bread, food, for us, which we eat.

Sadly for most of history, the Mass, the celebration of the Eucharist, has been separated into two parts, with the emphasis being placed on the first part, the consecration, the bread and wine becoming Jesus, while the second half, the ritual meal of Jesus' body as food, seemed to be almost an afterthought.

The Light of Easter

This was written at Easter in 1993. It is part of Sebastian's lifelong attempt to understand and convey the mystery of Jesus' passion and resurrection. In it he tries to understand what is meant by 'the reign of death' and how Jesus overcomes it.

The only background against which we can know what we mean by saying that 'Christ is risen' is the deepest theological understanding of the meaning of death. The suggested source for this understanding is the Greek patristic tradition. According to this tradition the human being, designed and destined for union with God, is 'fallen' out of this knowing of God, and of all things in God, into 'the knowledge of good and evil'. Phillis Trible, in her superb book, *God and the Rhetoric of Sexuality*, understands this as 'a knowledge of which God is not the source', that is, a non-knowledge.

Fallen out of God and communion, man finds himself alone with death his ultimate horizon and survival his top priority, so that violence and war become justified. This 'reign of death', death in place of God as the ultimate perspective in which man lives, is terrible. In it, death becomes the symbol of that frightful 'nothing' that draws us to sin as a black hole sucks light into itself without trace.

Jesus was man as he originally – not in history certainly, only in the divine intention – is. But he was absolutely part of our history, he was totally under the reign of death. Death swallowed him up and introduced him into the ultimate negativity into which we are fallen. Hans Urs von Balthasar was right when he said, years ago, that the 'descent into hell' was going to be the central Christian mystery for modern man. Every Holy Saturday, I feel more deeply this tasting of *Sheol* by Christ. In it I learn more about the ravages of death-as-ultimate in my own way of thinking and being in the world.

But this swallowing of Jesus by death is, perforce, death as it is for un-fallen man, that is, the removing of the final obstacle of finitude to union with God. There is thus a trans-valuation of death. Everything that death means for fallen man, all the horror of history, all the concentration camps, emblems of the cynical reply of mortality to all claims to be Godlike, and all the depths of my own affair with the bottomless pit of my own life, all this, and nothing less than all this, is to be understood as the death that Jesus has undergone and changed from the gateway-to-nothing into the gateway into divine union.

The 'death' over which we celebrate, with a great candle in a darkened church, the triumph of Jesus, comprises far, far more of us, of
our history, of our self-approval, of our compromises, than we ever
admit. It is real death, death for fallen man, death for the spiritual
being fallen out of God into the reign of emptiness. It is this darkness
that we hardly begin to acknowledge in ourselves, of which the light
of that candle symbolises the dissipation.

All this darkness is swallowed up in God. If we do not feel
the darkness, feel its caress in the small hours of our despair, in the
hopelessness of the teenage suicide and the loneliness that covers
the world, we do not know what is its dissipation by the light.

But how can anything so momentous, so unbelievable, as the divine
displacement of this darkness, be shown to us? The answer is:
dramatically.

This is the drama of the empty tomb. The absence of the body is the
sign of something that cannot possibly be seen or imagined, and only
conceived in a mind-transforming faith, namely the coming of Jesus,
through death the god of fallen humanity, into the fullness of the
Godhead. The corpse, sign for fallen man of the triumph of his god, is
not there! And if you think you know what is there, you've got it wrong!

But if we do not understand, if we do not remember to be human as
we contemplate the Easter Mystery, then the empty tomb immediately
becomes trivialised. It is then understood as the sign of something of
the same order essentially as the sign itself, namely, an imaginable
enlivening of the body, the whole anthropology of death forgotten, 'a
conjuring trick with bones', as David Jenkins said. We have moved –
such is the human capacity for inducing total unconsciousness – from
a world glimpsed by Dostoyevsky, to a world confidently envisioned
by the creator of Sherlock Holmes.

Aquinas, in a cooler way, introduces us to the same dynamic. For
him, the empty tomb is a fact. And at the same time, for him the
resurrection itself is a mystery, strictly so-called, that cannot be witnessed or imagined. There is no way to combine these two ideas other
than to say that the empty tomb is the *outside*, the historical deposit,
the drama, of what on the *inside* is ineffable.

What that ineffable reality is I have tried to hint. It is the realisation
of God's original intention for this mad being that we are, a realisation
that takes into its sweep the last depth of our alienation and proneness
to the nothing whence we are drawn, and, with Easter, drawn all the
way into infinite being.

God forbid that we should think we can imagine as a corpse in the hands of a divine mortician the darkness that the light of Easter dissipates!

And finally here is a grisly example of the kind of preaching that has not grasped the above principle. It is taken from *The Virgin in the Garden* by A. S. Byatt:

> Mr Ellenby preached on St Paul. He assured his congregation that if Christ had not risen there would be no church and they themselves would be condemned to eternal death. 'If after the manner of men', said Mr Ellenby, adjusting his glasses, licking his dry lips, 'I have fought with beasts at Ephesus, what advantageth it me, if the dead rise not? Let us eat and drink; for tomorrow we die'. 'A terrible saying', said Mr Ellenby, beating his fist on the stone edge of his pulpit, smiting it, 'if we were not assured that Christ is alive now, that the natural processes, so terrible, were thwarted and changed, a dead heart beat and dead feet walked, decomposition was stayed and reversed, and therefore we rejoice, in fear, because we too live forever'. The people nodded and smiled as they nodded and smiled annually and Stephanie felt every stage of rejection, from embarrassed discourtesy to frozen hate.

Fifty Days

The focus in this essay, which is much more recent, is on the effect of Jesus' resurrection on his small band of followers. The delirious joy that they experienced, the 'making of all things new', their new community consciousness in 'the body of Christ' – all of this is the real meaning of the resurrection.

We take fifty days to celebrate Easter, not only because it takes that long for this revolution to sink in. We take fifty days to remember that it took that long for the nascent community to become attuned to a new state of affairs constituted by the victim of Calvary now alive among them differently and more fully – among them in this world of ours, upsetting it.

The life to which Jesus has come is not what we call life after death, 'on the other side', the life we never take quite seriously (hence all the silly jokes about the pearly gates) that the Hebrew mind was appropriately gloomy about. No, it is among the disciples *as they are* that he is alive, shaking them, appearing now and then and here and there, strangely, not recognised at first, then recognised with delirious joy. They were subjected to this *now* of Jesus, of 'still here but otherwise', for a stretch of time of crucial importance for the Church, for the new togetherness called *ecclesia*. They were called together by him who, 'in terms of the Spirit and of holiness was designated Son of God in power by resurrection from the dead', as Paul puts it in the opening of his Letter to the Romans. There is a new togetherness, of God's love among us in place of the mimetic glue that holds societies together but always on the edge of violence.

This new togetherness or *koinonia* is the reason for the ambiguity that a great scholar has found in Paul over the phrase 'the body of Christ'. Is he talking about the body we killed or the body we are? They are hardly distinguishable, so intimately are we the body of Christ. Robinson got it right when he said that the word 'body' has to be understood 'not corporately but corporally'.

Now it is this total takeover of community consciousness by the new risen presence that accounts for something often remarked on in the gospel accounts of the resurrection: that they don't add up, that they can't be harmonised. As Rowan Williams trenchantly puts it: 'If the evangelists were trying to make the resurrection credible the way they make the story of the passion credible, they did a devastatingly bad job.' They did devastatingly badly what they weren't trying to do at all. They were doing something else. They were telling us what it was like to have Jesus among them in this new way. And because they were totally possessed by this new awareness, it did not occur to them to wonder how the body got from its cadaverous condition to Jesus now. And do you know why this bothers us? It's because we have so very little sense of Jesus now.

We need to hear again, as if for the first time, the question of the angel to the women at the empty tomb: 'Why are you looking for the living among the dead?' What's in the mind of the evangelist is the contrast between Jesus then and Jesus now, because the sense of Jesus now is so overpowering. We don't feel the *now* of Jesus because we don't feel ourselves as a new community, which is the same thing as feeling the now of Jesus, Jesus as the focus of the power of now, Jesus as what he has now become. So if God hasn't yet made Jesus now for you, you find yourself trying to imagine him getting out of the tomb – 'emerging'. The fact is, we have no image whatsoever of a glorified body. Fr Aelred Watkin used to say that as *we* have him under the appearances of bread and wine, he came to *them* under the appearances of hands and feet.

A text which wonderfully conveys this contrast between Jesus *then* and Jesus *now* is a text I've never bothered with and I bet you haven't either: 'He was put to death in the flesh, but made alive in the Spirit' (1 Pet. 3: 19). You might even have seen it as confusing matters – there was that business with the former Bishop of Durham. Don't let's get bogged down in that again. The transition from the body dead to the body alive was swept up for the disciples in the transition from the body we killed to the body we're in. God doesn't go about things in our plodding way. Put to death in the world we know only too well, Jesus comes alive in a new world still barely visible. 'Behold I make all things new.'

And what is meant by 'all things new'? It is our original making made plain. It is when we love one another absolutely, unconditionally, at the cost of ego and its complex claims, and with the joy of this creature finding itself at last. Jesus is the way we're made, our *ratio*, our *logos*, made visible and crucified to draw all things to himself. This is what they knew when they saw him again. This is what they are trying to tell us, what it was like when he returned to them. The eternal genius of Christianity is this making visible of our human meaning as love, our word made flesh. And that is what will persist in a Church transformed out of recognition, the Church of love, shown us unmistakably in our first fifty privileged days.

> Visibly God, he would not walk on earth
> But show himself in moments, they together,
> His incarnation in a church of mirth,
> A people they, no more birds of a feather.
>
> For sacraments are signs and not disguises,
> They show what is: so how will God be shown
> If not by us in a way that surprises
> As a community, man not alone.
>
> So how can we church mandate loneliness
> For some who are innately different?
> Taboo the cuckoo in the church's nest
> Proclaims that it is we who are the bent.

What all this comes to in time's melting-pot
I do not know, though God untied our knot.

My Body for You

Here is another necessary revision, concerning our understanding of the
Eucharist. We have to move from the traditional emphasis: 'bread becoming
Jesus', which has led to all sorts of ingenious theological speculation, to 'Jesus
becoming bread' – Christ offering us his willingly tortured crucified body as
food for our new life in love. The point may seem subtle and the piece may not
be an easy read. But the implications are far-reaching, particularly in how we
offer our bodies to each other – not least in our sexual relations.

I want to try to talk about love, realistically, politically, which means
with the Eucharist as my exemplar, for, as William Kavanagh says in
Torture and Eucharist, 'Torture is the imagination of the state. Eucharist
is the imagination of the church.' Let me start with a good formulation, by Tad Guzie from the beginning of his book *Jesus and the*
Eucharist: 'The real Jesus took real bread and identified himself with
it.'

What a self-identification! We cling to life, such as we understand it,
and this weds us to a system that preserves life by violence and thus
has its victims. We cling to life, as thus secured – even under a tyranny
such as that which Jesus lived under, of Rome and its instrument of
order, the cross. We view with guilty horror the system's victims.
They are on the other side, the underside, and we keep on this side.
And here is Jesus, our leader, we thought, taking a piece of bread and
saying: 'Take this, eat it, it's me hung!'

This is his choice, so it is of love, of a new and frightening kind. Do
those at table with him get this? Well, they taste and smell fear, which
is the first taste of invading love. And when the whole drama has been
enacted and he is showing himself in the breaking of bread, the truth
comes through. When we eat this bread and drink this cup, we
become assimilated to the love that undermines the system we live by
and opens to us another living that changes everything.

'Jesus took bread and identified himself with it.' Unpacked, this
excellent formulation describes an act of love that is unique, revelatory, and world-changing. Jesus becomes bread. The statement of
Jesus over the bread, 'This is me, hung, for you', puts him, as I say, on

the feared other side, the underside whence, through his choice to be there, he undermines by love the system we live by. And this system had ritualised itself, for Jesus, in millennia of bloody sacrifices to appease a supposedly angry God. All this, too, Jesus is undermining with that simple gesture with bread and wine – and in a way that takes one's breath away. For the context of the slaughtered paschal lamb reminds us that animal sacrifice was a benign substitute for human; so what he is doing is going back to this bloody human origin and stepping into that role – the first victim in the history of religion to speak of 'my blood'! And the love that alone puts him there finds expression in the breaking of bread among friends. So, willingly broken by us-in-our-world, upon the cross, our instrument of world order, he expresses this love by breaking himself as bread at a *convivium* with friends: a love-feast that thus subsumes a million years of bloody sacrifice, which vanish in the presence of a God who is love. That's quite a self-identification on the part of Jesus! He, the loving one, self-given to murder, becomes bread broken for us to share.

Now Jesus becoming bread involves bread somehow becoming Jesus. But how different is the question provoked by these two descriptions respectively. Jesus becomes bread. The question: 'What does this mean?' takes me right into the politics of torture and love and Peter's terrified denial with Jesus looking at him from the dock, from the dreaded other side, and the cock crowing, and Peter weeping (pope-training, Jesus-style!). It challenges everything in me. Whereas the question: 'How does bread become Jesus?' challenges only my ingenuity, a challenge to which Aquinas rose with magnificent aplomb, and reached an answer that required 'transubstantiation', a neologism for a change totally unlike change as we know it, and a presence that is 'not local'.

So if you think 'bread becoming Jesus', you teeter on the edge of nonsense, whereas if you think 'Jesus becoming bread', you come up against yourself in all your cowardice and triviality and hunger for love.

Alas, theology chose the path of ingenuity, and I recall Mary Gordon describing how, as a girl, she had to freshen their drinks for Jesuits as they explained to her father what happened to the eucharistic accidents. There is a kind of Catholic inauthenticity that is beyond the tolerance of some stomachs!

So the direction, the sweep of the Eucharist, goes from him crucified to bread and wine. He says as much: 'this bread is my body'. 'This is what I am for you, through my flesh given as the bread of life.' Joachim Jeremias, in his magisterial study of the eucharistic words of Jesus, has pointed out that the original sense of those words is that this, *this* piece of bread, is what I, crucified, am, for you to share. He regrets that theology, heavy with its own agenda of controversy, has shifted the emphasis from 'this' to 'is'. 'This is' does not merely symbolise my body. So what we have is a total derailment of the words of Jesus in deference to religious controversy. Jesus is *Alpha* and *Omega*. Get him wrong and you are wrong from start to finish.

This derailment has been fatally influential in our theology. The emphasis on the '*is*' in 'this is my body' – Aramaic has no word for 'is'! – changes the ritual role of the words. They become a performative utterance, like 'I declare a state of war'. They effect the eucharistic change as 'I absolve you' effects absolution. Aquinas actually asks at what moment the change occurs, and answers 'at the word *est*' – though it has been suggested that he had his tongue in his cheek, and the intrepid balance of his eucharistic theology suggests this. Transubstantiation is, as I say, a neologism for a change unlike any change that we can imagine or even conceive, so that his elaboration of it teeters on the edge of nonsense.

So a heavy price is paid, in intelligence itself, for not hearing in their own right the terrible words of Jesus.

It is not a question of de-emphasising the words of consecration. On the contrary, changing them from their whispered form to being declaimed emphasises them. Audible, they demand to be heard as the words of love by an ear that can hear love speaking; not, as they were when whispered, with the tin ear of theological polemics.

Make no mistake! I do not doubt transubstantiation. It is what you get if you insist on swimming intellectually upstream on the torrent of Jesus' terrible words of love for you. I can't help thinking that Aquinas somehow knew this. If you really work through his great sequence *Lauda Sion*, you find him saying over and over again that we don't break 'him', or move 'him' or do anything to 'him' except eat him and become part of him in his love for the world. Also, a presence that for Aquinas is 'not local' enables us to say: 'He is not there on the altar, with us here, sacrificing him to God'. He is 'here', and this 'here' is focused there on the altar, the Eucharist known as his 'mystical body' – with us the 'real body'. There's a pay-off from the brilliant reasoning of Aquinas, in the right hands! A young Dominican, fresh from his studies, preached a sermon explaining Aquinas' teaching on the

Eucharist. An old lady was heard to mutter: 'The man's a black Protestant!'

For only the Catholic theological tradition has had the nerve to contemplate, with the concept of transubstantiation, the joke that philosophy has to see lurking in the mystery that God has told us we must celebrate. History is important here. Aquinas came at a time when theology was teething rationally with the help of Aristotle, pulling free of the powerful rhetoric of Augustine – and incidentally preparing for modern science by asking questions of the ultimately mysterious, to which you only get probable or helpful answers.

Yes, but how does the Mass, as we have it, take us into the heart of Jesus and his love-revolution? As I take part in our daily concelebration at Downside, I try saying: 'I am not engaged in doing decently something we don't understand' but: 'I am letting myself be dragged kicking and screaming into an act of love that terrifies me'. Or, more sedately with Bernard Lonergan: 'I am about the inauthentic mediation of an authentic tradition'. It's a matter of letting him speak for himself at the Mass as he did at the supper table: 'This bread is my body for you. Take it and share it and become, for each other, my body for you.' For nearly two millennia in the west, these crucial words have been whispered inaudibly (it was a 'sin' if you could be heard more than five yards away!) by a priest crouched over the bread and then, hey presto, it's no longer bread. It has still not been understood what a revolution was effected by the reform, initiated by Vatican II, of *proclaiming* those once-whispered words. For what they say is: 'I love you as God loves you, to bloodshed. I break myself as bread for you to share and become bread that is broken for each other'. These dramatic words are God's de-mystification of religion by love, and we have used them to re-mystify it around a magic moment, a conjuring trick.

Of course the main reason for this monstrous derailing, even de-sacramentalising of the Eucharist, was this. To say that Jesus identified himself crucified with bread and wine is equivalent to saying that he created a symbol: and the word 'symbol' was taboo for Catholics, who saw it as Protestant. Thus we learned our religion in what Cardinal de Lubac called the worst possible way – against someone else.

'My body for you'. Once we really hear those words of Jesus in the Mass, and eat and drink him as he there gives himself, his words find a resonance right down to the depths of our bodily being. And if we do open up to this resonance by asking the most basic question about ourselves, then we do not know what hits us. We are reborn. We begin to taste the fulfilment of our most foundational desire: to be for another and for others. Though we don't realise it until we really fall in love, this desire is what we're made for, and we are frustrated until its release in us. Jesus, says Paul, 'died for all, so that those who live might live no longer for themselves, but for him who died and was raised for them' (2 Cor. 5: 15). To live for myself is that ultimate misery that we call hell. To live for another and for others is what Jesus calls heaven. We only partially know this about ourselves, but congenitally we are *lovers*, and only so do we have a hint of happiness.

All of this includes our sexuality. For you can't talk about love without getting into sex, love in the flesh. Don't forget, what we're doing is tracing the resonance of Jesus' love words at table down to the roots of our being, to see how they work there. Paul gives us the clue here when he says: 'The body is not for fornication but for the Lord'. What this does not mean is: the body is not for sex but for higher things. What it does mean is: sex is not 'your body for me' but 'my body for you', that is, love, of which Jesus gave us the supreme demonstration in those very words, when he took the bread, blessed it, and broke it, saying, 'my body, given to the torturers and broken as bread for you'. That's what Paul means. The body is to go the Lord's way, of love, of sacrifice, of self-gift – which, because God knew what he was doing when he made us, is the way of good sex. Forgive me this celibate glibness!

What Paul archaically calls 'fornication' means 'your body for me'. This is the logo of our sex-obsessed culture. 'Your body for me' means your body serving my needs, meeting a requirement of mine. What requirement? The sexual, but now seen simply as a part of me that has to be satisfied. Now the worst thing about this inversion of Jesus' words into the logo is that it powerfully reinforces a tendency of the western psyche to have its sexual energy trapped in the lower part of the body, what Hindu philosophy calls the second *chakra*.

There is no release of our sexual energy from this low-entrapment except through the recovery of love as the heart of sex. The other formula, 'my body for you', has to be recovered and lived by, an attitude, in which sex can take root and live out the full meaning of the Eucharist.

Our whole fulfilment is to discover love in a culture of death, so that the weary pursuit of 'your body for me' gives way to 'my body for you'. Then, and only then, do we understand the Mass, of which those words, spoken by the to-be-crucified for us, are the key words.

At Mass

Why are we bored as we proclaim the death
Of our own victim till he comes again
If not because, deep in our underneath
We seek relief in visiting of pain

Upon those who disturb our settled way,
Ignore the sacrifice that is required
Of everything from Tesco's day-by-day
To how our civilization is wired.

Before we can come at this source of grace
That we call Eucharist, we need to think
More deeply, join anew the human race
And meet ourselves as killers on the brink.

At Mass today I was allowed to feel
A numbness whereupon his grace may steal.

The Eucharist and Liturgical Reform

For most of history the liturgical form of the Mass has tended, wrongly, to emphasise the transformation of the bread and wine, rather than its sharing among the Christian community as the body and blood of Christ in a ritual meal. The changes introduced by Vatican II finally restored the balance. Reintroduction of the Tridentine rite should be seen as a backward and theologically mistaken step.

The history of the Church can be seen as the history of fragments of a big picture, of *homo ludens*, humanity in celebration, centred on a dangerous memory, of a murder whose echoes are the material of history, victims everywhere, violence everywhere, all the stuff we learned, in chaotic dissociation, as history in school. One continuous element of the tapestry is 'the Mass', variously called and celebrated – for important occasions, for superstitious purposes, and even sold to pay for the sins of the rich. As we attempt to piece together this ritual action, the Church at worship, we encounter a split. On the one hand, there is the *transformation* of bread and wine into the body and blood of the victim slain by us humans. On the other hand there is the

sharing of the bread and wine thus transformed. Now the bread and
wine are thus transformed *to be* shared, but this is not what we see in
the rite as performed for most of its history. The action seems to be
arrested at the transformation, with the sharing almost an afterthought
that for most of the history of the rite did not happen, the elements
being consumed by the priest alone.

The transformation was everything. Where the eating was concerned
(never the drinking, that was for the priest alone) this was private, a
devotion for the single communicant, not the completion of the rite
itself. Even Aquinas said that this sacrament is perfected before it is
eaten. There was of course much emphasis on *what* is eaten by the
communicant – creating the rumour that Catholics eat flesh, so that it
had to be explained that this was not cannibalism, which made us
emphasise *what* is eaten rather than *that there is eating*. And I recall, the
way I do these days, that as I tried to make sense of the Mass talking to
the old monk who was teaching us these things, he suddenly said,
exasperated: 'You seem to be wanting to attach importance to the *eating*.'
Damn right I was, though I understood next to nothing at that stage.

The split between priest and people seems to stem from a split in the
Mass itself between the Founder's instruction to 'take bread and wine'
and the instruction to 'eat and drink', the former swallowed up in
complex explanations that juggle with Aristotelian categories, the
latter either forgotten or done in private.

The Mass has a history. But the one thing that Christianity is about,
the divine response to man's cry for ultimate meaning that gathers
people and peoples into one in love, does not stand out in the history
of the Mass. So liturgical reform, if it is deemed necessary, is not done
by choosing a 'good' period in the past and taking this as a model.
Nor, however, can it be done *without* a model, a basic idea of how
Jesus' action at the Last Supper is to be done today. Jesus gave them
the bread broken with the words: 'My body for you'. Liturgical reform
has to be based on a model that is none other than the ritual meal
enacted and spoken by Jesus, and past forms of the Mass used as
models in so far as they are faithful to his ritual as a meal whose
content is his crucified body and his blood shed.

Thus, for instance, if a given form makes it clear that the Mass,
though it does not look like a meal, is one, and is unlike an ordinary
meal *because* it is his ritual, a unique ritual meal bending to his mysterious purpose the universal significance of food and drink shared,
then that way of doing it provides a model for this reason and not

because it is deemed to come from some liturgical golden age. Such is, for instance, the Eucharistic Prayer of Hippolytus said for all to hear. By this same token the Tridentine Mass, that does *not* make clear this essential character but obscures it, is to be deemed deficient, even if it has persisted for a near millennium.

And if it has to be admitted that the Church has been wrong on the vital matter of eucharistic worship, well, this was conceded when Pius X had to recall the Church to frequent communion after a millennium during which communion was normally infrequent. It was conceded when the same pope in a *motu proprio* said that our rites, including the Eucharist, had become 'squalid'. When I was young, the participation of the people in the Mass was a novelty, promoted by a 'liturgical movement'. This movement was made necessary by the fact that it had long, very long become normative for the people not to be actively participant. During that long tract of time, the Church had been in error over the practice of the Eucharist, not of course in its belief in the bread and wine being really the body and the blood of Christ, but in its way of doing things in church.

Any restoration of the deficient form, the Tridentine, to virtual parity with the Vatican II reformed rite, would also be an error, since doing so denies the need for *real* reform, with the model of Jesus' own special ritual meal in the forefront of the mind. And if this action leads to a situation where you have some churches that advertise themselves as based on the old rite, there will be a state of virtual schism.

No! *Real* reform is needed for the sake of the Church's spiritual life and not as the restoration of a supposedly 'good period' of liturgical practice.

> There is a hunger for our liturgy
> That nothing ever will eradicate,
> It seized upon me once, an other me
> Who could not know our planetary fate
>
> Which knowing now makes it more urgent still
> To recognize the Godhead in our bread
> Reminding of the God we had to kill:
> The thought that anything will do instead
>
> Is typical of our time's throwaway
> Which makes a bin of our created home

And when we learn again to body pray
We shall want landmarks, what better than Rome

Where Peter sleeps who once his truth denied
And honoured him by being crucified.

The Mass before Vatican II as I Remember

They let us see they'd cut the Mass in two
When High Mass opened for communion,
People's communion, now a separate 'do'
They stitched on for the eyes to fasten on.

'Confiteor', the clean-up of the crowd
For its admission to the priestly lane
Now must be sung – the error cried aloud
As though the thief had waited to explain.

Did Jesus at his final supper think
That what he made so clear we'd so obscure?
What could be simpler than to eat and drink
But how could he have reckoned with the pure

Split in the church itself between the priests
And those outside with ordinary feasts?

CHAPTER 5

Church, Theology and Culture

The Church came into existence as a community that preserved the dangerous memory of Jesus – the memory of his public crucifixion and his subsequent return among his frightened followers in a way that was totally without reproach but was rather utterly new and beyond anything that could have been previously imagined. This new radical community has held together over two thousand years, as a community based, at bottom, on mutual love and not, as with other human institutions, on fear.

The Church's contemplation of this dangerous memory is what we call 'theology', which is actually founded on the marriage of sacred Scripture with philosophy – particularly classical Greek philosophy. This is important. A religion, whether Christianity or Islam, that is without theology quickly becomes fundamentalist as it begins to interpret Scripture in a literal way, full of cultural bias and with little rational underpinning.

Fundamentalism is always culture-bound, whereas, although the story of Jesus is historical, set in a particular time, place and culture, his teaching is essentially transcultural. So, too, should be the teaching of his Church.

This chapter reflects on these issues, and, although no definitive conclusion is reached, there emerge three themes that must be pre-eminent in any Christian dialogue with other 'faiths', notably Islam.

First, the dialogue should be theological, therefore transcultural, in so far as this is possible, and should recognise that Islam too has its own fruitful theological tradition.

Second, and most important, the Church should not minimise the radically different nature of its revelation. Christian revelation is founded in the person of Jesus who invites us into the freedom of God's love; that of Islam is a revelation through God's dictation of a text to a man who then imposed this text on others.

Third, nevertheless, for too much of its history, indeed since the time of Constantine, the Catholic Church has not in practice demonstrated this God-offered freedom but has rather been associated with worldly power. If inter-faith dialogue is to be ultimately fruitful it is important to acknowledge this historical failing of the Christian Church.

Saving Blood

This short homily reflects on the need to rediscover 'church', not as institu-tion, but as the ongoing community of love that was first established by those who witnessed Jesus' crucifixion and resurrection, and ever since has con-tinued to hold this memory throughout human history.

'No one can say "Jesus is Lord" except by the Holy Spirit' (1Cor. 12: 3). In the Spirit, we know that the Church is the difference Jesus of Nazareth has made and makes in human history. And what is the Church but a society held together not by power but by love? This polity of love stems from the self-consecration of Jesus as our lover nailed to the cross of our power, manifest in his resurrection to draw all things to himself. This is the secret of the Church, the ripple effect of Calvary.

Here is how one of my American theological colleagues has just expressed this:

> It was in fact through the church that Jesus of Nazareth became an historic figure, an agent of history. It was Christians who pre-served the memory of his mere existence, who remembered his words and his deeds, who proclaimed him to have conquered death and to have become Messiah, Lord, and Saviour, who interpreted him as the enfleshment of the very Word of God, who understood their own communal experience as a fellowship in his Spirit that made them members of his very Body, who undertook to bring others into communion with him and with his Father, who invited those to whom they spoke to make him the principle and the criterion of a redirected personal and collective history. The church made Jesus of Nazareth an historically significant figure. (Komonchak, 2004, p. 30.)

This kind of writing assures one that theology is destined to survive the vagaries of Church management.

Now what does the Church give as her credentials? A man put to death by us and brought to life by God. An act of political bloodshed that otherwise would have been lost in the great mass of human injustice. But focused upon through the Spirit, political bloodshed is a universal language. This language is elemental. Everyone who witnesses the killing feels a barrier being crossed. There is this awed hush, a sense of having gone fatally too far. And a very important and most easily forgotten aspect of this elemental insight is, that all of us, those for and those against the victim, are being brought together, and this not only as in the bonding of Caesar's killers, but as men involved simply as humans, all our loyalties forgotten with the sight of the fatal blow. At the end of the film *West Side Story*, when Tony has been shot by someone in the rival gang, and his gang lift his body onto their shoulders to carry it off, one of the arms falls over to the side, and one of the rival gang lifts it up and lays it across the breast, and there is a moment of shared understanding, of something bigger lifting them all together to its heart.

This is an elemental, transcultural perception, much more available to the child than to the scholar. The then Cardinal Ratzinger, whose boyhood coincided with the Nazi nightmare, recalled how it was obvious to him as a child that the blood of Jesus meant reconciliation not blame of the Jews. The true theologian is one in whom the vision of the child is alive at the heart of all his learning.

So that is the given of our faith: a public murder held in focus by a continuing community who owe to the victim a love that is the fulfilment of our humanity to change this cruel world. For all peoples and for all times, a dangerous memory.

This new humanity, born of God in the blood of old, being in time has to grow. And since this life is God's in us, the law of its growth is the Holy Spirit that endlessly completes the relationship between the non-manifest Father and the manifest Son. And since love is the formula of this new life, its growth will be, as with each of us, a succession of breakthroughs in loving. And there's no going back on a breakthrough.

John Stands the High Priest on his Head

The small community of love brought into being by the resurrection of Christ was the beginning of a new humanity, which stands 'religions' – all world religions – on their head, and ultimately will transcend them. This essay was written in July 2005.

What Jesus died for, *pace* Caiaphas, was 'to gather into one the scattered children of God'. To understand how that death could have this result, we have to engage in a radical diagnosis of the human condition. The most radical one I know is that of René Girard, who differs from Freud in where he places the root of our trouble, not in guilt over the murder of the father, which he sees as a cover story for our real fall from grace that is *fratricidal* not parricidal. What this means is that our radical flaw is our fear of one another that it is not in our power to get free of, and that submits only to the control of *victimage*. In one way or another, the one stabiliser of our historical humanity with its insidious memory of wrong done us is the sacrifice of the one, or of the few, or at least of the fewer and less powerful, for the sake of the many. Caiaphas' judgment that Jesus, in the situation he is in and is provoking, has to die is a dramatic instance of this principle at work.

It is now upon the followers of this man that we have to concentrate. The narrative makes it embarrassingly clear that their reaction to his arrest and its grim sequel epitomises that in us which will save our own skin; even, as in their case, at the cost of a man who, they thought, had changed their lives. *They* preferred the safety of conformity rather than whatever it was that he seemed to demand. It is in the desolate condition of having succumbed to the fear that keeps us together only on the terms dictated by the mob and their rulers, that he showed himself alive in a way more powerful than any sort of miraculous survival, which, for instance, made it hard for them at first to recognise him. Breakthrough is the only word here.

There is in his self-showing after the resurrection no trace of reproach. Why so? Because he is lifting them out of the despond of shame, and empowering them. The note of empowerment, of commission, of mission, predominates in all the accounts of his 'sightings'. And this empowerment cancels the disempowerment that has led them into such an abysmal role as Caiaphas' plan went ahead. And what is our disempowerment for the flourishing to which we are called, to which all charismatic leaders call us, to which Jesus preeminently called them, but our fear of one another? Mutual fear is the cement of what Augustine calls the 'City of this World', where those who dominate confer the benefit of being enabled to save one's skin at the expense of others, as Jesus points out at the Last Supper.

Thus the ending of mutual fear is the direct consequence of Jesus showing himself, and the end of mutual fear is the constitution of a new humanity, encouraged out of all self-reproach at their cowardice by the mission they are receiving. Their cowardice is thus revealed as the failure not only to have the guts to support a friend but of our common humanity in face of a beyond-human challenge. What we have is a dismantling of the insecure structure of society under the rule of death.

Now 'the rule of death' is the very name for a society forced to cohere short of mutual love, and this in a very practical sort of way. The enemies of every sort who abound in the psalms are deadly because they can kill us, and if all we're about is staying inside our skin, then unhappy we who live under the threat of death. When the author of the Letter to the Hebrews says that Jesus has saved 'those whom the fear of death has made slaves all their life', he means *everyone* till Jesus comes and takes away the fear of one another which is the fear of death. So when we hear from Paul that death has no more dominion over him, we must not understand this as referring to a mythic hero triumphant over mythic death, but to him triumphant in us in the mutual love that replaces the cement of mutual fear.

Strangely enough, before I had worked any of this out, I became convinced that the encounter with the risen one created a community that will never disappear from the earth. It felt intuitively obvious. Now I think I can fill it in a little.

What this makes clearer and clearer is that the love of people for each other, finally sloughing off the complex investiture of mutual fear, is the sufficient description of what has happened with Christ. It will demand such an understanding of the name of Christ that will totally de-sectarianise it so that no conflict of world religions is involved. I find myself talking these days of the necessity to invent Jesus, *à la* Voltaire.

The Disciple Speaks

The death of Jesus grew us into God
Out of the uselessness of sacrifice
Which labours under death's conducting rod
Whose rule is just that nothing will suffice.

One dies for all, the world well understands
And Jesus dies by the High Priest's decree
His followers enduring both demands
Of our own skin and love that makes us free

Until he came alive and showed his own
Our life as children of the loving one
Who are not born ever to be alone
But be to one another as the sun.

And this shall be, though planetary ruin
Take all but love that we never yet knew in.

Revelation and Philosophy

Theology, as it emerged from the beginning, was a happy coming together of Hebrew revelation with Greek philosophy. Philosophy tries to be transcultural, so to abandon philosophical reflection on revelation, as some Christians now do, is to risk falling into fundamentalism and cultural bigotry. This piece was an Advent homily.

As we prepare once again for the coming that changes everything, here is something that Christians all over the world are forgetting to their and our peril: that those who worshipped the God of Abraham met with the philosophical tradition that flowered in Greece, what Lonergan once called the 'Greek miracle', for which God is the infinite, the incomprehensible, the unimaginable. And when the biblical revelation climaxed in Jesus killed and revealed as the life of this world, this fusion between revelation and thought took a huge step forward with the Greek and Latin Fathers. Hence was born that wonderful use of the mind that we call theology. Theology is the great achievement of Catholic Christianity – eastern and western. I like to think of it as God's playground for the faithful mind, on which we are never allowed to forget that God revealed is still God the unimaginable.

But when this Catholic link between Scripture and philosophy is broken, revelation's almighty God becomes the omnipotent oriental despot described recently by Anthony Flew, whose sensationally recovered belief in God does not lead him to Christianity for this reason.[1]

He is absolutely right, if we mean by Christianity that which now increasingly goes by that name. The Christian religion de-philosophised is lethal. It is capturing the world's one superpower. The God of Abraham, deprived of philosophy, becomes the God of fundamentalists both Christian and Muslim. And, by way of example, fundamentalist views on sex are those of bigots, so that the issue of homosexuality, for example, which a theology alive to Aristotle will class as a third-order problem, assumes centre-stage and tears apart the worldwide Anglican Communion. We are being terrorised not only by fundamentalists but by fundamentalism itself.

Let us pray to hear again the Christmas gospel: 'In the beginning was the *logos* and the *logos* was with God and the *logos* was divine by nature.' No oriental despot there, but all-embracing and all-loving mystery. The fourth gospel is the first big theological adventure. 'Oh', say the worldly opponents of fundamentalism, 'that's when the Palestinian rabbi got divinised'. But we, who know him in his ritual of tortured flesh in bread and wine, know otherwise. To confess Jesus as God is to know that God's revealing man who speaks in all our gospels is all-revealing, believing those who have 'felt with our hands the life itself'. We tire of this belief because we do not focus at Mass and bring to its victim our own vulnerability, so that our *'amen'* to the priest's words, 'The body of Christ', means: 'That is me'. These are the words of Jesus' enlightenment. Pray to hear them.

Of Culture and Cultures

Christian belief is beyond any particular culture. Failure to think transculturally is to open the door to culture-bound fundamentalism.

Belief in a transcendent deity is belief in a God beyond cultures. Now, all fundamentalist belief in God is culture-based. That is to say, its promoters conceive of God as an all-powerful master of the world as

---

[1] Anthony Flew, the philosopher, might best be described as a 'deist'. He believes in god as a 'first cause', but in no way associates this with the God of revelation or of love.

they understand it, that is, their world. As Wittgenstein brilliantly says, the limits of my language are the limits of my world. The error of fundamentalism is the inability to think transculturally.

But the failure to think transculturally is not confined to fundamentalism. One can be quite sophisticated in one's ideas and still not have recognised that the word 'culture' has to have an article before it and is something there are many of. The human animal, which nature does not take care of after weaning, spawns 'cultures' for this purpose. The meaning of Vatican II, according to Lonergan, is the acknowledgment of history, that is, of the existence of other ways of being human than that cultivated in the west. Both the Catholic Church and the World Council of Churches have felt inspired to 'think cultures' as an indispensable step to promoting the teaching and life of Jesus. The latter, of course, is culture-shaped. But the execution of Jesus by the culture that shaped him, and its issue in the resurrection and explosion of the Spirit makes him for the believer the representative 'word' of the transcultural God.

And this leads to the interesting result that the pronouncements of the Church, in so far as they express the kind of absolutism that Vatican II was destined to dissolve, are themselves short of real transcultural belief. In these pronouncements, 'relativism' is regularly deplored. But cultural relativism is the indispensable requisite for real belief in God. In so far as the Roman authority harks back to its pre-Vatican II hegemony, it is failing to represent the true, transcultural God. I think it could be shown that the doctrine of the Trinity is transcultural, but this would take time.

The fatal ambivalence of culture is shown by the fact that the highest form of western culture, that produced Kant and Goethe and Beethoven, could nosedive into the abyss and come up with Auschwitz. By contrast, the life that Jesus by his crucifixion and resurrection has made possible consists in loving the other irrespective of culture, even to the sacrifice of one's own life, as Maximilian Kolbe did when, in Auschwitz, he volunteered to be starved to death in place of a man he'd never met.[2]

---

[2] Maximillian Kolbe was a Polish Catholic priest, sent to Auschwitz in 1941. In July of that year he was murdered by the camp authorities, having volunteered to take the place of another man who had been selected to be killed as a reprisal for an escape from the camp. He was canonised in 1982.

On the Pope's Lecture in Regensburg

In September 2006, Pope Benedict XVI delivered a lecture in which he seemed to endorse an opinion that Islam was an inherently violent religion. This prompted a violent reaction in many parts of the Islamic world. The Pope subsequently apologised for any misunderstanding he may have caused. This piece reflects on the incident – a real clash between theology and culture. But is our classic Christian theology up to the task?

Christianity, the movement that was born, in a sense full-grown by reason of its divine origin, out of the execution of Jesus and his self-revelation as the Body of a new humanity, is subversive of the old humanity that is based on the power of death as controlling political threat. Death's bluff had been called by God, successfully for those who were touched by the emergent Spirit, giving us 'a dangerous memory' that will leave nothing the same again. We have glimpsed a humanity free of death that still preys upon us and our world.

But this new humanity in Christ, a polity of love not power, was far beyond the culture in which this extraordinary Jewish sect had to take root, the then universal Roman Empire that had adopted Christianity as its religion. Once thus empowered politically, and in a matter of a couple of generations, the *ecclesia* of Jesus the un-accusing all-embracing victim of world-justice ruled its subjects the way the world rules, not the way love rules. I ask the reader's forgiveness for these simplifications, which I hope will later justify themselves.

If now we look at Islam, we see that *its* rule *also* is a rule imposed, does not rule as love rules and 'should' rule according to Christianity. So there is a certain similarity between Christianity in its political infancy as an order imposed from above, what was to become 'Christian civilisation', and Islam. The fact – *later* to prove crucial – that the Christian order is an order *not* imposed but born of love does not distinguish the Christian order from the Islamic in the ages pre-ceding the break-up of Christendom. The difference, evident to theology, between the Christian revelation and the revelation to Mohammed, is very clear to our theologically informed minds: it is the difference between a divine revelation born of the Spirit out of the dangerous memory of the bluff of death divinely called; this on the one hand, and on the other, a revelation dictated to one man and imposed by him on his disciples. Revelation the Christ-way has implicit in it an enormous *freedom* awakened in the believer, which is the opposite of the idea of God's law *imposed* on man via one man.

Now before what we call the Enlightenment, this radical difference between revelation Jesus-style and revelation Mohammed-style does not appear in the cultural political world, because in both you have order imposed from above, from the imperialised Church and from the rulers in Islamic lands. It is only when the Enlightenment has achieved the separation of Church and State that Christianity is able to embrace this separation *as implicit in its own free-making revelatory structure*. God never did impose his law on us, he came among us as love comes, on our cross with its amazing sequel, but this fact of divine non-imposition only shines before us as we 'come of age', at least relatively (for this conscious image of God that we are is forever growing). Thus, in our post-Enlightenment, modern world, Islam and Christianity stand over against each other in the stark contrast between, on the one hand, the divine will directly translated into a human polity, and, on the other, the will of God as the mysterious transforming force of love in society, wooing not imposing.

This is a stark and bitter contrast. And I'm afraid that this theologically sophisticated pope is pointing to it. He can, for good measure, ask how Christians fare, as regards the public practice of their faith, in Muslim countries, and point to the fact, on the Christian side, that the claim of brutal national-security states in Latin America to impose their will in the name of 'Christian civilisation' is a cancer diagnosed by liberation theology.

On the other hand, though, has the pope taken into account the less-than-Christian shape of medieval Christendom, under 'the sword of Constantine'? In other words, to be a little arch, has he read his René Girard, who is quite unique in combining a new realisation of the mysterious source of Christian faith with high praise of the Enlightenment as a maturing and enablement for its scientific embrace of tradition?

So is the pope theologically sophisticated enough? Lonergan comes in here surely. When told to teach theology at the Gregorian in Rome, he said that the theology he was supposed to teach was seven hundred years out of date. It had allowed Scotus to reduce reason to logic, and then failed to see that Kant's *Critique of Pure Reason* is only the critique of this lamentable resultant. It had forgotten the revelatory power of symbol and poetry.

So, to repeat, is Ratzinger's theology, which has led him to discern the painful incompatibility between Islam today and Christianity today, sophisticated enough to understand fully what Christianity today implies? Has his theology taken on the immense task of integrating the birth and growth of historical consciousness into theology, which Lonergan saw it as his life's work to restore – hence that devastating observation about the seven-hundred-year gap. Does not Ratzinger's theology show a certain timeless brilliance which was adequate to expose the timeless dullness of the old guard at Vatican II, but was and is not adequate to give a full account of how the Christian fact is showing itself today as growing out of *and* outgrowing the Enlightenment?

There certainly is something timeless about his theology. It is brilliant at a cost. John L. Allen, for his book on Ratzinger that preceded the latter's election, enquired of his German contemporaries among theology teachers, and learned that none of them saw his work as seminal or used it as a class-book for their students. Surely what they were finding to be lacking was a grappling with the implications of the demand made on theology by the development of historical consciousness. The faith that springs from the wounded side of that executed challenger of all things human is a vibrantly alive and changing and growing thing, and one hears too much of the clarity and brilliance of Ratzinger's theology to be reassured when one confronts the demands of faith today.

Lonergan had that dense definition: a theology mediates between a culture and the role and significance of a religion *for that culture*. The battle between growing Christian belief and the 'non-historical orthodoxy' brandished by the old Cardinal Ottaviani at Vatican II was only half won by Ratzinger the reformer, who came out 'brilliantly theological' and far too ready to castigate Küng and the many other theological attempts to deal with modernity and, *a fortiori*, its postmodern sequels. His handling of liberation theology was insensitive and that of 'the love that dare not speak its name' was described by Paul Cullen as difficult not to describe as vicious. (He is still stuck with 'sodomy' and named very recently the 'sin of Sodom'!)

If my critique is on the right lines, this brilliant theologian on Peter's chair may not be able to measure up to the subtler problem of Islam, that, in spite of the theological poverty of its origin in a revealed-to teacher as opposed to a universal fruitful victim, was able in its cultural heyday to rule a society more tolerant of Jews than was the abysmally intolerant Christian culture of the time.

For a study of this I would cite *The Popes Against the Jews* by David Kertzer, whose father was a rabbi who had worked with Catholic priests on Jewish-Christian relations, and whose book has the strength of lacking resentment. The book details relentlessly the Catholic sins against the Jews, silence about which on the part of the pope at Auschwitz was clearly heard by Jews. The careful argument, in *that* blood-soaked context, to the effect that Nazism was 'really' a sin against Catholic Christianity, was surely symptomatic of the *lacuna* to which I am pointing. And surely, when in his attempt to deal with the situation created by his Regensburg lecture, he chose to cite the great Pauline text about the cross as a scandal to the Jews, he was putting his other foot in it.

In short, I would say that the pope, vis-à-vis the powder keg of Islam today, has seen the point but not in sufficient depth. He is trying to face those raging crowds of Muslims who are suffering what is in fact a failure to catch up with history, a failure in religious sense, with the brilliance of a theology but which is short of what our theology now requires.

It all comes down, I think, to the implicit theological wealth at the birth of Christian faith, in which the folly of God proved wiser than the wisdom of men, in a way that pushes beyond the bounds of irony and sends shivers down the spine. Now this is dynamite, not to say nuclear. To make it mean 'our religion is better than yours!' is a ghastly abuse of an awesome mystery, and to this abuse theology, which spells out the implications of the event, is prone.

A good theologian resists this temptation. He or she realises that presiding over the drama of Jesus in Jerusalem and its rapid spread in the world is the tender Holy Spirit who is inward to all the varieties and cultures and sins of humanity. With the aid of this Spirit, the philosophers of Islam and Judaism and Christianity were able, for a short golden period, to form a three-ring necklace, in which Aquinas could get his favourite definition of God, as *ipsum esse subsistens*, from a Muslim scholar, Avicenna. The Holy Spirit was prompting, perhaps, a non-emphasis on the theological poverty of Islam, of God dictating to a man, versus God giving his Son as our victim to reveal us to ourselves and lead us into eternal life. As a result of this discretion, we had the brilliant Islamic culture that gave us Aristotle and the whole achievement of what Lonergan called the *miraculum Graecum*, and an Islamic civilisation noted, as Christian civilisation was not, for its tolerance of minorities, especially of Jews.

Oh dear, there is so much in our history that dictates against making a triumph of our theology, especially as even this was muddied up in vindictive notions of what Jesus did for us on the cross. One could go on! But there is, I think, a kind of last word to these ruminations, and it is the word of a pope, spoken by John XXIII on opening the Second Vatican Council. He told the assembled Fathers about some of his advisors who were listing the modern errors that the Council had to condemn. This thinking in terms of modern errors is what you get when you apply theological conclusions from the truths of faith directly to the contemporary situation and find in it errors to condemn. This is the short circuit to which the present pope, as a professional theologian, is liable in the tortured situation of Islam today. Of these 'prophets of doom' Pope John said that they lack knowledge of history, 'which is the true teacher of life'.

Some further reflections

And what difference does it make to these reflections when we factor in the consideration that the aggressive Islam that is forced upon us, and is Islam as far as we are concerned, is of the Wahabi sect, which accounts for two per cent of the Muslim population? Is the pope, or any other Christian authority, conscious of being threatened by two per cent of the huge world of Islam, and that the desire for peace which we presume we have is shared by the vast majority of our 'enemy'?

Not only do we ignore the ninety-eight per cent of the 'enemy' on the side of Islam. We also neglect to notice how large a section of the Christian world is a prey to fundamentalism and does not want peace any more than our enemies do. They do not see our two per cent any more than we perceive theirs! Some kind of a call to consciousness for both Christians and Muslims is not inconceivable.

It gets trickier and trickier. The huge strength of the Christian faith in God is that the human mediation of it is not a prophet to whom God dictates his law, but a man stripped naked and crucified by the world and showing himself beyond the power of death, inviting us into his eternal life. Now what is implied in this mediation-through-crucifixion, as opposed to mediation through a dictated word, is that the believing mind is not constrained by the words written in a book, but is free to work as the mind works, intelligently and reasonably. So far, top marks for Christianity.

I fear that what the pope was doing in that lecture was identifying

Christian belief with good theology, and ignoring the fact that we've got buckets of bad theology on our side. Yes, ultimately, a God who shows himself through a crucified Son is not ultimately a lawgiver, so his Church can welcome the separation of Church and State. But this has not by any means always been understood among us. Indeed it has been bitterly fought over as, in my memory, was the Vatican decree on religious liberty. Conversely, the Islamic world in its heyday has on the whole done better with a reasonable God, in spite of having a less radical, not to say devastating, idea of mediation through the crucified.

CHAPTER 6

On Mary and the Feminine

We live in a male-dominated culture in which women have tended to be 'objects' rather than 'subjects'. This is the case at least as much in the Church as in society as a whole. And yet Catholic tradition, perhaps inchoately struggling to give expression to the feminine dimension of humanity, has always given special place to Mary.

The three important Catholic doctrines in relation to Mary – the Immaculate Conception, the Virgin Birth, and the Assumption – should be seen as the attempt by the institutional Church (the Church of the head) to keep open a mystical contemplative space for the feeling, praying Church (the Church of the heart). In this contemplative space the Church deepens its awareness of the feminine in God's plan for humanity, and indeed of humanity's active co-operation in the act of redemption through Mary's free and conscious 'Be it done to me according to thy word' of the Annunciation.

Yet the institutional Church is still deeply entrapped in the patriarchal androcentric culture of our time, to the extent that, while happy to celebrate the 'feminine', it remains, for now, deeply resistant to the 'female'.

Contemplation of the Virgin Birth

We start with an essay on our understanding, or rather our contemplation, of the Virgin Birth. There is a fascinating possibility that, at the moment of the Annunciation, Mary had already consecrated her virginity to God. Of course this may just be a beautiful story, but it emphasises Mary's conscious assent to participation in God's redemptive plan. At some level she clearly understood that that was what she was doing. In other words her assent was much, much more than just a 'submission' to God's will. And, as subsequent essays

*will demonstrate, this conscious assent on Mary's part is an important key to
(re)discovering the feminine in God's created humanity.*

*This is a long essay not always easy to follow. A short, very recent, afterword
may help to clarify the argument. What is important is to surrender oneself to
the mystery in contemplative prayer!*

For as long as I can remember, I have had this idea that I now see to be
stupid that when Mary said to the angel, 'How can this be since I
know not man?', she means, 'How can this be? I am a virgin.' This is a
stupid projection of belief in the virgin birth back onto the dialogue, as
though the dialogue were merely putting the belief into dramatic
form, Mary obligingly inviting the angel to say how she is to be made
pregnant. But the angel's statement that she is to bear an important
child is simply a statement about the future. No specified time. One
day, you're going to be the mother of the Messiah. So Mary's problem
with this must refer to her indefinite future. It must mean that she had
committed that future to be manless, a vow of virginity in fact. 'You're
going to have this child.' 'But I'm committed not to have children.' I
have always despised this interpretation as the projection of the
Catholic idea of the vow of chastity onto the story. But it is the only
sense the story can make.

Now, it is generally maintained that, in a Jewish context, the idea of
such a vow makes no sense. But according to Bargil Pixner OSB of
Dormition Abbey, Palestine, a commitment of this kind has been
found among the Essenes. There is a regulation to the effect that if a
father discovers that his daughter has made the vow unknown to him,
he can void it. Pixner argues that Mary might have made such a vow,
as an Essene, and that Joseph, already a widower, could have taken
her under his wing. Hence his surprise when she became pregnant.
This is of course the eastern Orthodox interpretation of 'the brothers of
the Lord' as sons of Joseph by an earlier marriage.

What you could have, then, is a vow of virginity on Mary's part,
offering her womanhood to God, and God's acceptance taking the
form of having her enflesh his Word. Ignoring the credibility of this for
the moment and simply assessing its value as a story, it is an extra-
ordinarily good story, for the following reason. It unites the two
aspects of Mary that keep coming apart in Mariology: the spiritual and
the biological. Mary's consecration of her womanhood to God is the
spiritual side and God's 'use' of her womanhood to produce the Christ

is the biological side. This undoubtedly would be a holiness, a conformity with God's will, unique in all history: an obedience that
became a gestation of God. And, as Eckhart says, total obedience to
God does bring his Word to birth in the soul. Of this, Mary is the
historic archetype. Hence the liturgical statement that giving birth to
the Son increased her holiness.

It is a story that has ravished the imagination of artists more than
any other. Is it true? And could it still be true, even if Mary had
conceived in the ordinary way? Not if Joseph had been the father. For
then her holiness must have been a wifely, a spousal holiness, not one
with God as spouse. She could not be – in one of her titles – Spouse of
the Holy Spirit if she had been the spouse of a man. But an extra-
marital pregnancy would not carry this commitment at the human
level. Irregular and untidy no doubt, but who said God had to be
regular and tidy? Raymond Brown betrays this penchant for neatness
when he warns theologians that in dispensing with the literal interpretation of the virgin birth they are admitting an 'unpleasant' possibility. But my main point here is to invoke the authority of Brown
who finds the paternity of Joseph exegetically out of the question.

I have spoken of the archetypal uniting of the Virgin with the
Mother. What the story, properly interpreted as above after a lifetime
of me-typical inattention, is anything but a violent imposition of this
combination of roles by the archetypal realm on the historical. It is a
simply superb story of consecrated and uniquely fruitful womanhood.

Is everyone to whom I propose it going to be as impatient with it as I
have been all my life? I feel the need at this stage to 'fight off' friends
who are going to force on me the either-or approach, the binary
opposition that besets the modern mind and is, after all, the basis of
our formidable computer technology. So, I am neither for taking the
virginal conception literally nor against it. I seek more understanding
here.

What has shed new light for me is the Essene connection. For this
affords the possibility of a consecration to God of the woman's vital
role in life which is to make life – a consecration that becomes especially meaningful in the circumstances of Mary's life. We are thus able
to distinguish two acts of Mary's will: the surrender of her procreative
womanhood by her vow, and her acceptance of God's acceptance of
this vow and his turning it to his own purpose. Without the first act,
the second would be the surrender to an overriding supernatural
purpose – and the supernatural does not override, is not thus violent.

You would have Mary sitting in her room and presented with a role in God's plan that makes sense to us with two millennia of Christianity behind us but that could have made no sense to her, a role accepting which would involve the denial of her sense of herself – of that sense of herself that blazes forth in the Magnificat.

In point of fact, her sense of herself does object to what the angel has said. And what is fascinating is that her objection is based on her consecration to God. It is not: 'I want children of my own, not your child.' It is: 'I have vowed to you to forgo children, and you seem to be contradicting this vow. What's going on?' And just to reiterate the importance of her double consecration, if we only have the one – 'I want you to bear my Son. Do you accept?' – then her question is simply: 'How are you going to do this?' In other words, it's a question formed retrospectively in light of the virginal conception, as though the incident were simply didactic, putting into story form the doctrine of the virginal conception. The doctrine says: 'She conceived of the Holy Spirit.' So the dialogue runs: 'How am I to conceive?' Answer: 'by the Holy Spirit'. Indeed, if we accept the theory that the virginal conception is a theologoumenon,[1] this is precisely the way we are going to read the dialogue. But the Essene possibility suggests a 'straight' reading of the dialogue.

Thus the doctrine of the virginal conception has stilted, as above, the dialogue with the angel, so that the doctrine – itself reduced to theologoumenon – dictates the dialogue.

Let me step back now, and think about the virginal conception and theologoumena. To say that the virginal conception is a theologoumenon is to say that, once Jesus was accepted as 'Lord and Christ', it was seen to be appropriate that he have a very special birth, which was accordingly provided. The objection regularly levelled against this way of thinking is: 'Where are you going to stop? Why not say that it is appropriate for this sort of person to have a resurrection?' This objection, however, ignores the fact that it was as *risen*, and only as risen, that Jesus was acknowledged as Lord and Christ and thus deserving of a special birth. So resurrection could not be among the qualities appropriate to a hero known from some other source. The disciples did not start by deciding – God knows how – that this man was all that it takes, and then proceed to deck him out with grandiose

---

[1] A theologoumenon is a doctrine held to be true because it is considered 'appropriate' and traditional rather than because of any direct scriptural evidence.

titles concerning birth and death. The resurrection came upon them.
'The risen one addresses the community from the outside', as Rowan
Williams puts it, and this constitutes a luminous centre for our theo-
logical thinking.

Now if the virginal conception is a primary emanation or offshoot
from this luminous centre, we shall expect it to be ambiguous, in the
sense of partaking, in part, of the light and, in part, of the mundane
reality into which the light is being refracted. The question: 'How far
can you go in theologoumenising the events?' is misplaced, as indeed
is the Catholic moral question of the sixties: 'How far can you go?' For
it is not the more or less daring intrusion of the light of reason into an
arcane mystery that we are to be about, but on the contrary an
opposite movement of trying to follow the supernatural light of the
mystery of Christ as it pulses out into our darkened world. In this
process, the virginal conception seems to be on the cusp between the
blinding reality of God in Christ, and the world where we try to
explain. All we can see is that it reads much better as a story when we
don't read it as a doctrine taking story form. A woman comes to life in
it, and makes a surrender of her life in which we can all recognise
what we are called to, a surrender that is to the forming of Christ in us
as in her womb.

On the other hand, biological objections to a virginal conception are
formidable. And this is not to deny to God the power to work miracles. What I clearly have to do next is to ask myself why, accepting
miracles as I do on the first-hand evidence of totally trustworthy
friends, I tend to jib at this one. And I think the reason is that this
miracle is in no sense a restoring of a natural process as in all healing
miracles, but is more like the cheating of a natural process, a divine
conjuring trick of doing without what is normally necessary. Now it
may be that I only see it this way because I am not seeing it from the
point of view of a humanity transformed by the incarnation, a
humanity appropriately grounded in a *nova nativitas*. The incarnation
is still, for my unregenerate mind, an object not a perspective, an
exception rather than a fuller norm. Precisely what we have to learn
'at the cusp' is to cross over from the old perspective to the new,
within which the new birth is not exceptional but normative. If this is
correct, the reason for finding unworthy of God the miracle of conception without a man collapses, and with it the objection to taking
literally the virginal conception.

And yet! Of course, 'and yet'! One cannot manipulate the mind as

easily as this. Perhaps the most we can do is to point out the above
conditions for thinking at the cusp, and observe that this kind of
thinking is learned slowly in prayer and not imposed – not even
proposed to a mind that is coming newly to the faith, a frequent
occurrence today. And perhaps this is the proper meaning of 'theologoumenon': not 'a doctrine expressing itself as a story' but 'a to-be-
expected gap between what the mind can take and the luminous
reality present to it'. And now I see, as if for the first time, the significance of the Christmas liturgy's reference to the birth of Christ as
nova nativitas. It's a new way to be born, started by Christ and
extended to us. This curious floundering of the mind over virginal
conception seems to be what God 'meant' in saying to me in answer to
my rude question: 'I'm not telling!'[2]

To prevent the above idea from lapsing into mystification, let us not
forget that the child into whose making no man has gone would have
to be without the very chromosomes that differentiate a man, namely
the Y-chromosomes. At this point, people have an irritating habit of
saying that biology is not the point, of warning against 'biologism'.
What I seem to detect here is a having it both ways, wanting to cling to
the orthodox understanding 'without getting bogged down in biology'. But if you accept the orthodox interpretation, you are bogged
down in biology. You are stating that a baby was conceived without
the aid of a man. You are making a statement with chromosomic
implications that are self-contradictory.

On the one hand, virginal conception makes much better literary
sense of a most wonderful story that is at the heart of the Gospel and
that speaks to the artist in all of us. On the other hand it looks like a
contradiction in terms biologically. But is there such a thing as 'a
contradiction in terms biologically'? Is not a science that comes up
with such an objection to miracle told to find some new terms?

The problem seems to be this. What compels me to take the virginal
conception with a seriousness approaching awe is the aesthetic love-
liness of a woman's gift to God of her procreative womanhood and
God's acceptance of this in a ravishment that is his own Son's con-
ceiving as human; I mean, that it is a new understanding of beauty, of

---

[2] After Stephen Mitchell's reduction of Mary had produced in me something like a crisis
of faith and my faith had unaccountably deepened by the experience, I asked God:
'What did happen?' What I heard in reply was: 'I'm not going to tell you. My ways are
not your ways.'

the aesthetic, as criterial here. But then the aesthetic seems to be offended against when we would have to speak of God 'supplying Y-chromosomes'. And I repeat, it is no use saying: 'Oh don't go into biology!' This is a way of avoiding the unavoidable collision between divine myth and human fact. Nowhere is this collision more acute than in the Christian story. Nowhere is the divine more divine, the human more recalcitrantly human. And the place of the collision is the Virgin's womb. Hence the old anthem: 'Rejoice O Virgin Mary, you alone have demolished heresies throughout the world!'

Does not the Christian psyche require a ravishment of the flesh by the Godhead? The mystery of the incarnation cannot be kept at the belief that God is incarnate in Christ. It has to go on, with imagination, to consider that the taking on of our flesh has been felt happening in our flesh, in the experience of the Virgin. In the fourth century, the test of whether you really believed became the question whether you could call Mary the Mother of God. I seem to be pushing this test further, in the direction of the Mother's experience: a thing not to be speculated upon, but thought within the rhythms of prayer. Only the personal experience of surrendering to 'nothing in particular (which is God of course)' could 'pick up' the experience of the Virgin Mother.

Afterword (some years later)

Can I say in a less mystificatory way what I am trying to say here? I am saying that when we are looking at a story that bears the weight of divine revelation, we should expect the following untidiness. What we are reading about when we confront the gospel narrative is, simultaneously, a divine mystery beyond our comprehension, the self-disclosing Absolute, and a reality involving 'the girl next door' – to quote an article on Mary that I published in the *Irish Theological Quarterly*. So there is bound to be a 'cusp' where these two totally different kinds of communication overlap, and at the cusp science with its Y-chromosomes, without which there wouldn't be men at all, overlaps with the divine other. So if there is such a thing as 'cuspmanship', this demands a high tolerance of ambiguity.

I think my point can be illustrated by an experience reported by, and of, William Temple, one of Anglicanism's giants, and a churchman noted especially for his impatience of pious twaddle. As a young ordinand, he had difficulties with the virgin birth, but was urged to go ahead regardless. Then, one evening, during an orchestral concert, he knew in a flash that it was true, and he never had any subsequent doubt about the doctrine. But what did he thus 'know' in a way that, as he took it on, doesn't sound at all pious, another kind of certainty altogether? It may be the kind of certainty on this matter that came to me: an acceptance of the cusp with a tolerance of ambiguity which is not the tolerance of the liberal. How about that? – as they say in Liverpool!

> You make it well with me about the Virgin
> Mother of him we know as your own child:
> Only discouraged by your church's urging
> I have to face the dark and touch the wild.
>
> How you have ravished her I cannot know
> Save in my heart where you may ravish me.
> How deeply in me your love's probe may go
> Governs what, looking to her, I may see.
>
> There, beyond reason's reach, though, what may come
> To mind, the mind cannot stop puzzling
> over: supplying the Y-chromosome
> Hardly a theme to bring the heart to sing!
>
> That night, though, when you told me all was well
> And I asked how, I heard: I do not tell.

Virgin Mother – Five Essays on Mary

Sebastian comments that these five short essays formed part of his own personal recovery and conversion of recent years as he began to discover, acknowledge and accept his own bodily self and his feminine side. They were a kind of 'tour de force' as he kept going over the same ground trying to enter deeper into the mystery. They are now perhaps a little repetitive but still worth keeping together as a single piece.

First Essay on Mary
Faith in and devotion to Mary is a belief that works!

One thing is clear about Mary. She could never have reached the status she has as a worldwide religious figure on the credentials required for this by the ordinary, intelligent and uncommitted mind.

These credentials are not able to mediate this kind of religious reality. In a similar, though not the same way, John Robinson once suggested that were the evidence for the fact and impact of Jesus undeniable and unavoidable, the relative number of believers and non-believers would be what it is now. A different way of claiming and holding attention is involved than that of any other historical phenomenon.

But what is this quality that gets the mystery 'believed in throughout the world' (1 Tim. 3: 16) – a clause in the great encomium of the mystery that I have always loved? In the case of Mary, it is a unique combination of universal psychological need (and consequent popularity, the need met) with intellectual rigour. The psychological need for a universal mother goes without saying, but the accompanying rigour is notable. Whatever is said of her as a 'perfect' being must be compatible with the belief that there is only one such being, Christ, on whom we all depend for our perfecting. A way was found to deal with this problem, in the build-up to the definition of the Immaculate Conception. Mary could be initially exempted from the human flaw retrospectively in view of the transformation effected in the sinner by the work of Christ which hadn't been done when Mary accepted her role.

What I want to stress at this stage is the contrast between the psychological pressure for a universal mother and the meticulous way in which this pressure is allowed to prevail. Yes, you've got your universal mother, but she's had to clear our test! She's a one-off, yet not an exception.

The papal definition of the Assumption is interesting in this regard. For the official reasons given for it leaned, dangerously heavily in Abbot/Bishop Butler's opinion, toward making psychological need the justification for the definition. Nothing was appealed to except the persistence of the traditional belief. And for good measure, Jung greeted this dependence on psychology enthusiastically, when he described the definition as the most important religious event of the century. Here was Rome promoting the Great Mother from the depths where archetypes reign to the status of formal Catholic belief in one who was 'the girl next door' – Catholic *chutzpah*, you might say!

Now is there a category for what I am describing, for this curious combination of psychological need and meticulous respect for the implications of revelation? Let me make a suggestion. It clearly is not satisfactory to make the psychological need the justification. The justification has to come from faith, from the mysteriously held belief of the Church. But how about 'the psychological fulfilment that follows on the acceptance of this belief' as the category we are looking for? This would mean that we were basing her extraordinary universal and unique status *neither* on the faith of the Church alone *nor* on psychological satisfaction alone, but on the two combined; and not combined as two forces added together, but interwoven.

Faith in, prayer to, confidence in Mary is a psychologically proven tenet of faith. It is a belief that works.

But its base is ultimately mysterious. It is not psychological except as confirmed psychologically. Whatever faith involves, in the way of re-orchestrating our experience around a new transcendent centre, includes a key feminine element. Personally I am very conscious these days of my faith as stripping off a lifetime of what I call woman-proofing, heavily endorsed by monastification (get the echo of 'mystification'!) What my therapist will call the recovery of woman, faith will call the opening to Mary.

Let me try to be exact here. I have for a long time been convinced that things that appear in religious myths – e.g. virgin births – show up in Christian belief 'as historical'. But what does 'historical' mean here? Does it mean that the myth of virgin birth is replaced by scientifically verifiable parthenogenesis? This would involve not a deepening of our response to myth but a dispensation from it. The literalist interpretation ignores the psychological reception of the myth. It says that what the pagans dreamed of the Christians know as historical fact. My understanding, on the other hand, emphasises psychology: it points to the extraordinary phenomenon of a doctrine accepted in faith and then (and thus) satisfying a universal psychological need. It is not accepted because it satisfies this need. But accepted, it does satisfy the need, and very much so.

This psychologically proven act of pure faith fascinates me. For, although the virgin birth is not accepted because it satisfies the psyche, its satisfaction of the psyche when accepted is a powerful existential reality. The classical apologetic distinguishes between 'this is believable' (credibility) and 'I must believe this' (credendity). I am adding a third notion that straddles these two: 'this is believed, and fulfillingly so'. Hence it 'is believed on in the world'. Not only does this faith 'overcome' the world, it 'makes it' in the world, where psychological fulfilment by this mystery is the mystery itself operating on us.

Does all this 'do anything' with Y-chromosomes? Well, at least it takes the spotlight off this sensitive area, and it does this not by saying: 'I wouldn't touch this if I were you!' but by talking about something else which is manifestly the essence, namely the psychological consequence of believing. In other words, the mystery of Mary, contemplatively and intelligently entered into, takes us away from any scientific 'reconstruction' of the virgin birth. It is taking the virgin birth seriously that discourages taking it literally.

But of course it will be objected: 'Come off it, you are saying that the virgin birth is to be reduced to an enriching myth and not an alleged fact. It is what has been called a theologoumenon.' But this is precisely what I am *not* saying! I am not saying that the doctrine is believed because it satisfies. I am saying that it satisfies because it is believed. That is to say it satisfies when Mary is allowed to be Mary and to speak to our silence. I don't know why the mystery of Mary, held in contemplative focus, discourages biological probing, but it certainly does.

So, finally, why is the mystery 'believed on in the world'? What has seized the world's imagination and will not let it go? It is an unimaginable consent that embraces everything. 'Be it done to me according to your word.'

> Young Mother now my sweet incestuous
> Release between my pairs of opposites
> Over a lifetime missing every bus
> While all the time the tireless pattern knits.
>
> I don't know how you let in the sublime
> To Nazareth on a dull afternoon
> But the world knows enraptured for all time
> By one your son whose coming is too soon.
>
> Sweetness and light meet in the body's Now
> In which I know you and am known of you
> Who asked not if, but wanted to know how
> And got an answer we may not construe.
>
> Fine edge between indulgence and the fire
> Lying between the sheets of new desire.

(The first line evokes Louis Malle's superb film, *Murmurs of the Heart*.)

Second Essay on Mary

A way to understand the doctrine of the Immaculate Conception is that the woman, Mary, being unencumbered by the karmic weight of 'original sin', was enabled consciously to assent to, and actively to co-operate in, God's work of salvation, as done by the man, Jesus. So Catholic Marian theology fundamentally excludes sexism, even though the Vatican's culture-bound psychology remains deeply sexist.

There is only one saviour of the world, and he is a man. Yet Jesus' question: 'Who do you say I am?' receives, in orthodox doctrine both eastern and western, an answer that is gender-neutral, namely 'a divine person'. Now this does something interesting at the level of gender. The humanity of him who is a divine person has about it an openness that it would not otherwise have. This humanity, though male, uniquely embraces the female. This suggests, to say the least, that what is said of the agency of Jesus in salvation is inclusive of the female.

Now, in Luke's gospel there exists a strong implication that there is just one consent to life over death that is made, first, by the Virgin to the Angel of the Annunciation and, later, by Jesus emboldened by the Angel of the Agony. Luke's wording is virtually the same. 'Be it done to me according to your word.' 'Not as I will but as you will.' One 'Yes' to the inscrutable starts in the woman and is completed in the man.

The later theological development that sees Mary as co-redemptress has its roots in this double agency that follows from the divinity of the saviour. This rooting is instinctual rather than conceptual; conceptualising has taken centuries. But the instinct is enormously powerful. It urges through praying, worship and liturgy, art, music, poetry – not excepting 'the eternal feminine' of Goethe, whose Marian overtones have been noted.

It is the pressure of this quasi-instinct that is at work in another, modern Mary doctrine: the Immaculate Conception. My friend Geoffrey Hill, one of our greatest living poets, has strongly objected to this doctrine as implying a sort of protection for Jesus. He couldn't be born of a normal mother; it had to be of a mother 'travelling club class'! With respect, and recognising that too many Catholics have thought this way, I don't think this is the logic implicit in the doctrine of the Immaculate Conception.

Let me suggest what the implicit logic is. How can we see the act of the Virgin saying 'Yes' to the start of a new and forever humanity as psychologically credible? How on earth can 'the girl next door' have in mind something inconceivably innovative in respect of any world she could have known? Now theology, with its centuries of homework, has a suggestion here. To be able to consent to the wholly new, she would have to be unencumbered by the old, by the enormous, karmic weight of 'original sin'. What the new doctrine was securing was the *conscious* agency of Mary in the coming of a new and inextinguishable human life.

But why was this necessary? Why shouldn't Mary have been the mother of someone who turned out to be what Christians believe him to be? The answer is: no reason at all, unless there is operating a felt need to bring the mother significantly closer to the operation, to make her as consciously responsible in it as Jesus was.

With a clarity for which we must be wholly grateful, Karl Barth sees the Roman Catholic doctrine of Mary as the root of what he sees as the Roman Catholic heresy:

> In the doctrine and worship of Mary there is disclosed the one heresy of the Roman Catholic Church which explains all the rest. The 'mother of God' of Roman Catholic Marian dogma is quite simply the principle, type and essence of the human creature co-operating servant-like (*ministerialiter*) in its own redemption on the basis of prevenient grace, and to that extent the principle, type and essence of the church (Barth, 1936).

Congar comments that the question of humanity's co-operation in its own salvation is paramount, and: 'It confronts us with two contrary ideas: the entirely Protestant notion that human nature, in its very substance, is corrupt to its roots, and the Catholic belief that it is essentially and radically good, though wounded and disfigured' (Beattie,1999).

Just as the Catholic instinct unconsciously excludes the sexism implicit in the maleness of the one saviour responded to without sophistication, so the Protestant instinct is unconsciously sexist. To be a bit brutal, did any woman ever ask Barth, 'How can I be saved by the blood of a man and defiled by my own?'

Perhaps the biggest failure of the Catholic tradition is the failure to

exploit its radical freedom from theological sexism. The failure is
psychological not theoretical, and massively so. The agency of Mary in
our redemption, confessed by doctrine, does not show up, as it should,
in the image of Mary being a mirror to women's self-understanding, a
place where women could find themselves while the culture we are in
remains patriarchal. Here, above all, the Church fails to be counter-
cultural, which means that here she fails to be herself. There's a lot of
work still to be done here!

Of this work, Tina Beattie's book, *God's Mother, Eve's Advocate*, is a
prime example and exemplar. Taking up the suggestion of other
radical feminist thinkers, she uses the insight of Lacan, that 'the
unconscious' opened up by Freud and Jung is not a subterranean
menagerie accessed by our dreams but is in the very warp and woof of
our language, so that there is an enormous linguistic bias against
woman being the *subject* of thought and theology, rather than the
object. Through this bias, Mary has suffered what Marilyn Monroe has:
to be the object of male projection. But Mary's case is even worse, since
it is a 'Madonna-only' projection: 'alone of all her sex' etc. etc. etc., the
one sweet unthreatening woman, her revolutionary Magnificat
unheard.

A fascinating point made by Tina Beattie is that the reasoning
invoked by the Vatican for excluding women from the priesthood is
the way of thinking about women of which the Marian theology is the
systematic subversion. Take the words 'female' and 'feminine'. They
are, respectively, physical and spiritual. One can say 'in prayer we are
all feminine'; one can't say 'we are all female'. Thus women hear
themselves praised as 'feminine', their role in the Church indispensable etc. but when it comes to the sanctuary they immediately
become 'female' and are shooed off. The strong language used by
awakened feminists in the Church is faithful to a painful experience of
tension between a growing subjectivity and their Catholic identity,
still objective, which begins to look hollow and conformist.

> Mary you laugh with me as I enjoy
> Myself for the first time as God's own son
> Grown into out of the discarnate boy
> To speak at last the words: thy will be done
>
> That you spoke to the angel at the start,
> He with another angel at the end

With crucifixion as our healer's art,
Your wound only Assumption would mend.

But what of Barth's exposure of this dream?
Self-loathing tells a sterner story surely
Adapted to our life's own silent scream
Seeing a world of pain simply and purely.

But then he met his Mozart in a dream
Who met with silence his protesting scream.

(Barth's passion for Mozart was theologically subversive. In a four-page footnote to the *Church Dogmatics* he praises the music of Mozart as free of the distorted attitude to our creator due to original sin. In a dream, Mozart appeared to him, and he asked the composer: 'How could you have been a Catholic and accepted all that superstition and corruption?' Mozart was silent.)

Third Essay on Mary

Another attempt at the same topic. The doctrine of the Immaculate Conception, as formulated by the institutional Church (the head) creates a contemplative space that allows the praying Church (the heart) to feel and experience Mary as Wisdom and enlightenment personified, and hence, as the Wisdom Literature teaches, as co-operative in the divine plan. Yet this feminine wisdom, as personified in Mary, still has to find an accepted place in the institutional Church.

One way of putting the infallibility of the Church is to distinguish between truth apprehended in the head and truth known in the heart, and to go on to say that, if we are talking about the Church as an institution, the infallibility or reliable guidance will be located in the head rather than in the heart.

The imagery of head and heart is vital for a proper understanding of this matter. It is taken, of course, from the integral human being who is head and heart (and belly according to the Enneagram). The head does not dictate to the heart. It does what it can with what the heart knows. And so the infallibility that properly resides in the whole Church, in the *sensus fidelium*, exerts its pressure on the head to affirm it as best it knows and can.

Thus the role of the *magisterium*, or official teaching organ of the

Church, is to keep open the important spaces in which the heart may
live. It is not to dictate to the Church but to respond, after its fashion,
to what the Church in prayer and art and music and a hundred other
ways knows.

About the Virgin Mary for instance. Lonergan was asked why there
seems to be no creative theologising about Mary these days, and he
answered: 'I guess we're short on feeling'. On feeling which, between
writing *Insight* and writing *Method in Theology*, he realised to be central
to the intellectual enterprise, without which all that we write is 'paper-
thin'. Now if he is right here, we shall expect to find in the Church a
situation in which the *magisterium* does its job of keeping the space
open in response to the *sensus fidelium*, while the *sensus fidelium* finds
little creative theological expression. A middle is lacking between
what has to be said in the head and millions of rosaries. There is a
subtext here, which is Rome's appalling insensitivity to feeling, which
creates an unhealthy gap between rationality and sentimentality,
which have often been noted as the two salient features of official
Roman Catholicism.

Still, the head remains, with its function that is to keep open the great
spaces demanded by the believing, praying heart of the Church. And
Mary is the place where this drama is enacted. This was accurately
noted by the feminist theologian who told me years ago how impressed
she was to find that the Church that is so insensitive to women has,
throughout its history, bent over backwards to make a woman as nearly
divine as possible yet compatible with the unique divinity of Jesus
(which, the moment it gets attached to his gender, is misunderstood).
What she was naming was the gap between the head and the heart,
which is only to be filled by the heart – which, in the case of Mary,
means women – becoming more and more articulate in a patriarchal
culture that keeps women in mind as the object not the subject.

'... Which in the case of Mary means women'. The question is, how
are women, becoming the creative subject in culture, to see themselves
in Mary? Well, the gospel story appears helpful here, for it makes the
incarnation dependent upon the consent of a woman. But consent to
what? Mary's role in the incarnation cannot be seen as changing the
world for women forever (which it does) unless we can say something
of Mary psychologically that would make her an active and knowing,
not a passive and unknowing, participant in the incarnation. Woman's
power to change culture would have to be somehow foreshadowed
for her in Mary's: 'Let it be done to me!'

Thus we seek some sort of psychological conditioning in Mary which would make it possible for 'the girl next door' to say 'Yes' to the transformation of humanity, for the visit of the angel to constitute 'her moment come'.

Now obviously this condition is in the area of awareness, which is a subjective quality, for it is woman as subject who has been denied by our western culture. Nor is the Christian tradition, east and west, without suggestions here. Mary as the enlightened one has everything going for her. When I was a novice, the old office for 'Mary on Saturday' was mainly composed of a cluster of the Wisdom literature, describing the Lady Wisdom who assists the Creator as he fashions the world. I remember wondering: 'What has this to do with Our Lady?' Then there was the use of the Martha and Mary gospel, with its conclusion: 'Mary has chosen the better part', for the feast of the Assumption. Obviously the other big feature is motherhood, pre-scribed by the Ephesus title 'Mother of God'.

The question then becomes: Is there anything in the 'head' of the Church, amid the stuff that goes on there, that could respond to the popular and artistic pressure to have Mary as mother and wisdom personified? Is there any 'conditioning' she might be said to have undergone, to be described in the head's terms?

And of course the head obliges. It has a concept for the condition from which Christ crucified and risen saves us. Lagrange, the Dominican Scripture scholar who rescued Scripture studies from the ravages of the head, said, à propos of the Letter to the Romans, that we did not know what we had been rescued from until we experienced the rescued condition, of being 'in Christ'. This concept of the human plight is called 'original sin'.

It is, generically, the same as the unenlightened sleep condition named by Buddhism, the only difference being that it bears the marks of our western experience, moral, political, adventurous, dangerous, and is called by the name of 'sin'. But conceptually it is doing the same job as *samsara* in Buddhism. And in fact we are coming to see that the concept has become distorted in the west by emphasising the moral failure over that of blindness and sleep, which is much more emphasised, especially in Mark's gospel.

So 'original sin' is where we have to look, in the Church's 'head', for this sapiential quality in Mary that gives her the subject-shaped, active role in the incarnation that is hers once you take the title 'Mother of God' to mean what it says. One didn't become Mother of God by accident! The two things in Mary that have to be brought together are motherhood and wisdom: motherhood obviously, wisdom by the requirement of the universal *sensus fidelium*. This points to exemption from 'original sin', especially on the side of consciousness. 'Seat of Wisdom' is to be taken as seriously as 'Mother of God'.

And the head sets to work. Mary is 'free' of the original blindness of humanity from which only Jesus has made us free, so somehow she too must be thus free as Jesus' beneficiary before the fact of his redeeming deed. And now that the head has the bit between its teeth – to make haywire of the metaphor – it goes for it. Our Mary, 'from the first moment of her conception', must be untouched by original sin. Of course this is wild talk, inviting the bewildered smile of the people who deal in genetics. It asks for dismissal by the liberal who is ready with images of angels on the head of a pin. But it is only a caricature because it is trying to say in head language what the spirit demands and that, unless it is said in head language, will abandon us to common sense that keeps us in the night. The Immaculate Conception is the best of nice tries at keeping that great space of Mother Mary open to the soul of the praying Church. The head by itself, as the letter by itself, kills. The Immaculate Conception is as necessary as a reminder of who Mary is as the *homoousion* is as a reminder of who Jesus is.[3]

That was in 1865. And two years later, Mary put it right. She spoke as the archetype into whose psychological space the definition had put her, by saying to Bernadette: 'I am the Immaculate Conception.' She said it to all men and women, so we are to recognise ourselves as conceived immaculate in the mind of God before we succumb to the darkness of history into which we are to 'work out our salvation with fear and trembling'.

In the context of this fresh spurt of the revelation in Christ, Mary Douglas' plea for a women's commission on doctrine permanently in session with veto power doesn't look at all absurd, as the College of Cardinals gets to look like the Elders of Mozart's *Magic Flute*. The subject status of women in the Church is Mary's agenda, and we are only at the beginning of it.

---

[3] *Homoousion* is the word used by the Council of Nicaea to express the doctrine of the divinity of Christ, that Jesus was 'of one substance with the Father'.

Mary be me in bowels of abandon
With palms upturned to handfuls of the sky
And I with nothing of my own to stand on
Pray only so far up to 'Let my cry ...'

Deep subjectivity in me denied
With woman thrown into the dark as she
With shades of mother on and off descried
In the attempt, at half-cock, to be he.

Who in me knows you in your images
Sees you through eyes with some surrender softened
That let you in behind what the head says
To where deep space is all and I am orphaned.

And where at last you importune the church
You find me set up on her priestly perch.

Fourth Essay on Mary

Our increasingly stale patriarchal culture sees woman as an 'object' belonging to a man. Yet, in Mary, the seat of Wisdom, woman is a 'subject', who, by co-operating freely and consciously in his plan, belongs to God, not to man. This theological truth is the Trojan Horse of our culture, including the culture of the Vatican itself.

We can see virginal conception as a new creation, as creation anew, but could the Virgin have? Not if the knowing involved is thought of in objective terms, in terms of the idea. This would attribute to Mary a theological expertise which took centuries after the fact to elaborate. So we have to think of Mary's knowing not as scholarly and object-centred, but as a special condition of the subject, of herself as deeply called upon – which is precisely what has grabbed believers' imagination down the ages, the element of deep subjective consent. In other words, the realities of the situation, of a Jewish girl not a Christian scholar-in-advance, lead us to concentrate on the subjective state of Mary, to what begins to appear to us as the subjectivity of woman systemically avoided by an androcentric culture. Mary begins to appear to us as who woman is to herself as opposed to who she is taught she is by the culture. What begins to dawn on us is identity from God, identity from the unknown. This ordinary Jewish girl felt unaccountably different, called, as we can see, to represent woman the oppressed, woman the feared, woman the fled from into our brilliant phallocracy. God was speaking in woman before he would speak in the Son to be.

The Catholic sense of Mary has picked this up in spite of the androcentric pressure of the culture and felt compelled to emphasise the depth of Mary, some deep 'conditioning', a consciousness totally emancipated from the common sense that theologians have learned to call 'original sin' and, as a corollary, to see her as conceived free of it. The woman immaculately conceived is the woman for all women, hers the self in woman that woman has only latterly been allowed by our culture to have.

Woman, as so perceived, woman not as object but as subject, evokes the whole rich notion of wisdom, the automatic feminine personification of wisdom, and when we come to think of the transformation of humanity by God in Christ, she has a positive agency in this transformation. As the biblical author of the Wisdom literature has God consulting the Lady Wisdom while he worked on his creation, so we have to see God working on his new creation with Mary in mind.

Thus Mary, received by a culture androcentric and phallocratic, is subversive of this culture, is its Trojan Horse. The transformation in Christ totally restores woman to her neglected culture-shaping role.

Thus when, nearly twenty centuries later, science focuses on the genetics of virgin birth and looks for its Y-chromosome, the tradition has already focused us on the *meaning* rather than the curious alleged *event*. That meaning is the meaning of woman to herself. It goes to the roots of what we call grace, the subjective moment in the felt presence of the unknown.

Thus Catholic tradition has, long before the question of genetics arose, put the emphasis on the significance of the virgin birth rather than on the alleged fact. It has been led to ponder Mary's being 'equal', 'up to' this significance through the deep conditioning of being conceived immaculate. Mary is equal to this significance not by understanding it but by being it, being, that is, virginal to the unknown, whatever that means to our busy mind.

Long before science was to have problems with the fact of virginal conception, tradition was led to concentrate on the significance, and thus to enter the depths of the virgin consenting to the unknown. The consent to the unknown is unconditional and contentless, it is an absolute 'whatever', which each of us has to find within him- or herself. This for me has been the awesomeness of Tolle's experience which evoked my own feeling, 'I'll give him whatever he wants' and, much later, my own grace-given urge to celebrate my long-fled-from womanly form. Before science could have problems, tradition was led to explore, in Mary, the naked consent of the heart to the unknown, unspecifiable, unspeakable will, which could have embraced any source for the pregnancy. Thus to concentrate on the meaning rather than the curious fact is not a furtive ploy on being 'found out' by science in our pretensions, the reaction to the gibes of Richard Dawkins. Tradition anticipates the problem and leaves us with it – rather the way that a koan does. Ages ago, Eliot spoke of an obtuse mentality that would start the enquiry into religion by asking whether a virgin birth is believable.

We all know that consent to God is consent to life in its totality as all and nothing, for the contemplative to 'nothing in particular', and for this we look to Mary, Seat of Wisdom.

A woman belongs not to a man but to God, whose mission for her is for the healing of a phallocentric outlook and culture which is God-proof. She finds this destiny not in the 'biology' with which the culture identifies it, but in Mary – God's woman, woman God-conceived to open her womb to the absolute word. The call to Mary to be God's Mother is the call to her to be Eve's advocate, to represent woman as she frees herself from culture-assigned roles for culture's subversion and transformation. But the lens for the recovery of a Marian understanding of life as a flourishing rather than a conquest is woman's quest for her own subjectivity, her own denied initiative. For me it is the acceptance of the woman in myself. For all men it is this. She who foresaw that all ages would bless her marks an eschatological freedom from male and female which Paul saw as the character of all who are in Christ.

Thus the Spirit becomes more and more insistent, outside the Church if necessary, on the eternal feminine. The content of the 'already but not yet' of realised eschatology is the recovery by the woman of the culture-shaping power that she was robbed of with the birth of civilisation as we know it, of patriarchy. This recovery is not *over* the man in a reversal of the original male victory over her, but *with* the man, Eve with Adam. The version we have had so far of the redemption has it achieved for Adam as standing for humanity male and female. Innocence of anthropology has concealed from the propagators of this version the fact that in practice Adam has not been effectively both male and female but has been male, so that the whole story of redemption has been about our becoming sons – read Paul: it's obvious. 'Daughters too, of course' we limply add in deference to the other half of humanity, but the gap is glaring. This dropping effectively of woman from the would-be generic Adam is continued by a version of Christian theology that drops Mary. The virtually exclusive maleness of Jesus looks back to the maleness of Adam, with Eve left out in the cold. Scandalously, though absurdly and so harmlessly, the present Vatican polemic against women's ordination proposes as theological this dropping of woman from the generic 'man' where the sanctuary is concerned.

Fifth Essay on Mary
Once the mystery of Mary has taken hold of the woman believer, she sees in Mary her own freedom for God's purpose in the world.

I don't know any way to get clearer and clearer about something than to do so, chapter by chapter, and that is what I am doing as I focus my faith on Mary. This growing clarity is not simply 'in the head'. On the contrary, it consists in coming more and more into the body, into the discovery of Mary there, for me and for others I hope, especially for women. So let me embark on a final chapter.

How does Mary embody what Barth will not allow, namely humanity consenting to its own salvation? At first there seems to be no problem here. If we take Luke's Annunciation story as an account of what happened to Mary, the angel tells her that she, if willing, is to become miraculously pregnant and the child is going to be as wonderful as the manner of the pregnancy is 'out of this world'. So in consenting to this, Mary is consenting to the wholly new, to a *nova nativitas* as the Christmas liturgy puts it, and thus is willingly consenting to God's plan for human salvation. QED!

But how was she, on that showing, acting representatively for all humanity? How was she flouting Karl Barth? Only through the willingness of the story's believer to take her as so representative because of what the angel is reported as saying. But the contemporary believer, and certainly the contemporary woman, needs to see mirrored in Mary her own deeply buried, culturally obscured, being – a being called upon by the unknown to change the world – for the Christian is called upon to change the world, not to live in it keeping the rules and end up in heaven. She needs to see herself as the instrument of God's action, not by being told she is this through a story, but by knowing this role, however obscurely, as hers in the cosmos. Max Scheler's question, 'What is the place of the human in the universe?' is your question and mine, meaning for my life or none. And since the human being who is to have this transformative role is a woman, it is as a woman's coming-alive to herself that the believing woman takes it on board. She has to see Mary as what her own life is all about, to see herself in Mary, not as her alleged, even divinely alleged representative, but as mirror to her deepest self-searching. If the Magnificat means anything, it is a powerful affirmation of the role of woman in changing the culture. It is subversively feminist, and that this obvious meaning has not been seen only goes to show the power of an androcentric perspective to shape the language.

Now does this turn to woman as the subject reject the literal meaning of the story? No, it says that the literal understanding does not convey the mystery of Mary to her. If Mary does represent woman before God and the world, the believing woman has to feel represented, she has to feel awakened by Mary.

Once the mystery of Mary has taken hold of the woman believer, she sees in Mary her own freedom for God's purpose in the world, as opposed to the patriarchal story that her purpose is to belong to a man and raise a family. In her deepest subjectivity, a woman belongs to God not to a man, as a man does and not to a woman.

It is the personal presence of Mary to the believer as the one in whom she sees herself in surrender to the unknown and ultimately to-be-trusted that has called for a bold definition of Mary as 'cheating' where original sin is concerned. She had to be free of our vast and endless human karma in order to represent our humanity at its forgotten best, as immaculately conceived, as 'born for higher things' as Tennyson said, above all as willing to be forever changed and say 'Sorry!' to Karl Barth. Barth says I am totally corrupt. But I've tasted paradise, and Mary is my advocate.

For this interplay between the alleged fact and the meaning, the idea of the koan is useful. A koan-question – like 'what is the sound of one hand clapping?' – invites the hearer to hold two opposites in the mind in a way that will transform the mind itself. The koan seeks not solution but resolution, as does the practice of Focusing.[4]

In fact, the wording of the definition of the Immaculate Conception

---

[4] See Chapter 7.

is stingy. Mary scrapes in to her privileged paradisal place only in the
light of what Jesus was going to bring about. The framers had little
idea of the liberation of women that they were proclaiming. They
minimised the not-lost paradisal dimension of which Mary is the
luminous cosmic showing. That is the way of framers, and it is needed. Nevertheless, it secures the mystery against backsliding, even in
response to the needs of ecumenism.

> The end of time finds Mary in the gap,
> Gentleness total for the interim,
> Of new creation the immortal sap
> Softens our phallic bonding around him.
>
> How could a girl be the creation's self
> Assenting to the change to our eternal
> Life, the accumulating coastal shelf
> Not waste, as image of the near infernal?
>
> Good question! Barth has answered with the No
> Of eyes that see us only as depraved
> So that his Mary does not need to know
> The loveliness of what is to be saved.
>
> Not without ghastly phallocratic strife
> Depraved old Rome has known the girl as life.

Celebrating the Song of Songs

*The Song of Songs is a place where the masculine and long-unacknowledged
feminine come together in peace. But why was this beautiful love poem
between a man and a woman interpreted by the Church as a poem between
'the soul and its God'? The long shadow of St Augustine with his 'desexualising of love' falls here.*

*Part of this paper was delivered to the Guild of Pastoral Psychology in spring
2005.[5]*

What I have been given most deeply to understand about myself is as
a meeting place between a man and woman within. I can now look
back on my life as one of conflict between them, and I am only seeing

---

[5] See: www.guildofpastoralpsychology.org.uk

this now because they are coming to peace. I celebrate this peace in the Song of Songs that I read daily and always freshly. My guide through this text is Phyllis Trible's wonderful piece of biblical theology, *God and the Rhetoric of Sexuality.*

By way of paradigm placement, here are two definitions: sex is natural and universal, the same everywhere; gender is cultural, a huge array of what male and female mean respectively in different cultures. Religious interpreters always cheat here, slipping between sex and gender in a 'heads-I-win-tails-you-lose' way, praising women to the skies as feminine and keeping them out of the sanctuary as female. Now there is, I think, a universal common factor in all the cultural shapings of gender meanings: that man is a person, woman a place, and that to look to a cultural acceptance of woman as a person in the way man has always been so is to look ahead, to feel a realised eschatology. Keeping this personal, I am finding that I understand this need for psychological equality, of which Tina Beattie has the most radical statement, in myself, as the peace I am coming into between the man and the woman within. When Tina says that she was drawn to the Catholic Church as 'the most symbolised of all the Christian traditions' and disappointed on not hearing her body speak in the Church, I knew what she was talking about. (At first I didn't, and then to my shame I did and do.) The real equality between man and woman is psychological and is felt by its lack in the most intimate recesses of the soul, to some extent available to my introspection. Every morning I take up the Song, and feel the man and the woman as it were articulating me.

This ongoing meeting between the man and the woman is dramatised in the Song, in which Trible finds five movements, each of them ending with a statement about love, one repeated four times being a solemn abjuration not to stir love until it pleases. This injunction attributes to 'love' a final authority which takes us to Trible's fundamental thesis – echoed by Pope John Paul in his meditations – that the Song of Songs has to be paired with the account of the Fall in Genesis, her chapter on which she calls 'A Love Story Gone Awry', while her next chapter, on the Song, is called 'Love's Lyrics Redeemed'. The earthling's cry, on seeing the woman, 'bone of my bone, flesh of my flesh!' is love-language, interrupted by the Fall into thinking and dualism, the world we live in, and resumed in what I call the middle garden, Blake's *Garden of Love*. This is why Rabbi Aqiba, according to legend the only rabbi who saw God and in consequence got sex

straight, called this text 'The Holy of Holies' and accounted for its
having no reference to God by saying that where God is he doesn't
have to be referred to. How that observation of Judaism's founding
rabbi resounds for me!

The story of the Fall ends with God saying, 'You're on your own
now, sweated labour for man and subjection for woman, no more
Paradise!' How different is the absence of God from the Song! He's left
us to love. Only a prurient Church brings him back into the bedroom.
Love is to control the tempestuous moves of the flesh and to make of
sex a celebration of our unseen divine inventor.

And the Church, subtly but pervasively and devastatingly, has
inserted a distrust of pleasure, the pleasure people give each other,
into the very tone of its mediation of the Gospel. In his magisterial *The
Invention of Sodomy in Christian Theology*, Mark Jordan refers to 'the
nervous refusal of theologians to understand how pleasure can survive the preaching of the Gospel'. It is the last sentence of a powerful
book.

The obstacle, the boulder, between God's absence from the fallen
and his absence from the lovers is the massive ecclesiastical denigra-
tion of Eve. Eve bad, Mary good, is the way the Church has made
Mary insipid – and Tina's title, *God's Mother, Eve's Advocate*, is
appropriate. That is why Tina could not find woman's body in the
most symbolising of all the Christian traditions. She has found what I
would call a minority report in the feisty Virgin of a few Church
Fathers, as opposed to the male model of perfect submission. She even
suggests that the Council of Ephesus was taming an enthusiastic Mary
cult in making her the Mother of God as the logical implication of
saying that Jesus was really the Son of God. Interesting, and reinfor-
cing, but let's keep on track!

For the question I find myself asking, as I read the Song as celebrating the all-creator out of my felt fullness of life, is this. First of all,
it is a fact that the Song has been the primary revelatory text for the
monastic tradition of *lectio divina*. The question is: Does my understanding of the Song as celebratory, divine in that sense, match with
what was in their heads as they drooled over it? Surely not. Between
them and the text there is an unavowed, an unnoticed transposition
whereby the two characters of the text, the man and the woman,
become 'the soul' and 'God'. What dictates this transposition, I suspect, is an event crucial for western Christendom, the conversion of St
Augustine, the master of it. Conversion for him was the total

transformation that conversion always is, as a result of which, as he says: 'I talked with you as friends talk, of my salvation, my riches, my God.' But what conversion entailed for him was the liberation from the love of women. 'Are you sure you can do without us?' he heard them saying in his head as his moment approached. And the text that did it was 'Put on the Lord Jesus Christ, and make no provision for the flesh and its importunateness.' This conversion became paradigmatic for western Christendom, and Friedrich Heer is surely correct when he attributes to Augustine the 'desexualising of love' which he deems catastrophic. In a late soliloquy, Augustine was to write: 'Nothing pulls a man down from the heights like the embrace of a woman.' The long shadow of Augustine where sex is concerned lies across the Christian centuries. And this facilitates, makes to seem obvious to the spiritual realm, the transposition from that happy couple looking at each other in the sunlight of God into 'the soul and its God'.

'What was going on in the head and heart of the medieval monastic reader of this text?', it is important to ask. But it is not impertinent to ask: 'Does what seems to be going on with them mate with what goes on for me?' One of the things we never recognise is the way consciousness does progress through the ages. As we look at ancient texts there is a certain denouement going on, that is misunderstood when we let them look stupid to us. History is not a criminal investigation of the past, but in getting rid of this error we miss ways in which we do know more, are better off. Not better, but better off.

Lunch with Tina Beattie

This essay followed a lunch with Tina Beattie in April 2006. Most feminist writing is socio-political and leaves God out of the picture. But God is in the picture and is not limited by the prevailing culture. So a feminist theology has to go beyond merely incorporating women into what remains an essentially patriarchal, male theology – a sort of 'they-too-ism'. Tina Beattie is trying to change the whole symbolic language, and in so doing to turn everything upside down – as Christ did. It is not easy to explain.

Two things stand out as I try to follow Tina in her exploration of the patriarchal world from a woman's perspective. First, that that world is male, its mind male. Secondly, that that world is dealing with God the utterly transcendent and therefore the potentially destabilising of all the attempts of the male mind to build its world order. Woman shows

up only as man's complement, his completion: and however indispensable this makes her in the male mind, it does not make her a
person, a subject, an 'other', a self wondering about herself. Woman is
passive. She is creation personified. She is not a person.

Now the discovery by women that they have been, immemorially,
left out of the picture, is going to be socio-political. But socio-political
discourse is not going to look to God, to the 'big picture'. And a
woman such as Tina who is inspired by faith in the personal absolute
cannot accept that confinement to the socio-political. She has to
negotiate the God who is mediated to her – albeit by the narrow
channel of the male version of the drama of our salvation. So she
engages the difficult task of trying to say who she is, as a woman with
her body and its messages and prophetic dreams, in the 'big picture' –
that is unfortunately so thoroughly articulated by tradition without
her.

This does not make for an easy read! To make woman articulate *in*
the drama of salvation, not merely *named* in it as vital which of course
she is (look at the near-deification of Mary in Catholic dogma), she has
to resort to allusions, suggestions, images, to all the things that pro-
voke in the male reader the impatient reaction I found I was having
with her book last night. But Tina is attempting nothing less than to
say what it's like, or rather *could* be like, to be self-aware as a woman
in accepting the Catholic tradition by the skin of her faithful Eucharist-
consuming teeth – a tradition that sees nothing absurd in one group of
men (the Congregation for the Doctrine of the Faith) writing to
another group of men (the bishops) about women in the Church.

It all comes down to woman's self-estimate not as a complement, a
completion, an inspiration, etc. etc. etc., but as who she is – not a place
but a person.

And now I come to what looks to me like a 'breakthrough'. What
Tina is looking for is a theory which follows from the revealed truth of
God's transformation of humanity, known by supernatural faith, but
which is grounded in woman's subjectivity. Such a theory would
show the Christian fact as the death-blow to patriarchy, to the whole
of theology so far which is grounded in men's experience of woman,
not woman's experience, certainly not women's experience of men.
Tina wants tradition at its most emphatic combined with feminism at
its most emphatic.

Well, if you are looking for such a theory, then how about the self-
manifestation of Jesus after his death which is implicitly subversive of

world order as we know it? This is what Johann Baptist Metz has called a 'dangerous memory'. It is the witness of those who, having been dragged through the nightmare of Calvary, had met him and had 'our hearts burning within us'. To see Jesus after the nightmare is to be a martyr, a witness in every fibre of their being. It is to know by direct experience that the reign of death over us is vacuous.

And once we're 'through' the 'break' in the citadel in this way, then it widens and deepens and gives space for a thoroughfare. For Jesus represents *all* society's victims. But who are society's main victims, if not, in a patriarchy, women?

We can push even further. That naked man nailed to a cross with the assent of the powers that be is a man degraded, deprived of the privilege our society accords to the male, of being the dominant gender whose dominion has not so far been theologically challenged, certainly in the world of traditional symbols. That is, he is reduced to woman. The crucified is the one female subjectivity-laden symbol.

Further still, we do to him what we, as a society, a culture, a civilisation, do to women. We strip him of his male dominance. And so stripped, he is woman as society sees her, interprets her, and uses her.

> Once death is devalued in love's overspill
> It's game set and match to the Fool on the Hill.

(Recommended reading here is *Woman in Berlin*, just re-published, which is an anonymous account of being a German woman in Berlin as the Russians moved in. This woman survived by securing the protection of one rapist against his weaker rivals. No wonder Jesus liked and attracted prostitutes, the sourly recognised women victims of every culture there has ever been. This lovely apocalyptic man sees them sitting down at table with Abraham, Isaac and Jacob. On his cross, he draws 'all things', the whole cultural shebang, to himself.)

Women and the Church

This second attempt to explain Tina Beattie's theology is a bit more accessible!

I've just seen a way of explaining more simply what Beattie is on about. The story of our salvation is a story of men and women. Two things go into that story as we hear it and celebrate it and pray it in church. One is the revelatory saving word of God breaking in on the human condition 'from outside' as it were, as surprise. The other is our culture's way of thinking about men and women, what we grew up with, the things we take for granted. Above all, there is the assumption that underlies the way we think about men and women. Now this assumption is operative, automatically, in the way we think of ourselves as men and women. It is operative when in danger at sea the word goes out, 'women and children first', or when a man gives up his seat to a lady as I was taught to do, or in standard jokes of men about women or of women about men, or (and there's no difference here, why should there be unless we understand that the subject matter calls for unusual attention?) when as Church we tell the story of our salvation in Christ.

There too it is as obvious that women can't be priests as it is obvious that women don't fight in the army.

But the whole point of the Christian story is that it is *irrespective* of these cultural assumptions, it addresses that in us which is created *ex nihilo* by God for God's mysterious purpose which transcends our succeeding cultural phases, of matriarchy, and of patriarchy, and looks beyond these to a paradisal condition of union with God. So the Christian story is subversive of *whatever* culture it becomes articulate in, and consists in men and women saying things about men and women that are not automatically filtered through the assumptions of our culture. The mindset in which it is obvious that women can't be priests is not shaped by the story to be told but by the ruling cultural milieu.

The Church, being an institution embedded in a culture, is peculiarly resistant to the recognition of its own culture-subversive character, peculiarly attached to that weddedness to a culture based on male dominance which is the only one we have known. This shows itself in a tendency to be sensitive to the feminine challenge in so far as it stays political, urges the claims of working mothers and female political leaders. It is only when female equality is claimed in the *sacramental* area, the Church's province, in the area where women have subjective status in the sanctuary of sexual relations and in the sanctuary of the Church's ritual, that the Church clings anew to her assumption about 'women', unaware that this assumption has nothing to do with the Gospel and everything to do with my taught table manners. The Church lives in her two worlds quite incoherently.

What Tina is saying is that we shall not have a theology adequate to this time that is seeing the demise of a male-dominated culture until the facts just pointed out are faced and steadfastly considered. When this happens, we see that Church pronouncements in the area of women's issues express the attitude of men still dominant, with women as their problem not as subjects in their own 'rite' – let me spell it this way to make clear that this is beyond the politics of feminism.

The Smile of the Father

This was preached as a sermon on the feast of the Visitation. It is, in a way, a drawing together, and maybe a drawing out, of some of the themes of this and previous chapters.

Today we celebrate the Visitation, the birthday of the Magnificat, the authoritative voice of woman in the Church which, truly heard at last, prepares the Church for the end of patriarchy. God's Mother is Eve's advocate to retrieve the name of woman from the shocking press she has had in Catholic tradition so far. Now the most important thing that the mind of woman has for us concerns how we are to think of God as the Father. God as the Father of a co-equal Son in the abundance of infinite spirit as life is not the *paterfamilias* of the Roman family. The image is utterly counter-cultural, as Constantine discovered as the Council he had convened worked out the teaching on God as triunity.

But when, much later, the Church came to try to work out how we are saved by the blood of Jesus, good old sin assumed prominence and the Father becomes the offended one, the affronted. Sin, Anselm said, is an infinite offence by reason of the dignity of the offended one, and so the patriarchal image of God assumed centre stage. Infinitely offended, he calls for an infinite sacrifice, and that is the role of the Son. What is amazing about this account is that in it the resurrection does not figure at all, except as icing on the cake. And, thankfully, the Church, with unconscious wisdom, has never committed herself with a definition to that terrible imagery.

But how might the mind of woman, of the Magnificat, see God the Father here? As an infinite tender mercy toward his violent sons whom he will lead beyond the world of rivalry into a human polity of love. Far from expecting from his Son as man the repairing of offence taken, he exposes himself in the person of his Son to our violence at its most universal and worst, the killing, deemed necessary, of the scapegoat victim, in order to draw us, by the imitation of the victim, risen and not accusing, into the free way of love between us even to death.

At Mass we celebrate the true story. Liturgy is older and deeper than dogma, and his ritual given us commemorates God's rendering obsolete of the myth of dominance, the reign of death, by which the world is still controlled. 'In the world you will have tribulation', Jesus says at that last supper, 'but have no fear: I have overcome the world'. And God's Mother tells us of a tender Father who smiles on us sinners by raising his Son our victim from the dead. Let us thank him worthily!

Learn of Me

There is surrender in the universe
It coalesces in the Son of God
Who is our Father in the best and worse
And ill-associated with the rod.

Learn of me, the voice says, throb of the stars
I am who am meek and humble of heart:
I do not know how that voice never jars
But speaks entirely a creator's art

As Jesus murmurs Abba in the night
Unbounded worlds in resonance respond
Beyond our thoughts of *jouissance* and plight
This is the only meaning to beyond

That we can celebrate in Eucharist
Universal opening of the fist.

PART TWO

we desire to be
desired by one we desire
love wants to happen

desire is not sin
but love trying to happen
we are wired for love

CHAPTER 7

Focusing – Digging for our Real Desire

The practice of 'focusing'[1] or 'biospirituality' has become for many people an important way of deepening their knowledge of their 'bodiliness'. Through it we learn really to love ourselves, perhaps somewhat as God loves us, and not to allow the contempt which others may have of us to become self-contempt. Interestingly, genuine self-love allows us to flourish, which is God's desire for each one of us, and better enables us to open up towards others.

As always the model for this is Jesus whose corporal bodiliness we share in the Eucharist. And as we move deeper into our bodily selves, so we discover that our deepest desires are towards 'the other' and that sin is not, as we may so often have thought, a following of our desire but rather its frustration.

This chapter is mainly about focusing itself; subsequent chapters explore desire and love in greater depth. Finally, Appendix II sets out something of the practicum of focusing for those readers who might wish to explore further.

In Praise of the Body

There was a tendency, with the birth of modern science, and still today with some scientists, to reject any phenomenon that is not measurable. So it is important to stress that knowledge of the body in the context of focusing means much more than just those physical characteristics which are scientifically measurable. This essay was written in August 2005. It is followed by others which touch on the importance of focusing in daily life.

[1] For more information see: www.biospiritual.org

According to a philosophy in practice received by the culture of modernity, that of John Locke, I only know what my five senses deliver. However, all these deliver are the 'secondary qualities' of 'light, dark, dry or damp, chilly or warm', which are subjective and do not tell me of the world outside. But not to worry, for the primary qualities, of size and weight, are known to my reason building on the felt bigness and heaviness of objects. Such is the world in which the body is situated, a system voluminous and variously shaped, not seen as things are seen but there on the evidence of things that are seen and touched and so forth, and now revealed to science, by way of revenge if you like, as a world 'not only odder than we conceived but odder than we can conceive'.[2]

I try to become conscious of the abysmal poverty of this vision of variously arranged extension, presented as the environment in which I live. It is a travesty of the world known and witnessed to by poets and artists and musicians since the dawn of our humanity. And yet, in the name of what is called science, it is got away with.

Now we are not stuck with this lie, in which the body is only known to me on the scales, at the tailor's measuring it for a suit, on the trolley waiting to be wheeled in to the operating theatre. And the most striking systematic denial of this lie that I know is through the skill called focusing, discovered by Eugene Gendlin and developed in five continents.

What becomes *known* to this practice is a witness of the body to itself that is centred in the body and best thought of, at least to start with, at the solar plexus, above all (and this is the point) embracing at once the subjectivity of the body and the objectivity of the world it inhabits. In contrast with the curious divided 'knowing' of the body as felt extension and reasoned subjection to laws of motion, with taste and touch and smell and sight and sound their enjoyable selves only on the subjective side of the divide, while they afford evidence for the measuring of the mechanic on the other side, in place of all this, we have one evidence of the body to itself in its environment, the cosmic whole. This is nothing less than the philosophic vindication of the creative artists in every sphere of sound and sense against the crassness of a hopeless philosophy.

---

[2] The quotation is attributed to the English astrophysicist, Arthur Stanley Eddington (1882-1944).

Father it is by your almighty power
Alone I have been moved beyond poor body
To be some-body and no longer cower
But be for others fleshly and not wordy.

Poor body I know well, it's smacked and schooled
To be as nothing begging for attention.
By this most monstrous lie I have been fooled
And joined the crowd in hope of a stray mention.

Almighty power raised Jesus from the dead
To be the body of humanity
That does not need to live against the dread
Of death and be more than in theory free.

No coward soul is mine, one poet cried:
No coward body is the crucified!

Slings and Arrows for St Sebastian's Day

In the Downside monastic community it is the custom for each member to preach on their feast day. In this homily on his feast day in 2005, Sebastian points out the tendency we all have to put each other down, how focusing can overcome this, and in doing so how it is really an imitation of Christ.

Eleanor Roosevelt, that intrepid American lover of women who, as First Lady, did so much for her sisters, used to say that no one puts you down without your consent. Do we put each other down in our community? I'm sure we don't, but I wonder where we do put each other – not down, perhaps, but, well, nowhere. There is a failure, in most communities, to encourage one another, which is due to common moral cowardice – acronym COMIC, which is normal. And in the world that we meet in the newspapers, the put-down is rampant. Donald Nicholl was asked whether there is a liberation theology that this country needs, and he said: 'Indeed there is, liberation from contempt'. Contempt is our social virus, the intelligentsia's equivalent for the boozing culture of youth *en masse* which is now being discussed in Parliament.

But let us look at the ordinary moral cowardice, the failure to encourage one another. That we certainly suffer from. But we need to think about our response to it, the reaction to not being encouraged. How do I behave at being put down or at least not put up? This is what Eleanor is talking about when she says that no one does it to you without your consent.

How do we consent to being put down? It's simple. The offender is imposing on me his own low self-esteem and, prone to low self-esteem as we all are, I catch it and tacitly agree against myself. It's what Girard calls mimesis, copycat, the staple of society.

How do I stop doing this? The answer to this question is the most valuable life-skill I know, which we are teaching our pupils. It's called focusing, and it consists in becoming aware of myself in a negative confrontation with someone, and saying: 'You poor thing! Sorry for paying no attention to you, because really I love you, you're my body!' This is the antidote, this is how not to consent tacitly to the put-down: remember you love yourself as God's creation. Receive the put-down not with your miserable but with your loved self. That does hurt quite a bit, but it comes to feel right, because there is a true self-pity that is vital although our traditional spirituality still knows little about it.

And this is the imitation of Christ who, as St Peter says, 'being reviled, did not revile in return'. This does not mean that he accepted insults with what my old friend Tony ffrench-Mullen called 'a brave little smile'. Yuk! That's not how he reacted to being called a Beelze-bubber! No, it means he never forgot himself as God's beloved one, and received our onslaughts into that huge space where, in God's due time, he changed the world for those who awake to him in a new humanity that swallows violence in divine love. Nietzsche thought the brave little smile was the essence of Christianity, and he launched against this windmill the terrible force of his rhetoric. No wonder he didn't like *Don Quixote*! Try again, Freddie N.! Arise sleeper from the dead, and Christ will enlighten thee. The drama of this transforming reception of our fearful violence is documented, with unusual clarity for a pre-psychological culture, in what we call the agony in the garden.

The extraordinary thing is that it works! Well, of course it does! It's God's way in us, palpable in Jesus. When you feel put down by someone, remember you love yourself and don't catch their miserable bug of self-loathing. A friend to whom I spoke of this recently said immediately: 'Yes of course, it happened in the camps all the time, self-degradation of the victims in harmony with the infliction, a line of least resistance.'

In so far as I remember to put the more difficult way into practice, I am letting myself be drawn into the magnetic field of the Eucharist, in which Jesus' acceptance of injury was so total that he could make a party out of it. I must confess that I'm not getting far with this magnetic field as yet!

A Lenten Exercise

As we 'focus', that is, give attention to ourselves in our dealing with others, then we are fulfilling the commandment to love ourselves as our neighbour and in this we touch our deepest and most natural, i.e. God-given, desire. For all this, the Eucharist, the Mass, should be central, the magnetic field to which we are drawn.

Our culture lies to us about the self, telling me that I am a subject with desires to whose fulfilment I have a right. The self thus understood is confronted by the other, with whom he or she has to deal, with varying degrees of agreement. This confrontational model ignores a fact that some of us are discovering these days: that there is a tenderness in myself that, attended to as I am dealing with others, is toward the other and is naturally friendly. There is a certain skill in coming into touch with this tenderness. It consists in choosing, instead of my irritation and perhaps (and preferably for the exercise) rage at him or her, to drop back inwardly and notice myself all steamed up, and say something like: 'You poor thing, you really are in a state!' This falling back I call 'resiling' – a good word from which we get 'resilient'. You have to discover your own way of doing this, as you have to find your own way of praying, which is simply doing it with God there. But when it really works, you start to 'come alive'.

This new aliveness in you is toward the other or others. And this is the truth about us, of which our culture is in denial: feeling myself, I am inclined to the other, and whatever has been my ordinary extroverted view of him, whether of irritation or anger, becomes friendly. I think that this change is more likely to happen with those we do not easily find congenial. Certainly when it happens with the non-congenial, I am getting a glimpse of the love that Jesus enjoined, which is for my neighbour whoever he or she is, to whom I am so wedded by our creator and liberator that I am to lay down my life for them.

The point about this practice of self-attention when with the other is that it gives us an inkling of the commanded love of my neighbour as myself as the fulfilment of my most natural desire.

Let us look more closely at this attention to my self, my composure disturbed by another. It is pity for myself buffeted by abrasive confrontation. It is self-pity. And it is pitiful of the other. This true self-pity is a new arrival on the spiritual scene as traditionally described. Self-pity as commonly understood is the enemy of the spiritual life. True self-pity is a vital newcomer to our self-understanding. It is the discovery of what is the best spiritual discipline I know, called focusing or biospirituality.

Not so surprisingly, it finds its model in Christ agonised, crucified, risen, and Spirit-releasing. Jesus in the Garden of Olives became receptive of all the fearful hatred of the world, religious and secular, received it into a transforming tenderness that embraces the crucifier and, as Saul knew on the way to Damascus, turns him into a world-changing other Christ. How what Girard calls '*l'horreur humaine de la crucifixion*' becomes Eucharist has challenged theologians and exposed our radical human ineptitude.

Thus the exercise I try to remember to do – resiling into 'you poor thing!' said to me in life's confrontations (all of which exploit our natural low self-esteem and so easily endorse it, for 'no one puts you down without your consent', as Eleanor Roosevelt said) – can come into the magnetic field of the Eucharist.

Rowan Williams picks it up in an astonishing phrase: 'the festal abrogation of rivalry, the social miracle'. In *Good as New*, a 'radical retelling of the scriptures', John Henson gives his version of Gethsemani:

> Then he went a little way from them and talked with God. Jesus said, 'Loving God, please don't let me have to go through with this. But if it's what you want me to do, I'm ready.' As Jesus said this, he experienced a great upsurge of strength, and he knew *God had not left him on his own*. But the pain of grief and anxiety was so intense *as he opened his heart*, the sweat fell from him in great big drops.

The italics are mine, for the phrase encapsulates the *reception* of injury as the vital change in the subject.

With the Lenten Exercise

Jesus my self my brother and our war
Whose blood you change into a festive wine
Elation to make the spirit soar
And readily confess you as divine.

Self-pity we were taught always to shun
And now I learn to feel myself anew
With others as our business is done,
Find pity there for me and them in you

Whose vast compassion is the mirror to
My tenderness to me now uttering
Another language of our me and you
That is myself alive, can only sing

To you, your ritual alive again
The ready transformation of our pain.

My Wow!

In the new life that the risen Jesus brings, sin is not the breaking of a law but the frustrating of our deepest desire. To respond to this desire, which is to love and be loved, is to flourish as a human being. Such flourishing is goodness and we know it when we see it. In all of this the skill of focusing helps.

I have to tell you
My wow as it may touch you
For it is all I have.

We certainly know goodness when we see it, and the disciples had seen it in Jesus and followed him to the disaster that awaits goodness if it exposes itself too much in a politico-religious world. So when they saw him after his murder, this meant that goodness had not been defeated by our world order.

But how do we know goodness when we meet it? Because we see in it what we really want. Our real desire is to be a community in love reflecting a God who, in the disclosure of Jesus as who he really was, is also a 'we', later to be called Trinity. We killed Jesus because we couldn't believe in ourselves as a 'we in love' which he wanted for us, so when he showed himself to us 'beyond death' a 'we-in-God' came to be.

That phrase 'beyond death' does not mean 'in a state after death' that nearly all religions believe in. It means 'beyond death and all that', beyond the world as we know it which has death worked into it the way a painter will put flecks of red in a picture that you don't see as red, to make black more black: we meet death hiding in life. 'In the midst of life we are in death.' Now, as an oppressed people, the followers of Jesus, Jews, knew this presence of death in life not in the sophisticated way of us who like to think our lives are our own, but in the brutal form of a police state. So the death that is woven into life was there for them in Technicolor, in the shape of crucified corpses of troublemakers all along the *Via Appia* in Rome. Thus the beyond-death quality of the risen Jesus was, for them, 'one in the eye' for Imperial Rome. The point was more easily made for an oppressed people than when Paul tried to make it for the talkative Athenians.

But, the point thus made, the result is devastating. For a human world beyond death-and-all-that was able to be described by Paul as us 'sitting in the heavenly places'. Once we are out of death-and-all-that, we see how indispensable death-and-all-that is for keeping in place a God who dominates and demands cultic sacrifices – and fits into a substitutionary payment theory of atonement. Death is those flecks of red in God's robe that make him a dark God, meaning an unfriendly and untrustworthy one. Getting to know the risen Jesus is getting free of a God of death and sacrifice, and coming into a God who is love and whose pronoun is 'we'. 'Who will go for us?' Isaiah hears in his vision.

There follows a chain reaction of insights. With Jesus revealing us to ourselves as seated where he is in the heavenly places, we have a new definition of sin, not as the breaking of a law but as the *frustrating of our real desire*. This is paradoxical, for we have got used to thinking of sin as giving in to our desire. And *that* Paul had to deal with. The objection that these Christians were making everything permissible points to the paradox that leads to this misunderstanding.

And have we not already said that desire in us spots a good person whatever society says or does to him? It is this native desire in the hearts of Jesus' disciples that he has been coaxing to come out with parables and paradoxes and beatitudes, and that comes to shipwreck with the arrest of Jesus by the powers that be, because it had to be led through the horror of death-and-all-that which the powers that be keep in place. Their Jesus had to be in the dock, with that sickening total doubt that comes upon the disciple that sees him there. Has he, after all, led us on a dance that is against the law, which knows very well what to do with tiresome people? Peter finds himself in denial. Rocky got cold feet!

But what about this natural desire of ours which sees Jesus as goodness personified? Can we experience it in ourselves and not just as what must be in ourselves to be able to spot goodness in Jesus and some special people? Can we experience our desire to love all people that Jesus brings to flourishing in the *ecclesia* of the called? Yes: this is the discovery of focusing, now a worldwide movement known as biospirituality. It's the best thing on offer.

The best way I know to introduce this is as follows. Take any really strong feelings you have against someone. Acknowledge them. I hate his or her guts! Then very quietly – with a friend if possible – turn your attention to what is going on inside *you*. Look at your feeling about that person as something that's happening to you, a disturbance, a feeling not-good. Are you perhaps sorry for yourself being this way? Is it not you that are suffering from your bad feelings about this person? Now what people are discovering is that a moment can come when the 'you', that is the real sufferer in this affair of hating someone, 'speaks up', comes to life, and is friendly because it is naturally friendly. It is helpful – indeed necessary I find – to locate this new feeling in the body, around the heart. You might want to say: 'I am knowing my body for the first time.'

What is so fascinating here is that this lovingness that you can find in your body enables you to hear in a completely different way the statement that we are all members of Christ's body. St Paul's notion that we are 'members' of Christ's body easily gets bogged down in a crude literalism – am I, for instance, the big toe? What focusing does is to give us a knowledge of 'the body at first hand', which is at the opposite end to what the surgeon has under his knife – for which thank God: I have nothing against science! What I am talking about is the body lived-in, loved-in, loved to be in, that is so attracted to other bodies as to constitute with them a continuum. To be in Christ is to be fully alive, so that my body is extended into his body.

'Do not be afraid!' and 'Open now to one another!' are the same command to live in our new condition of human flourishing, for which Christ is the pioneer, as the Letter to the Hebrews says. What

Jesus does for us when he shows himself beyond death-and-all-that is that he lets us into each other. Mutual fear, that keeps so much religion going, stops desire flourishing; so with fear gone we open to each other. Notice that the one thing the risen Jesus keeps saying is: 'Do not be afraid!' Where desire is enabled at last to flourish, don't let fear say this is too good to be true – the disciples were saying that in their hearts when he showed up – the text says so. So here's a haiku:

> when Jesus is seen
> there beyond death and all that
> we feel each other.

It does all hang together beautifully. Original desire wants to become love. It does so successfully in the life and death and beyond-death-and-all-that of Jesus who in his horrible murder at our fearful hands made it to beyond death-and-all-that. And this elimination of the fear that frustrates desire does something to our idea of God, who ceases to be the untrustworthy unknown who tyrannises over us and makes us tyrannise over each other, and becomes instead our friend.

Practical summing up: by our nature we are likeable and lovers of one another. We are only mistakenly selfish. Our money-oriented culture heavily reinforces this mistake, telling us that to be likeable we must buy its self-enhancing products, from aftershaves to cars. The Church, when it's doing its job and letting Jesus speak in it, tells us that we are naturally likeable and flourish in loving one another. Sadly the Church is often not doing its job, but teaches instead in conformity with the biases of the culture: against women – even now, in spite of feminism – gay and lesbian people, racial minorities, Jews. This is the whole bunch of us that the gospel calls 'publicans and sinners', whom Jesus befriended and was crucified for doing so.

So we worship as God a man who let a tart wipe his tired feet with her hair. Do we worship this man, outside church on Sundays? Nietzsche said, 'Christians do not look as though they were saved!' He meant that you don't too often see on the face of the believer the unmistakable marks of human flourishing. For human flourishing is God's achievement. 'The glory of God is man really alive', as St Irenaeus taught us in the second century.

> Remember how you felt uncomfortable
> Hating a person whom you couldn't stand,

Stay in that place, your comfort and your stable
Where you are likeable and do not brand.

But I don't like myself, I hear you say.
It's what you have been taught and it's not you:
If you would learn to focus as you pray
For enemies, your Jesus would come through.

Our sin original is the mistake
Of listening to all the biases
We are brought up with, that we need to shake
Free of, a dog that's been baptised I guess.

When the church finds us likeable we'll know
That Jesus' second coming is in tow.

An Exercise at Mass

Focusing should help us bring our true, deeper self into our participation at Mass.

How do I think of myself as I take part in the Mass? Who is the self I bring to the celebration that is speaking of me as a sinner asking pardon and grace? I find that the self that 'answers' to this liturgical self-description is the beat-up habitual self, bullied at school, put down and resentful, the usual formula of practical low self-esteem in other words, the banal opposite of the self that the Spirit is looking for. This self is the resultant of routine life at my job and with people, and is probably not the self awakened by a love-affair or life with a great friend. It is probably not the self that waits on grace, which is the one the liturgy is really talking about. No, I am one of the people who were 'unfaithful' when God 'put them to the test'. I don't identify enthusiastically with those hangdog people the Israelites in the desert grousing at Moses, but participate routinely, because this is Mass and Scripture is now 'important'. This is who the Mass is telling me I am, and it's the same as who I'm told I am by the people I routinely interact with. So of course the Mass is a bore. I never or seldom come alive at it.

Now I can change this situation by 'focusing' it. I come into the right kind of self-pity, in which I attend to myself as 'you poor old thing', confused as you remember a problem you're having with someone, really upset at what he or she said or did and what I didn't say or do. You poor tired old reactive me! The point of focusing is that this 'me' thus attended to, thus listened to, what Tolle calls my 'pain-body', is where desire resides and wants to grow into loving. OK, so I go there and let this happen. With practice it comes easily.

And it is this self that is invited into the huge vulnerability of the Christ-self, to be transformed into the real sinner that Jesus loves and dies for.

Of course in this exercise I am recovering from Church attrition, which is simply an extension of world-attrition. The huge psychological error of average half-baked Christianity – the inoculating 'small dose' Bernard Shaw referred to – consists in concentrating on 'sin' as opposed to desire, of which sin is the derailment. Remember the young man in *Equus*, coming upon men at a porno movie: 'They were like people in church!'

So Mass is the time when I am to let my real, life-desiring and vulnerable self come into contact with the ultimate expression of our nakedness: my body for you.

Could this address the infinite boredom that the Mass means to young people today, to those who still go, probably with family? Bring to Mass the row you're having with that asshole of a teacher. Learn to be really sorry for yourself, and remember Gethsemani and the wonderful party Jesus got out of it, with the bread and wine.

That bread and wine become his body and blood is the simplest description of a transformation that cannot be got into words, of all the violence of the world taken into the heart of its victim whose acceptance demands a party like nothing else does, what Rowan Williams calls the 'festal abrogation of rivalry, the social miracle'. People who throw themselves into peacemaking come to recognise in the Eucharist its compact expression.

A Focused Sonnet

You never told me this was dead-sea fruit,
Its garden of resentment my own space,
Left it to praying to be more astute
And sink into my body and its grace.

Yet it was possible, for half a life,
To cull these poisoned products of the mind
Whose space was laid out by surrounding strife
In which I sought and never was to find

Until the body not the spirit spoke
A language long denied it by belief
Which saw my members as not there to stroke
But use for worshipping without relief

Epitomised, God, by a reining pope.
Faithful awake, and learn how you may cope.

(no misprint in couplet!)

CHAPTER 8

Desire is Love Trying to Happen

In the previous chapter we saw how our real desire, for which God made us and Jesus saved us, can emerge through the practice of focusing and discovering our true selves. In this chapter we explore how 'desire is love trying to happen' – a favourite Sebastian catchphrase.

God is a god of desire, not of power and prestige, and Jesus knew God as the object of all our deepest desires – for joy, for laughter, and the love of friends, for sexual fulfilment. All of his life and teaching can be summarised as encouraging us to allow our innate desire, which is also God's desire for us, to break through our fear and self-loathing. And sin is that fear, fear of desire, fear of life and fear of falling into God.

We are wired for love and we only flourish when we love. Our most ambitious desire is to be the cause of joy in another. This includes our strongest experience of God-given desire towards another – sexual desire. But in some ways the Church is still in thrall to Augustine's ideas, perhaps appropriate for his age and culture, that set love of God against sexual love which he regarded as greedy and lustful. It took the erotic amour courtois *movement of the twelfth century to discover the godliness in sexual desire, and later the theology of Aquinas to arrive at a deeper understanding.*

Good Friday 1993

This first piece was published in The Old Gregorian *(the magazine for former pupils of Downside School) in 1993. It still seems worth keeping.*

The Letter to the Hebrews urges us, in conclusion, to fix our gaze on 'Jesus, the pioneer and perfecter of our faith, who for the sake of the joy that was set before him endured the cross, disregarding its shame, and has taken his seat at the right hand of the throne of God.' (Heb. 12: 2.)

But how are we so to fix our gaze on him? The image of Jesus, in our mind's eye, is like a very old painting, blackened with candle smoke. How is this image to be restored for us?

Well, there is a big difference between it and the ancient painting. In a deep part of ourselves, we know the original. We do not have to apply the restoratives of scholarship, though these have their uses. We have only to look into ourselves. So let us do that for a moment.

The best sermon I ever heard as a boy at Downside was by the then headmaster, Fr Anselm Rutherford. He said that a person's desire is without limit. Nothing will satisfy us. We reach beyond ourselves. And being a man of faith, he knew that this infinite desire is never satisfied because it has an infinite object, a state of proffered bliss that haunts our dreams.

Although most of our education and training for life has fed us to ignore the fact, the real and essential self, the real you, wants all, dreams a human world that is otherwise than this, where all is light and people see the light in one another's eyes, dreams the infinite excitement which a young boy might catch a sense of in a book like *The Lord of the Rings*. Desire, at root, is infinite. And the mind, at root, conceives the question: 'Why is there anything at all?' So this infinite desire we have is not only never satisfied; it has an infinite object, the why of there being anything at all, the other side of everything, the source of the light in another's eyes.

Here, then, is how I have come to think of Jesus. Jesus knew God directly as the object of all desire. For him the object was not just a hint, 'flattered in sleep and deceived in waking' (Eliot, *The Family Reunion*), it was the most certain reality. He knew the ultimate as his Abba, which, according to one Aramaic scholar, is best rendered 'loving birthing parent': he knew all the desire in himself, for joy in all its forms, for sexual fulfilment, for laughter and the love of friends, as the multi-faceted single thrust of eros toward its absolute origin. And thus he dreamed a society ruled by desire as he knew it, and not by the myriad forces that come to rule the world forgetful of real desire and forever sinking into its counterfeits. What we call sin is the enormous darkness everywhere, the worldwide conspiracy to turn our back on what we most deeply know about ourselves.

Jesus had a name for society as he dreamed it, society ruled by our real desire. He called it the Kingdom of God. It is interesting that none of the early Christians used that phrase, 'the Kingdom of God'. They seem to have understood it as his special phrase, like 'Son of Man', and they didn't quite know what he meant by it. Of course they didn't! For they didn't know what it was like to have the inner God-track open, clear of all the junk with which we make it impassable. Essentially he was alone, with the peculiar aloneness of knowing what is in everyone else without their knowing it. That is the essential loneliness, and it is terrible. You get an echo of it in that line of Baudelaire quoted in Eliot's poem *The Waste Land*: 'You hypocrite *lecteur! Mon semblable, mon frère!*'

Jesus was wedded to his 'Kingdom', to the way his people had to be if only eyes could be opened and hearts unburdened. Everything he said and did had it in view. Lenin's wife said that he breathed, ate, slept and dreamed the revolution, and this is the way it was for Jesus and his Kingdom. It's like this, he would say, it's like that, or try this. These are the parables, stories not moral precepts – it is almost shockingly indifferent to moral teaching, for moral teaching accepts as normal the fact that people want everything except the one thing they need, and tries to restrain them in all these vain pursuits. Bonhoeffer opens his *Ethics* as follows:

> The knowledge of good and evil seems to be the aim of all ethical reflection. The first task of Christian ethics is to invalidate this knowledge...Already in this possibility of the knowledge of good and evil Christian ethics discerns a falling away from the origin. Man at his origin knows only one thing: God. It is only in the unity of his knowledge of God that he knows of other men, of things and of himself. He knows all things only in God, and God in all things. The knowledge of good and evil shows that he is no longer at one with this origin.

Bonhoeffer's statement is stunning. It means that when infinite desire is in touch with its infinite object, a person knows, by this light, how to live, is not dependent on rules. We have fallen out of this in-touch-ness into the knowledge of good and evil, the condition of original sin. In Jesus we encounter original humanity. Still, each of us has a kind of corner of original humanity, out of which we recognise Jesus. One of the Reformation theses most strenuously rejected by the Catholic tradition was the idea of 'total corruption'. When Paul fell in love with Christ on the road to Damascus, he came to know that we are 'not under the Law' and told this to his people. He saw that he was opening himself to the objection: 'Well, in that case I can do whatever I like.' His answer is, no, but if you fall in love with Christ you will learn what you really like, and that will be God. In the Sermon on the Mount, original humanity speaks. It opens with – and I retranslate under good advice – 'Lucky are the poor in spirit'. What this means is: 'The new time is here, the time of the liberated heart, and lucky are the marginalised people who haven't learned society's ways of ignoring the heart and its real hunger. They've really lucked out, in this new age when the God of desire is supplanting the God of power and prestige and respectability.'

A few years ago, a New Testament scholar said that it was hard to see what Jesus did to deserve crucifixion. That scholar should really find other employment. He's in the wrong league. The Jesus-vision of the God of desire and his goofy people is the straight way to crucifixion. The Jesus-vision, the world seen by the unencumbered heart, is the original of what in the sixties we called the counter-cultural. The crucifixion is how the world punishes the Sermon on the Mount.

So the dream came to a bad end. A revolting public death, at the hands of an impressive and oppressive imperial power, wiped out the dreamer, the Jew who knew God by desire alone and in consequence dreamed up a new Israel.

Nothing should be of greater consequence for us than to understand and make a judgement on the events that followed his death. For if you say, 'Yes, he was raised from the dead by the one we call God', then you are saying, 'Yes, my deepest desire which I know is everybody's, is who I really am, is what the world is about, tells me more about reality than all the science there is. Jesus' Kingdom is the reality, whatever signs there are to the contrary.' And if you say, 'No, I don't believe he was raised from the dead', then you are saying no to a great deal more than that. You are saying, 'Hold the child in you who dreams another world.'

There's nothing like putting the options of faith and unbelief before people in a thoroughly manipulative way, as I've just done! But I have to tell you what I am becoming more and more certain of. The story of the empty tomb does not read like a story invented to persuade us of the resurrection. There is an unmistakable element of shock, of disorientation, of terror; something new and unmanageable is breaking in. And who is this figure that people don't recognise until something happens inside them? Sounds familiar? You don't know him till the real you wakes up, and then he vanishes, leaving you with the breaking of bread, the light in the eyes, the heart on fire, the Kingdom, the world the way it is meant to be. And then the shock of the empty tomb reveals its secret. It is the shock of recovering from a sickness as old as the world, the new breaking-in on the oldest thing we know, the place of the dead, emptying the tomb and the mind to receive him, the man of our desire, the true shape of the world.

Any other way of reading the events following his death breaks down. History supplies a catalogue of alternative explanations, improbabilities offered in place of the mystery that holds it all together.

The latest wave of alternative explanation is represented by A. N. Wilson's new book, *Jesus*. Preaching, one has to be terribly careful not to lie. No, I have not read Wilson's book, only the reviews. But I do know him in several previous forms, going back to Reimarus in the eighteenth century.[1] Curiously, under the impression that he is being radical, he says that the real Jesus would have been strongly opposed to the Church. I would only change 'would have been' to 'is'. Jesus is the man of desire, the man of total spiritual risk, at the right hand of God, whence he upbraids us in the words of the Lord of the Book of Revelation:

> You are selling me short. I am the real you. Wake up to yourselves with my Holy Spirit in you, and change the world. Don't you remember that I said, 'I have come to bring fire to the earth, and how I wish that it were blazing already!' To what purpose has my Father raised me from the dead but to show you that in choosing life as opposed to its many counterfeits you have him behind you, our Spirit in you, the world at your feet?

And the greatest mistake of all is about Good Friday. Jesus is the man of passion, and we have made him the enemy of passion, the pale Galilean of Swinburne. The cross represents all the power of this world slung against the great dream which God vindicates in raising him from the dead. We have shifted the emphasis, fatally, from *why* he suffered, to *that* he suffered, and thus in his name we have canonised

---

[1] Hermann Reimarus (1694-1768) was a German 'deist' philosopher who believed that the existence of a benevolent creator God could be inferred from the natural world without the need of revelation.

suffering. What have we made of the cross, bearing on it the man who chose life and changed God from the projection of our fear to the object of our desire? Where has the passion gone? We have made of Good Friday a sad day. It is a sad day, but in the sense of that prophetic man Georges Bernanos when he said that the only tragedy is not to become a saint. It is a day to mourn not the pleasure we have taken but the life we have not chosen. The word from the cross is, 'Go for life, it will cost you everything, but you will be changed, will utterly surprise yourself, and change the world!'

The key to Calvary is buried deep inside you, inside me: it is the same key that unlocks prayer, for it is desire. It is in some moment when you knew that nothing would ever satisfy you, and knew, at the same time, 'This cannot be all there is!' Indeed we are far short of the desire that 'for the sake of the joy which lay ahead of him, endured the cross, disregarding the shame of it'. But that is not the point. In fact the point is that we must be short of this. For this is desire, coming from a self that we hardly know as ours. It is seated in what mystics call *la pointe vierge*, the core of our being, whence alone we may restore that image, blackened by the candle smoke of centuries. This is beautifully expressed in a poem by Charles Causley, *From a Normandy Crucifix of 1632*.

From a Normandy Crucifix of 1632

I am the great sun, but you do not see me
I am your husband, but you turn away
I am the captive, but you do not free me
I am the captain you will not obey

I am the truth, but you will not believe me
I am the city where you will not stay
I am your wife, your child, but you will leave me
I am that God to whom you will not pray

I am your counsel, but you do not hear me
I am the lover whom you will betray
I am the victor, but you do not cheer me
I am the holy dove whom you will slay

I am your life, but if you will not name me
Seal up your soul with tears and never blame me.

How Love Tries to Happen

This longer paper was the first of the two delivered to the Guild of Pastoral Psychology in Spring 2005, under the more prosaic title, Sexuality, Uniting the Masculine and Feminine, Part I. *It draws out the theme that 'desire is love trying to happen'.*

I want to start with a story. It was told me by my old friend Chip who was invited to a literary week sponsored by the government. At one session, a roomful of poets was given an exercise for the morning. A poem was read, *Love* by George Herbert, and they were asked to spend the morning together over the question, 'To respond to this poem, do you need an acquaintance with theology?' Let me now read you the poem.

> Love bade me welcome: yet my soul drew back,
> Guiltie of dust and sinne.
> But quick-ey'd love, observing me grow slack
> From my first entrance in,
> Drew nearer to me, sweetly questioning,
> If I lack'd any thing.
>
> A guest, I answer'd, worthy to be here:
> Love said, You shall be he,
> I the unkinde, ungrateful? Ah my deare,
> I cannot look on thee.
> Love took my hand, and smiling did reply,
> Who made the eyes but I?
>
> Truth Lord, but I have marr'd them: let my shame
> Go where it doth deserve.
> And know you not, sayes Love, who bore the blame?
> My deare, then I will serve.
> You must sit down, sayes Love, and taste my meat:
> So I did sit and eat.

They were given some time to ponder the question before they discussed it. As he pondered, Chip recalled how he had first read the poem aged seventeen, as an amazingly exact and simple description of a good sexual encounter, 'a good lay', overcoming all his inhibitions.

He was totally without religious upbringing, brought up by agnostic and very cultured parents. What Chip wondered was: 'Dare I tell them how I first understood the poem?' He was by now, a budding PhD, well aware of the poem's high status in the canon of metaphysical poetry, and so he dreaded putting his foot in it with these sophisticated strangers. Then he said to himself: 'Well, Sebbie would!', and with my presumed encouragement jumped in.

At first there was a frisson. Then someone murmured agreement. Soon the whole room was alive with an extraordinary excitement, a tidal wave of insight. Of course! Herbert's simple symbolism of the meal filled with the delights of love became clear to them for the first time. And as the discussion proceeded, it became clear what an astonishing poem this is. Coleridge said that while good prose is the right words in the right order, poetry is the best words in the best order, and F. R. Leavis used to talk of the 'inevitability' of a good poem. Herbert's poem registers at every level, from the nervous adolescent having his first sexual experience to the divine. Some critic, I remember, said that Herbert was one of the very few who had taken poetry itself, as characteristic of its time, and lifted it from the then fashionable love-lyric to the spacious world of the mystical. Leavis, I remember, himself religiously agnostic, rated Herbert above Donne, whose wrestles with God are self-conscious and dramatic. Contrast *Love* with *Batter my Heart*, and the point is made.

I want to take this poem, and what happened to it on this occasion, as my text for this paper. My young non-religious friend had no difficulty in identifying with the poet's sense of unworthiness, dust and sin. Contrary to the modern bias, this sense is not induced by religion. Rather it is pandered to by it. This is a crucial distinction. The sense of personal unworthiness is also identified, by religious misunderstanding, with humility. In reality, the sense of unworthiness, a poor self-esteem, is most deeply rooted in us by a culture concerned to mould us 'after the pattern of the present world'. Forget the Church: it is the mere chaplain to the culture. Ernest Becker, in *The Denial of Death*, could make the astonishing statement that Hitler sacrificed six million Jews on the altar of his unworthiness. So, back to my friend. He didn't need theology to tell him he wasn't worthy. He only needed the way he had come to think of himself, as a poor prune. And so the 'love' that the poem describes as cajoling him out of this self-loathing appeared to him quite naturally as what he would have called a good lay. And he was able to see, in the simple metaphor of being invited to eat, the whole process whereby someone else loving me breaks down barrier after barrier of self-disapproval in me. (To take a risky leap: was the resistance that Tolle was ordered to desist from the 'I'm not worthy' voice? Not put in that way. Rather a primitive 'Not for me, this is frighteningly un-me-like.' Yes, I think so.) The way a person has learned to hold himself together is of a slowly-acquired worldly self-dislike, in my case an acute tendency to self-punishment. And this is most painfully challenged by the advances of a love waking up things in me that I can't manage. Damn right I can't! It is self-management for my own good that is threatened by someone loving me.

With all this in mind, I recall that the thing that fascinated me above all in putting together my theology class in the States was that when I feel really bad, depressed verging on hopeless, it doesn't help when I hear that someone loves me, or, worse, that 'everyone' loves me! This only helps, and is wonderful, when this person is someone I love. And I wanted to explain to my class why this is, and I never could, except in terms too easily understood.

The explanation was not forthcoming until I came to see, years later, that we are wired for loving, that we only flourish when we love because we are so designed, that our most ambitious desire, as Marshall Rosenberg blessedly saw and said, is to be the cause of joy in another. The notion of altruism is philosophically pernicious, because it implies that wanting the good of another even to the laying-down of my life is against my nature which, on this account, is selfish. No, my being is 'to-another' as my creator's whose to-each-other-ness in triunity issues in my creation as its image. 'In the beginning was relation', as John is actually saying, of 'God' and 'the Word'.

Now I have to warn you that as I feel myself zeroing in on a human dynamic that is universal, I enter that area which philosophers sometimes write in, a kind of universal first-person. What I am trying to share with you is a universal first person with a lot of me in it! So, I am a failure, and my only cure is to love someone with all of myself, to carry on the baby's first smile at the beckoning mother. To experience myself loving, as Auden did in 1933, is to come alive. There was no particular person in this case, just his teacher friends on the lawn.[2] I do

---

[2] Auden described the occasion as follows: 'One fine summer night in June 1933 I was sitting on a lawn after supper with three colleagues, two women and one man. We liked each other well enough but we were certainly not intimate friends, nor had any one of us a sexual interest in another. Incidentally, we had not drunk any alcohol. We were talking

not come alive on being told that someone loves me. I stay inert. If I love him, ah that's different, then we have it all, knowing myself loving and being loved, what Augustine described as his youthful joy. But this misses the mark by way of excess, a luxurious overflow of the essential, which is that I come alive when I feel myself loving. The very meaning of 'a human failure' is the inability to love, because that's what we're made for. And the failure-child, the child left as unloving, can be a menace to the world, as Becker said of Hitler and Alice Miller gave all her writing life to warning us of. The badly abused child is a time bomb. Something has been taken out on the child that the child must take out on others. And at age eight to ten I was remembered as 'the worst bully in the school'. Here I'm doing-me in the universal first person, as when I recall the verdict of a woman who fell in love with me, that I had never loved anyone in my life. In falling in love with me, she had come slap up against my inertness.

So the concern of saving grace is to get us loving, and this happened to me in 1944, my turning point when I stumbled on contemplative prayer and started visiting a sick old monk whom I did not know.

All men are lovers by nature and liars by sin.

I am discovering/inventing Jesus as I discover in myself the need to love another absolutely, the alternative to which is to be a human failure, a soul damned. My need creates this slot which Jesus fills. God 'arrives at' Jesus through me as failure which he redeems by making me dead no longer, no longer the failure I somehow inherited myself as, like Harry in Eliot's play *The Family Reunion*. This is telling the salvation story backwards, starting with being saved, asking 'what from?' and so on back to the beginning.

The notion of myself as an inherited failure becomes clearer and clearer as I come to another place in which a true self becomes available to focused prayer. It is only in this context that the sense of being an inherited failure becomes useful and enlightening,

casually about everyday matters when, quite suddenly and unexpectedly, something happened. I felt myself invaded by a power which, though I consented to it, was irresistible and certainly not mine. For the first time in my life I knew exactly – because, thanks to the power, I was doing it – what it means to love one's neighbour as oneself. I was also certain, though the conversation continued to be perfectly ordinary, that my three colleagues were having the same experience. In the case of one of them, I was able later to confirm this. My personal feelings towards them were unchanged – they were still colleagues, not intimate friends – but I felt their existence as themselves to be of infinite value and rejoiced in it' (quoted in Kirsch).

exemplary in fact of what theology calls the fallen condition. I wake sometimes these days to my past as a parade of absurd posturing, as though I was getting a look at *The Puppet of Desire* of Oughourlia's important book by that name. And in the vulnerable, horizontal time of early waking, this is overwhelmingly depressing until I see where now I am, write a sonnet or two, and get up for the day. This depression is induced by 'the Accuser of the Brethren', one of Revelation's names for Satan. This demon of hindsight has his poem, *Warning*, by the Australian poet James McCauley, which begins, 'Beware of the past!'

Now none of this makes sense except in the perspective of some 'success' in being human, which I am experiencing an unmistakable glimpse of. (I remember that it was part of the crazy orthodoxy that Rahner had to deal with, that divine grace could never be experienced! It was something the Church told you that you were getting if you went to the sacraments.)

So the connection that was still waiting to be made, as I lectured those young people in Boston, was a matter of finding, in the roots of my own desire, the orientation to another that would be total. Until I knew this, I could not see the command to love as referring to the fulfilment of desire. Until I felt in myself the desire to be for someone else even to death, I could not give real assent (with Auden in his memorable *Vision of Agape* in 1933) to the desire I had been teaching about for years as the desire 'to be someone for someone'. And let me repeat, there doesn't have to be a particular person involved; there wasn't for Auden. It is a matter of realising that I am a lover, and readily seeing Christ as the focus of this self-understanding, what I call inventing Jesus.

To think of myself apart from other people is sheer illusion. There is nothing we have, starting with language itself, that has not come from, or joyously with, others. And into this essential mix we have to factor desire that keeps us going. So desire is an affair of myself with others. But desire is for 'life more abundantly', philosophically it is infinite, and when I conjoin this infinite reach of desire with our relatedness to each other, our neighbourliness, it becomes clear to me (at last!) that the fullness of life, its flourishing, is the heightening of our inter-dividual existence to the love of one another to the point of the laying down of a life otherwise meaningless.

This reasoning is how I would spell out an intuition I have had recently, of another self, not needing to be specified, as the test of my attitude to life as between heaven and damnation, as Jesus makes plain in the parable of the sheep and the goats. And what becomes clear when this is clear is that to love my neighbour as myself is not only to fulfil a command but to experience the fulfilment of our radical desire. The Christian story is the story of desire becoming love through all the violence and pain of history, the pioneer of this evolution being Jesus the willing victim of our violent way of association which, with his resurrection and the explosion of the Spirit, issues in the new humanity whose polity is of love, the politics of the Kingdom. I shall keep coming back to this story as the magnetic field in which the pattern of my thinking shows itself.

What I have been waiting for in all this rumination is to experience, in the roots of my own desiring, the orientation to another that would be total. Until I knew this, I could not see the command to love as referring to the fulfilment of desire. And now that I can feel in myself the desire to be loving, I can give real assent to another of my key axioms: desire is love trying to happen. It was this axiom, seen by an intelligent fanatic in a paper of mine never published, that impelled him to take the paper to the CDF in Rome. He had the intelligence to see that this formula creates insuperable problems for the official line on homosexuality. It was as though I was onto the Higgs boson particle for theology!

If the desire that moves me about my day is love trying to happen, there is a radical resistance to this development. The notion of an original desire naturally evokes the concept of original sin. Original sin is our anti-desire, on the analogy of anti-matter. It is our original resistance to the tendency of desire to bring us together. It is the anti-desire that is the root of un-love. As our whole tradition sees original sin as on the side of desire, we have a problem. And interestingly, Catholic orthodoxy defended desire against the Lutheran idea that it is totally corrupt. And the work of Karl Rahner on the notion of concupiscence comes in here, but this would take us too far afield.

Above all, the problem I had as to why it is only being loved by someone I like that lifts me up finds a solution. To flourish, I must experience myself loving, because a lover is what I am, just as I am, according to Lonergan, a knower. When I already love the person who is offering me a helping hand in my depression, I am responsive to his loving with my loving, my already halfway there state which he is enabling me to go all the way with. His love cannot get to me when I am still inert. The big truth here is that loving is our flourishing. We can go on till the cows come home having our needs met, but this is useless unless we can cease to be inert, and this only happens when we love. We have an unforgettable example of this awakening from inertness in Victor Hugo's *The Hunchback of Notre Dame*. When he falls in love with the obviously unattainable great lady, he lies on his back as usual to ring the bells with his whole body, but this time the whole town is filled with sound and everyone is saying: 'What on earth's with Quasimodo?' He's in love. He's alive. The ugly elephant man is dynamite. His enormous ugliness only serves to bring out the essence of love, which is the adoration of someone else. I'm sure that the same intuition has grabbed Marshall Rosenberg, the man devoted to conflict resolution at its most resisted, that our supreme joy is to cause joy in another or others, seen in the new light in people's eyes when they come through the sharing of their fears to a mutuality that is of hea-ven. That I have recently found his axiom so fascinating indicates something encouraging in my approach to life.

Radical desire trying to be love and most often failing is a far better description of the human condition than goodness marred by original sin. It is preferable, because with the traditional notion we have to ask 'what is, of ours, the original sin' and this is problematic even if you don't take the story of the Fall as historical, which no one does except some bureaucrat in Rome. And as I say, there is the worse problem that original sin is the succumbing to desire whereas it is the refusal, the resistance to desire that is the root of all our troubles. Blake expressed this truth in a mad way when he said, 'Better to kill an infant in the womb than kill a true desire'.

With the theory I am coming up with, there is no difficulty in naming the negative, what we call sin and then wonder what this is. It is fear: fear of desire, fear of life, fear of growth and change, fear of process, hunger for the eternal status quo. Erophobia is the root of gynophobia and homophobia and all the other phobias.

Now once we have understood that desire is everything, we find ourselves confronted with desire in its most exciting and universal form, the sexual. We understand why, on the one hand, sex is the theme of a host of taboos that vary from culture to culture. For with sexual desire, we are nearest to generic desire. With sex the desire which is our essential energy devotes itself to mating and family and the building of civilisation. Sexual desire is dangerous because it seems to offer, as in the bewilderment of orgasm, desire in its mystic meaning. It is in a way a fake radical desire. The Church is certainly not alone in trying to hedge around this wild joy in us. And when it associates two persons of the same sex, the Church gives up, which means it gives up on gay people, who represent my axiom in its most critical form, as the CDF understood when it saw my formula. That this formula was described by our secretary of Campus Ministry at Marquette University as 'the only thing you've said that I've understood' and is for Rome the undermining of its sexual teaching is aesthetically pleasing!

The best exposure of the false claim of genital desire to represent generic desire is that offered by Oughourlia, whose book *The Puppet of Desire* argues that the notion we naturally have that our desires are our own is illusory. My desires are desire at work in me as their puppet, and it is an arduous process, called by Jung individuation, that brings a person into full responsibility for his or her desire. Individuation is the emergence of a self that 'owns' all desire as opposed to normal consciousness that is desire's slave. This development is not dissimilar to that envisaged by Freud as the goal of psychoanalysis: *Wo Es war, soll Ich werden* – where there was 'it', there shall be 'I'.

Here we have to invoke the seminal idea of Girard, who works closely with Oughourlia, that the evolution of the animal into the human involves the switch from instinct to desire as the director, and desire is mimetic. We see our desires in each other, so that desire is our involvement in the huge game of life in which we are involved, each player pathetically trying to absolutise his or her role in the grand dance.

Now let us look at the formula that desire is love trying to happen in the broad perspective opened up by René Girard. The desire that is love trying to happen begins on the earth at the beginning of the breakthrough whereby desire succeeds instinct as the animal's guide. Desire in its beginning is an entirely 'inter' thing, the beginning of the interdividual animal who only sees what he wants in another wanting it. It associates the new animals through their seeing each its desire in the other and others, and this is the source of rivalry and conflict so that love has somehow to prevail over this human maelstrom. So desire's attempt to become love does not start with you and me, but with our ex-animal beginnings, and it brings its implied violence to a climax in the crucifixion. This is the 'invention' of Jesus in the full bloody context of our existence. Desire becomes love in the body of Christ, the new community of humankind, *cosmopolis*, *philadelphia*, the Kingdom. This happens in the heart of the man Jesus, whose acceptance of the world's fearful hatred of God in the loneliness of Gethsemani issues in the festivity of the new man.

Which brings us back to George Herbert's poem *Love*, with its simple symbolism of feeding. 'You must sit down, said Love, and taste my meat/So I did sit and eat.' I simply never understood the poem, because I thought it was about sitting down to dinner 'on the other side'. My non-religious friend got it right. It is a love poem that outstrips Donne.

But another huge obstacle stands in the way of our revelling in the poem in all its dimensions, secular and divine. It is the serious derailment of the Church's understanding of the Sacrifice of the Mass that lost sight of the fact that the Mass is a meal that takes a long time over grace. Jesus said 'take, eat, my body for you', but the 'take' got isolated from the 'eat' and referred to something to be done to the bread and wine by the priest who now has in his hands the body and blood of Christ to offer 'in an unbloody manner', the sacrifice of the cross. This distinction, between a 'bloody' and an 'unbloody' sacrifice, became classical, and it is quite pernicious, obscuring the fact that what happened on Skull Hill was a horrible murder done by a lynch-mob with government and Church approval.

So what happened to the 'eat' bit? At a High Mass, said to be the full Mass, that was a cleaning-up operation by the priest – no one else communicated. The Last Supper, the divinely given enactment of 'the Lord feedeth me' as meaning love wherever it 'works', was lost, and so the primary symbol of the creator satisfying the deepest hunger in the human spirit, the love-hunger that works at every level, was lost, and religion resumed its usual violent self.

It is not far-fetched to see this travesty of the unbloody sacrifice as significant of our reluctance to being loved, to being 'sat down in the heavenly places' (which has got nothing to do with the pearly gates of a joke in the pub). The inability to read the poem 'naively' as showing the luxury of loving is not unconnected with the failure to see the meal as the total experience of God's love. Resistant to this envelopment of us by the arms spread abroad on the cross whose symbol is the principal one of being fed, we have preferred to hold on to a male, violent, sacrificial Mass monitored by a Roman congregation. And when it came to the Reformation, the split between bloody/ unbloody/muddled sacrifice and the meal took the form of the Catholic Church clinging to this 'sacrifice' and the Protestants holding on to the meal which in consequence of the split became insipid – 'Take this bread and remember Jesus!'

The drama of original desire has acted itself out in the blood and sweat of history. It has acted itself out in my life, fought for against the too-simple demands of love. It is in the laboratory of myself that I have investigated a self-hatred that fears, and desires above all, to be loved, a desire that is love trying to happen and that is restless till it loves and, loving, is enveloped by the beloved. So wholly other-oriented is our original desire that as long as I am inert and dead as I have been for so much of my life, I only wake up in loving, and loving is the ability to receive. Though the great lady is herself unavailable, the hunchback revels in himself as lover, and 'tastes' her 'meat' even though his love is not reciprocated.

I don't want to be loved until I love. And when I love I open to the sheer luxury of being loved. Nietzsche saw nothing of this luxury in the eyes of believers, so he easily mistook his travesty of Christianity for Christianity itself.

Note on the Herbert poem

I looked up the poem in the standard Oxford Clarendon Press edition with the commentary of F. E. Hutchinson. The commentary of course has no suggestion of what my friend read into the poem. I am sure this editor would have been horrified, perhaps even revolted, by Chip's response. It is quite clear to him that the 'love' is divine love. As it always has been to me, though the poem has never done much for me, I now see because it was confined to pious allegory in which I am being admitted at the pearly gates. The implied banquet was purely symbolic and – what is important – it was not working on me and for me as the symbol of the meal now does; and a symbol only releases its power through a radical change in my own infrastructure such as I am now getting some sense of. Resisting Chip's interpretation, I would have said, 'Look, you can't get round the clearly theological intention of "who made the eyes but I?"' Well now I think I can get round it. Getting into the experience – which I have never had – of that good 'first time' (I recall a gorgeous moment in Gabriel Garcia Marquez's *One Hundred Years of Solitude*), 'love' is something that's in charge, beginning to happen as in my formula, and saying to the young lover, 'I'm giving you the eyes you're looking through now.' 'Love' here is 'the real thing' and answers to a theological description. Flourishing is itself and doesn't make distinctions. There is a two-way traffic between agape and eros. Eros teaches agape not to be 'humble', and agape teaches eros to plunge beyond sex as we know it. And nowhere is there room for anything prudish. The love of the other as myself, even to death, takes into itself all the eros in us. We should pay more attention to the experience of love breaking in on an already active sexual relationship, as with Donne's 'I wonder, by my troth'.

Inhabit now the body that I am
From top to toe, from finger tip to tip,
Spread to the fuller body, some by name,
This loosens up a never noticed grip.

Remember now how I become ecstatic
On hearing that our supreme happiness
Is to give joy to someone – it's dramatic
As news to me, the good news drawing yes.

This yes is Jesus who inhabits me
As he has promised if I keep his words:
Be there for someone else practically
And my desire, by him awakened, stirs.

Sleepless to pray for people who are dear
Opens perhaps to love my deepest fear.

Aquinas Clarifies Augustine on Desire

This is an abridged version of the second paper delivered at the same conference. The amour courtois *movement of the twelfth century celebrated, for the first time in western culture, sexual desire. This was a challenge to Catholic orthodoxy which was then steeped in the writings of Augustine who could not reconcile sexual desire with true love. Yet Aquinas, writing somewhat later, with his notion of* cum-placentia – *pleasing-together – seemed to get it right, although the official teaching of the magisterium still has to catch up. Perhaps it is all there in the Song of Songs.*

In the theological world shaped by the Church Fathers, there was, on the one hand, love as in 'love your neighbour as yourself' and, on the other, love meaning 'desire' and associated with the disturbing motions of the body ('irregular motions of the flesh' even survived into the old penny catechism). Not that desire was absent in the 'good' sense, but then it was something that good people felt for God and heaven, and the, to us, loaded word 'concupiscence' was liberally used for this. *Concupivit anima mea.* My soul lusts for thee.

Into this theological world there burst what C. S. Lewis called a revolution in feeling compared with which the Renaissance was a mere ripple on the surface. This was the *amour courtois* of the troubadours, which was desire coming into its own. The strong desire, which till then was only good when it was for God and heaven, became an ennobling force between two people issuing in sleepless nights and endless serenades. This was the first wave of the romantic movement, long before our time.

This absorbing culture of desire, nourished in the rich land of the south of France, issued in what was called the gay science (*gai saber*) which challenged Catholic orthodoxy and provoked the most savage of the crusades, with the unspeakable barbarities inflicted on men and women, with copious burnings.

I have always been fascinated with this movement, but now I have to look at a further implication of it, as it coincided with the monastic renaissance around Bernard of Clairvaux and the Cistercians. Bernard was the leading commentator on the Song of Songs. The men and women, like Héloise of *Héloise and Abelard*, who entered the new monastic life tended to be young people already versed in the new meaning of the love that had to do with desire, and not desire for God and heaven, so you had the makings of a first-class theological controversy. This was not to do with 'gay' relations in monasteries – just forget all that as it will get us hopelessly off the point of what I'm writing about. No, it meant that into the conversation about the love of God and neighbour and its duties there was introduced the idea of desire as a force between people giving new meaning to love.

Over this debate there brooded the gigantic figure of Augustine, for whom desire had both meanings, and strongly so: the hunger for God and the allure of women, and of course the first overcoming the second in one of the most important conversion stories we have.

Well, imagine the new restoration of desire to honest living thrown into the world inherited from Augustine, torn between divine love and lust, and you've got quite a brew. For here is a love that is desirous (not just obedient to the Christian commandment) and is spiritual and pertaining to the good human life. And it is the desire-bit, the erotic bit, of love that Augustine is leaving out of the converted state he has come to (all those whispering voices saying: 'Are you sure you'll be able to do without us?' just before the *moment critique* in the garden). Love as ordinary people know it is getting a look-in on the spiritual, the new Cistercian movement.

The response to this vital new claim on spiritual attention was divided between 'Augustine right, the new love nothing to do with divine love' and 'Augustine wrong, the new love all-important'.

Actually, though, the desirous love between people, that gets this look-in with the *amour courtois*, neither is to be dismissed as not spiritual nor is to be unfittable into the world of Augustine: what is needed for this is a more sophisticated account of love than Augustine in his time could have had, and that Aquinas, much later, came to. In other words, deepen Augustine and deepen the *amour courtois*, and we may come into a significant advance in our own understanding of ourselves and our loving. This was the achievement of Aquinas.

One of Aquinas' key words is 'complacency', *cum-placentia*, pleasing-together, something found between friends, and *amicitia* is also key here. It is perhaps significant that we only know complacency as a bad word, a thing to accuse rulers of. What it means for Aquinas is the delight of friends resting in each other, totally at ease with each other. But what's that got to do with desire?

Aquinas' clarification of Augustine on desire, which I think is irreversible, is one demanded by a large shift in the culture: in this case the shift brought about by 'the gay science' and the *amour courtois*, especially in view of the vicious reaction of Rome. A new state of affairs, of new feelings in coalescence at that time, called for a 'refinement' (a weak word – try *approfondissement*) of our understanding of desire as a force between people and not only to be directed heavenward, good, but when earthed, to be viewed with extreme pessimism. The clarification then required was an important deepening of our self-understanding in affairs of the heart, no longer content to judge desire by what it pursued – the self denied for the sake of heaven, or the self affirmed in contempt of heaven – but needing to understand desire itself and the luminous paradox of its rooting in the creator-given orientation to others in God.

Augustine did not reconcile sexual desire with the love of God. He didn't have to. There were no troubadours around, no *amour courtois*. It was a less sophisticated world. Life grows and sets new problems. But with each new problem and its solution, the eternal in man, as Scheler calls it, resounds. The orientation of a man and woman to God, to one another and to the cosmic whole reappears at greater depth as the intention of a creator who is Trinitarian harmony. The resurrection of Jesus is the triumph of love as the human formula.

What Augustine never saw was 'loving the other as yourself' as the heart of sexual loving. With the whole Church tradition following him, he saw sexual loving as greedy and lustful, dragging the soul down from God, as did John Paul II when, asked by a journalist what he thought of sex, he gave a 'Darby and Joan' kind of answer. And he put up for canonisation an old married couple who had given up sex long ago.

The strategy for reform of the official teaching is for the *magisterium* to catch up with Aquinas in seeing the great commandment at the heart of sexual loving. Sexual love is still not acknowledged by the Church as communion with God, embodying the love between persons unconditionally and to the laying-down of life. At one moment, during a meeting of the papal birth-control commission, one couple described the experience of love-making with its mystical dimension, to the surprised gratitude of the priests. But the challenge of the *amour courtois* to the Church's understanding of the mystical as the only divine intimacy, pressed since that medieval renaissance, still awaits the approval of the Church, which admits it only as legitimated by canonical marriage. It goes without saying that a love that requires legitimation is not being recognised for what it is.

Notice that in this quasi-manifesto nothing has been said of sexual love among gays and lesbians. It does not need to be. For the real issue here is, and always was, the Church's distrust of Eve, the erotic complement of Adam. Once that is abrogated, the whole scene changes, and Augustine's mystical desexualising of love, described by Friedrich Heer as catastrophic, is diagnosed in its full significance, and finally disavowed.

Conclusion

It is very exciting that what Aquinas discovered to be the formula to solve the subtlest problem with love, which is, how to understand the unrest of loving, its sleepless nights and serenades, as rooted in 'complacency', the serene delight of lovers in each other, is 'willing the good of the other' from his or her existence upward into the sound of the voice and of the 'step upon the stairs', which is precisely to have my neighbour as myself. The ultimate subtlety of loving is named in the great commandment of love.

Reading the Song of Songs again after taking on board the Aquinas insight, I am struck again by the delight of the lovers in each other, stillness that is the secret of the storm.

Stillness that is the secret of the storm
Unites the lovers as they rest their gaze:
The mind in search of love's explaining form
Finds it, and it continues to amaze.

Augustine found it, and not yet in sex
But in his liberation from its ways
And left us a millennium of complex
Research to find a clearing in the haze,

Which found turns out to be the commonplace
Of both our Testaments: other as self
Sexless Aquinas got the saving grace
And took the old commandment off the shelf.

Lovers' delight in presence to each other
Eye of love's storm that any sound will smother.

Desire is the consent to someone else
Revealed to the self growing in the boy
As heart unknown until that moment melts
Into a new complacency of joy.

I am in love, he absolutely says
And knows his God more closely than the church
That only gives him space wherein he prays
Not knowing she may leave him in the lurch.

The church has still to learn the formula
Implanted in his growing by its God
Who wrote a song of love, while near and far
She learned and taught her children how to plod.

And to distrust what he at first instils:
Consent as secret of the man who wills.

Afterword (some months later)

It has just occurred to me that there are two big failures to connect in the thinking of the Church as we pick it up today: the failure to connect God with desire, and the failure to connect love with sex. And there is a connection between these two failures. If desire is not reaching out to God for a share in his life, it cannot have the vigour to shape sex, as the pope is hinting in the new encyclical, *Deus Caritas Est*, which, cautiously and for the first time in such documents, introduces the concept of the erotic into spirituality. In the Roman theology I knew at Sant'Anselmo, the teaching of St Thomas that there is a natural desire to see God was flatly denied, for it was thought to impugn the strictly supernatural character of union with God.

At my age, as you see, one thing leads to another – just when one is becoming incapable of doing *anything!*

CHAPTER 9

Love, Sexuality and the Church

Desire is oriented towards love. Nowhere is this more obvious than in the matter of sexual desire which, although it can also be turned towards violence and domination, powerfully draws us into loving relationships – as God intends. However, the teaching Church, which is largely celibate, has difficulty in understanding this.

A consequence is that official Church teaching in this area is focused on faithful procreative marriage as the perfection of loving sexual relationship and rather passes over, or has practically nothing positive to say about, how sexual relationships can contribute to human flourishing, which in fact is God's desire for us all.

So the Church needs to reorient its approach and to explore, not what is or is not 'permitted', but how we should subject our sexual urges to the demands of fidelity and love in relationship.

This applies also to that significant minority of humanity whose sexual orientation is towards the same rather than the opposite sex. Here the magisterium faces a collapsing social taboo, which may have served a social purpose at one time and certainly still does so in celibate monastic communities. Its current reaction to this collapsing taboo is to retreat to ever more convoluted formulae – not 'sinful' but 'objectively disordered' (whatever that means).

Other churches are faced with a similar issue. But it is the Catholic Church that is more likely to get it right in the end. For Catholic moral teaching is based on 'the natural law', that is on consideration of whatever supports human flourishing, rather than on a literal reading of the Bible that is constrained by the cultural environment in which it was written – the approach of 'evangelicals'.

So, under the guidance of the Spirit, we can look forward one day to a deeper Catholic understanding of all of sexuality. This would point towards sexual desire being fulfilled through faithful, loving relationships, whether hetero- or homosexual. Indeed the challenge in the latter case is all the greater, since homosexual relationships are not covered by the grace of marriage, nor by the natural attraction of emotional complementarity that exists between male and female.

Love and Longing

Desire is love trying to happen, and sexual desire is love's strongest driving force. The 'faithful' may instinctively understand this, but the teaching authority of the Catholic Church does not 'get' it. Somehow the Eastern Church manages better.

Desire is love trying to happen. Desire is what drives us, it is our life's energy, and it has two channels it can go in. One is envy, because desire is mimetic: I recognize my desire in another, and this puts me into competition with my model. But this mimetic shape of desire has also a positive channel, of admiration, of wanting to be like my model, not to dis-empower him, as in the other channel. Now this admiration can grow to love, and this is how desire becomes love and thus realises its meaning as love trying to happen.

Now the most important human area in which this happens is sex. Sexual desire, like all desire, has these two channels it can take. It generally goes in both at once, so that two persons can fall in love and even get a taste of the love that is larger than life which we call God's love, the creator as it were unable to contain himself in heaven and appearing in lovers on earth. But almost always the sexual love between people has in it a lot of violence and the urge to dominate, just as happens to people with their other desires.

Now God is love. This is why desire, which is the creator's dangerous mark in the conscious animal, 'is love trying to happen'. So the fulfilment of desire in the sexual realm is to become a love between two persons that makes manifest the principle that desire, God's initial signature on us, is love trying to happen. The principle is most manifest here because sex is the area in which desire between people is most evident.

It follows rather clearly that if there is to be a teaching on sexuality that implements the principle that desire is love-oriented, that teaching will have to have an implicit definition of sex as relationship, of sex as attraction between people, which of course everyone knows that sex is.

Everyone, it seems, except what we call the 'mind of the Church', for that mind, as teacher, is celibate, and so it tends to have a bias against understanding sex as relationship. For the committed celibate, sex as relationship is forbidden. It is, at least, very difficult for a celibate teaching authority to see wholeheartedly as God-implanted, and thus relational, the desire which it must know as temptation.

Surely what I am accounting for here is the increasingly evident absence of communication between official Catholic teaching and the faithful in this most common human area.

Does it follow from this that the teaching authority has to be married? This is not the case in the eastern churches, where the bishops are all monks. But the Eastern Church has been non-aggressively monastic, the Western Church aggressively so. In the east, the bishops, the teachers, were monks and still are, and perhaps they have something to teach us of ecclesial celibacy as representing a perspective wider than marriage. In the West, the great reforming pope Gregory VII, monk himself and monastically advised by Peter Damian, monk and mystic, imposed monasticity on *all* the clergy, making them into celibate secular monks with breviaries. They in turn imposed a monastic sexuality on the married, with the disastrous consequences I have been looking at.

Nothing like this happened in the placid (?) East. The eternal meaning of man and woman could suffuse marriage from a mystical distance through monastic bishops, not invasively, aggressively, interferingly, as in our Western Church. Above all, a married clergy secured married life in its own right, common sense and kids and all, as normative, not subject to the noxious tinkering of celibate clerics.

Reflections on the Church's Sexual Teaching

The Church's sexual teaching is expressed in very 'black and white' terms: sexual expression is only permitted in the ideal situation of faithful married love open to procreation. But such teaching lacks understanding of the importance of physical sexuality for 'human flourishing' – across a whole range of committed human relationships. Yet human flourishing is God's will for us all. Fortunately the pastoral Church frequently manifests a deeper understanding.

I am easily understood to be dissenting publicly from the teaching of the Church on sex. I am not doing so. What I am doing is crying out: 'Let's think again!'

The very thing that is of the essence of sexual love, namely the becoming-love of desire, is something that the *magisterium* 'wouldn't know'. It is something that happens to the laity, that a zealous pastor will do all he can to 'allow for'. That phrase is revealing. It refers to creating a space in one's mind for an experience one does not have but that the laity do have. As a consequence there is a huge lack of communication.

If now we are asked to say in what consists this lack of communication between the teaching Church and people in the area of sexuality, the following occurs to me. For the laity, sex connotes four things: pleasure, relationship, babies, and, of course, marriage. That 'of course', for the laity, is a large spectrum that ranges from humour to the most serious. But when we pass from the lay to the official perception, that rich 'of course' gives way to the lean 'only'. And a chill comes on the air in which communication is attempted. In the teaching, only the last of these four is approved of, and enthusiastically. This obviously distorted valuation, indeed caricature, on the part of officialdom, of something that is the staple of human experience, has to be looked at rather mercilessly.

We might say that this order – pleasure, relationship, babies, and marriage – shows a progression from the worst to the best, with pleasure the worst. There is a word whose translation always puzzled me: *luxuria*. It's worse than lust; rather it connotes sheer self-indulgence, the heart aswim, and it plays an important role in moral assessment. An innocent lay word for it is 'fun'. The thing to note is that the moment it appears on the scene for moral assessment it is assessed, very negatively. It is something that has to be justified, paid for, compensated, and there is an unavowed dependence on the old Stoic idea that sexual enjoyment is only permissible as involved in procreation.

Now this is a downgrading of sexual pleasure that assumes massive proportions in the idea, not quite but nearly defined as 'of faith' – by the great Jesuit general Aquaviva – that in the matter of sexual sin there is 'no light matter': one impure thought deliberately held in the mind merits eternal damnation if not repented and absolved. So low is pleasure in the official account that in the course of a large and compendious book, *Man and Woman He Created Them, A Theology of the*

Body, John Paul II never observes that sex is enjoyable. One argument against contraception in the debate preceding *Humanae Vitae* was the comparison between this practice and the old Roman *vomitorium* where at a dinner party you could go and vomit and begin again.

When we look at this pleasure as shared generously or not at all, in other words at *relationship*, what is striking is how much this counts for people and how *little* for the official moral assessment. And clearly the people – as any good confessor will agree – are right. The difference between a relationship of totally shared pleasure and a relationship that is cruel or exploitative is, for people, vast, but it does not show up at all on the official chart. A friend of mine who was gay (now dead) told me that when as an adolescent he finally gave up on the losing battle between 'falling' and confession, he found himself for the first time noting the difference between generous and manipulative relationships: he became a moral being only on leaving the required Church practice.

Now obviously, on the lay side of the gap, sex improves morally as we pass from selfish to *shared* pleasure which exists in its full form as the sexual expression of loving the other as the self in committed Christian marriage. And this is clearly right and exemplifies the *sensus fidelium*. Yet this development from mean, cruel exploitative sex to *caritas* sexually expressed only shows up for official approval when it reaches this end! The best becomes the *only* permissible, when the babies are prepared for.

The whole failure of the teaching so far is the inability to observe the difference between the exemplary and the mandatory, between the 'facticity' of sexual love, unitary and fertile, and the appeal to it as the ground for declaring sinful all others. As James Alison keeps pointing out, according to the official teaching, married people who practise contraception are living in sin just as much as same-sex couples, only the Church never says so. Rather charmingly, Archbishop Beck of Liverpool, in his version of the cushioning pastoral that all the Church's bishops came out with after *Humanae Vitae* (what Bishop Butler described as 'protecting their flocks from the chief shepherd'), noted that the encyclical never spoke of sin 'except in a gentle pastoral kind of way'!

Going back now to where I started, the implicit need to justify, to render permissible at all, sexual pleasure, it becomes clear that the way in which sexual pleasure is justified is through shared-ness in a loving relationship. This contrast between, on the one hand, the way people come to realise that sexual pleasure involves two persons together and thus pertains to morality and, on the other, the official view that sees all the steps on the way as sins, is glaring. And it states, in an extreme way, the big assumption I am referring to in this chapter, that sexual pleasure, fun, is something that has to be 'justified', paid for; that sexual pleasure 'unearned' cannot be approved.

And then the stark comparison has to be made, between this attitude to the most mutually bonding of human pleasures, and the human flourishing which God in his Gospel is offering to us. The Gospel, more than anything else, exposes the official attitude to sex in all its stinginess. Now this does not mean that the Gospel introduces a sexual free-for-all, though the fact that Paul found it necessary to clear his message of implying such a free-for-all is itself significant. Rather it introduces a huge transcendent perspective in which mutual love to the death is the basis – a perspective in which Jesus' attitude to prostitutes and that of religious society appear in the starkest opposition.

Now once we have introduced this deep perspective, let us try to bring out its ultimate implications in respect of desire.

Let us contrast, on the one hand – on the left, say – a person under instruction in any religious tradition and on the other – on the right – someone in the position that Tolle found himself in at the climactic moment when he considered suicide. At the realisation that 'There are not two of me, the "I" and the "self" I cannot live with', he felt himself sucked into a void, and heard the words 'resist nothing!' Now put that state of soul on the right. Now ask, what, for each of these states of soul, is the status of *desire*? How is desire in each case to be rated? Does it get a 'yes' or a 'no'? Is it 'a good thing' or 'a bad thing'?

On the left, it gets a 'no', at least a 'better not'. There are ways that seem good to men but lead to hell, as the *Rule of Benedict* says. Desire is at best suspect. On the right, desire is that which, if it is *not* yielded to, the chance of a lifetime is lost. What Tolle 'heard' at the critical moment was 'resist nothing' which means 'do not resist any movement of desire that now occurs to you by consulting an inveterate caution'. The God that Jesus shows us excites our desire at its deepest, and this has to be remembered when we try to cope with sex and the Church. The Holy Spirit seduces our spirit.

What is to be done? Plenty. The commission assembled by Pope John XXIII to thrash out the question of contraception was unwittingly providing a model for what is now needed. This need was vigorously voiced by Mary Douglas, a very conservative Catholic who is a world-class anthropologist. Asked about the position of women in the Church, she replied, 'absolutely iniquitous' and demanded the creation of a women's commission on doctrine with veto power over sexual pronouncements. This, of course, was merely the adversarial idea of an *anti-magisterium*. What she was clearly pointing to is a representative *magisterium*, a listening *magisterium*.

What the Roman authority has to do is to carry over into the area of sex and marriage the move into a consultative mode that happened with Vatican II, which has so far only been travestied by the Episcopal Synod. The kind of correction sought for, for such a lamentably lame set-up as the male celibate culture that continues to pronounce and put both feet in it, is of this kind. And indeed once you talk phenomenology you are talking conversation. Merleau-Ponty, one of the leaders in this mode of thinking, described this understanding-through-conversation when he said: 'When I succeed in making myself understood, I no longer know who of us two is doing the understanding.'

Finally, a theology that downgrades desire as such is going to make of the desire for God something rarefied and otherworldly, instead of being what it is, the hunger for the reign of God and his righteousness, the building of his Kingdom. In contrasting the joy of Jesus (*Jesu, Joy of Man's Desiring*) with the glumness of the Church where sex is concerned, I am easily taken to be wanting the Church to be more liberal, to go with the flow. Actually, I am saying something quite different, indeed almost the opposite. The contrast I am pointing to is not between a world of fun and a Church of gloom, but between a worldly sexual ethic that is recognisably coherent and a Church ethic that is incoherent. There *is* a coherence in a notion of sex as fun needing relationship to control it and seeking stability in the relationship of marriage, whereas there is *no* coherence in a teaching that allows sex only in marriage and has nothing to say about sex outside marriage except that it is more or less sinful. And it is a gross defect in an institution charged with leading men and women to God to have nothing enlightening to say about desire – the force that gets me up in the morning and moves me about my day – and puts on my road nothing but danger signals. The encyclical *Deus Caritas Est*, the moment it speaks approvingly of the erotic, hastens to name marriage as the latter's only proper place. The marriage-only teaching, reinforced with the distrust of pleasure quite evident in our moral theology, keeps this incoherent system in place.

So to anyone who says I am publicly dissenting from the teaching of the Church, I reply that the only charge I bring against the teaching is that it lacks understanding. It lacks understanding not only of how people are living but of what it is saying as it fails to observe the difference between the manifestly exemplary and the exclusively obligatory. As presently uttered, the teaching means that everyone ought to be heterosexual with no contraceptives in the bathroom cabinet.

The Church upholds marriage without knowing humanly why. This accounts for the increasingly complained-of silence of the Church now in this area. The culture now wants, needs, fears to know the 'why' of this thrilling experience. The Church doesn't know why, so resorts to a baleful silence.

If the Church is the Church of Christ, this huge anomaly has to be faced. And since I believe the Church is this, I know that it will be faced. The oldest institution in the world that owes its survival to the Holy Spirit will eventually be impelled to do so.

Sex and the Church: Make it New!

Traditionally the Church, in its teaching on sexuality, has placed too much emphasis on 'generativity' and too little on 'relationship'. Interestingly this parallels the old debate on the nature of the Trinity – is it generativity or relationship that is central to the nature of our God? The Church came down firmly in favour of the latter. Perhaps it now needs to rethink its teaching on sexuality in the light of its doctrine on the Trinity. This is the text of a talk given in June 2006 to a small group of students in Bristol.

The Church and sex are two huge facts, so we must first be as clear as we can as to what we mean by both. The Church is a pilgrim assured of who is leading and where this is going. Sex is two things, people attracted to each other, and babies being born and reared. Let's start with sex.

Any kind of story we write, and call this history, is inevitably biased, but if we are at all optimistic about the human condition we may usefully consider the story of sex as of a coming-together of these two things: mutual liking and procreation. In fact, these two partners have a wild and untidy history. Bits of the picture are got together unconnected with other bits. In the eleventh century in the south of France, for instance, there took place, for the first time, a fascination with this overwhelming liking between two people. This was the birth of the erotic, which C. S. Lewis described as a revolution in feeling compared with which the Renaissance was a mere ripple on the surface. And this had nothing to do with marriage! In fact, it was judged incompatible with marriage by a 'court of love' presided over by the Countess of Champagne. Still, there was the connection, not between sex and babies, but between sex and our deepest insomniac feelings about each other. Love larger than life engaged the creativity of poets, and saw the birth of the huge alternative to the poetry of war. And it would be a long time before babies and their care, the vast institutional self-securing by laws, got into the picture, and theologians could rhapsodise, for the first time, about Christian marriage as the full flourishing of the erotic.

And this brings me to the Church and its essentially exploratory nature.

A pilgrim is an explorer, not a moral policeman. There are things the Church has to get to know in this matter of connecting sex as generative with sex as relational. To get to know, not to know already. In the practice called 'focusing' or 'biospirituality' or *vipassana*, the thing we have to watch out for is called 'process-skipping', which is when the mind tells the body what it feels instead of listening to the body. A huge piece of process-skipping occurs when the Church says: 'We know how generativity and relationship work together: it's the good Catholic family with no pills or condoms.' That is the law, and we ignore it at our peril, but it is not, repetition not, the solution to the age-long human problem that each of us has: how do I come together as a sexual being? Here the Church has to share the question, and take part in the search.

Recently I have been awed by the discovery that our problem exists at the pinnacle of our theology: God the Father and God the Son in God the Holy Spirit. As we try to think of God having a Son, two alternatives present themselves to the mind: are we to think here of generativity or of relationship as the controlling idea? If we knew the answer to that we'd be dead and in heaven, but it is encouraging to see that our problem with our bodies and their strange emotional behaviour finds a reflection in the Godhead.

Nor is this a merely academic game. There is a Catholic theologian, Urs von Balthasar, who died a decade or so ago, whose massive work on the glory of God has become the inspiration of a new Catholic feminism that I believe, with Tina Beattie, to be in fact the old patriarchal thinking excitingly presented with God the Father as the patriarchetype (excuse, Urs!). What Balthasar is doing, according to Tina, with regard to the divine Father-Son relationship, is to see generativity as the basis of relationality, which gives you a magisterial God and not a tender participant in the suffering of his Son at our hands. I only instance this to show that we're on the money when we say that the problem of sex is: how to unite generativity with relationship? The believer, far from being a moral policeman where sex is concerned, hears God saying: yes, you're getting the problem right – we are its solution! It helps, though not immediately, with our sexual urges!

But it does help. It is God saying that as pilgrim-explorers we are striving toward that big connection.

To come down to some brass tacks. If I were one of the many people whose marital situation forbids me communion, what might my problem look like in this larger perspective? Or as a gay or lesbian similarly excluded? All these problems do begin to look different if the Church, to which these people deeply wish to belong sacramentally, is also seen as exploratory? Oh, come off it, someone is bound to say, this is simply a cop-out! Well if it is a cop-out it's not what I'm talking about. Isn't the cop-out a form of process-skipping?

The question becomes, not, 'What am I permitted sex-wise?', but, 'How am I called, here and now, to subject my sexual urges to the demands of fidelity?'

In other words, how do I bring my passions into the service of love as defined by Aquinas as wanting the good of another as my own?

The Gospel, so understood, is as demanding as and sometimes more demanding than the law of the Church. The divorced and remarried person, accepted at the Lord's Table, would find his or her present marital commitment more exacting than if she felt that, as far as the Church is concerned, it doesn't matter because she's wrong anyway. Two same-sex partners likewise, once they don't feel that the Church is washing its hands of them, would find themselves faced, with the Church's support, with the real difficulty of same-sex relating, that it has to achieve psychologically and spiritually and unaided by nature, that sense of the 'otherness' of the partner to balance the likeness, on which any close sexual union depends for its maintenance and vigour. Same-sex partners have to look to themselves in the grace of God for the stabiliser that marriage provides. Auden, who was gay, never forgave the infidelity of his partner.

These are only hints, but they are all based on the enormous task, which takes humanity as long a time as its full flourishing takes, of bringing our powerful sex urge into the control of relationship, rather than of law.

A Theological Stumbling Block

One of the greater stumbling blocks in the magisterium's misunderstanding of desire and love is its teaching on same-sex relations that effectively marginalises and alienates from the Church a significant minority of the human population. If, as Sebastian argues, sexual relations may sometimes legitimately express committed relationships of love, even outside regular marriage, this must be true pari passu *of homosexual and lesbian relationships also.*

About ten years ago, I noticed that the official teaching on homosexuality had changed, in the direction of severity. When I was a boy, I read a CTS pamphlet, *Purity*, by Fr Bede Jarrett OP, in which he said that some people were attracted not to someone of the opposite but to someone of the same sex, and that there was nothing wrong in being this way, which he described as 'worldwide and world-old'. He went on to say that only the action of following this attraction into sex with someone else was wrong. The implied inconsistency in this did not occur to me or to my monastic teachers; it was just one of those things. You can be it, but you must not do it. Then in 1986, the CDF came out with a statement that not only is the action wrong but the inclination is 'deviant'. I noted this change talking to a young confrère, who said: 'Oh, surely not!' and, somewhat impatiently, I replied: 'Oh, look it up!' Here is the statement:

> Although the particular inclination of the homosexual person is not a sin, it is a more or less strong tendency ordered toward an intrinsic moral evil; and thus the inclination itself must be seen as an objective disorder (CDF, 1986).

Now let me change the subject, almost, to the Council of Trent and its response to Luther and Calvin on the subject of our natural desires. This was the moral side of the new reformed theology that Trent took Catholic tradition to be opposed to. Both Luther and Calvin were what we would call pessimistic on natural desire, its theological name being 'concupiscence'. They said it was corrupted by original sin, so much so that we couldn't even desire to be saved. Salvation had to take us by storm, as a raider. Trent would have none of this. Our natural desires were raw, certainly, and had to be transformed by grace and discipline, and this applied to sexual attraction whether to one's own or the opposite gender presumably, but they were not depraved, evil, as they were for the new theology.

Now let us return to the change in the official teaching that I noted at the start of this reflection. The teaching on homosexuality given to me by Bede Jarrett was, it is now clear, upholding the doctrine of Trent in saying that there is nothing wrong with this unusual inclination, worldwide and world-old. It was like all our other raw desires, deeply in need of transformation by grace but, transformed, still the same desires. Transformable does not mean curable or remediable. Grace, I once read in a Jesuit essay on direction, will change a homosexual, but not into a heterosexual.

Now here comes the capital point, and it needs stating as clearly as possible. What concealed the inconsistency in 'OK to be it, never OK to do it' was that the teachers of the doctrine were celibate priests, and more often members of a religious order: vowed to sexual abstinence, they had a good reason for saying no to same-sex action, other than the Lutheran one that this action stems from a deviant desire. It was wrong for us because of our special commitment, and so there was no inconsistency for us to say 'OK to be it, never to do it.' It was OK to be sexually normal, and we weren't allowed to 'do' that either.

Thus the Catholic position on the same-sex inclination was protected by the celibate lifestyle for which sexual activity was forbidden, and manifestly inappropriate in a celibate clergy, especially a monastic community.

Now here comes the next vital step. This teaching was for us priests and monks etc. Homosexuality was, in this sense, our problem. It was only when the teaching was applied to people for whom sexual activity was appropriate that the inconsistency appeared between 'OK to be it' and 'always wrong to do it'. Like Italian wines, the teaching on homosexuality did not export well.

It was when the teaching authority found itself faced with homosexuality as an increasingly tolerated secular phenomenon that the teaching on same-sex activity had to be based on a new doctrine of deviant desire, which is implicitly Lutheran and eschewed by Catholic orthodoxy. Same-sex activity could no longer be forbidden 'because we're celibates', so it had to be forbidden because it stems from a corrupt inclination. The formulation of 1986, quoted above, is so awkward with its language that it is theologically embarrassing. To repeat: 'The homosexual inclination, though not itself a sin, constitutes a tendency towards behaviour that is intrinsically evil, and must therefore be considered objectively disordered.' 'Must therefore be considered' reveals the jam the formulator is in. 'I'm saying this because I can't say anything else.' James Alison finds in this a dexterity suggestive of an Olympic performer.

The contradiction is glaring, and will not go away. The inclination, the way the person is, is not a sin (of course), nevertheless (one of theology's biggest 'neverthelesses') it 'must be called' a deviance because of the forbidden things these people do (which we've been forbidding ourselves for nearly two millennia!) And, to keep reiterating with the dentist's drill here, underlying this awkwardness is the shift in grounds for the prohibition, from the celibate for whom all sex is forbidden, to the lay, where sex, at least in marriage, is part of life.

Of course the official teaching jumps in here and says something like the following: 'But don't you see? That's just the point! Some sexual activity is sterile, it doesn't make babies. That's what's wrong with it. Can't you see this? It's staring you in the face! What the Church is now onto is the real reason why buggery is wrong, not the superficial reason that it is not for celibates. There is a deepening of doctrine here, not the wriggling you're pointing to. What is really happening, in the change towards negativity in attitude to which you started off by pointing, is a deepening of the Church's conviction, upheld with such energy by the late pope, that sex is for babies.'

But this involves authority in a deeper problem. Sex is hugely varied, even among animals. As well as making babies, it unites people. It bonds. It keeps out the cold. It tenders people to each other. All this is part of that huge spread of life that we call creation. It is surely an untoward rethinking of the creation story to say that *only* in its pro-creative use is sex filling its creator's purpose. The labelling as deviant what is so untidily variant is a humourless rewriting of the story. Apparently there are deviant penguins. And the occasional swan. The victory of the official teaching appears as pyrrhic once we see the presumption of what it implies: sex for babies only. The creator is a very bad Catholic! And if he's a good Catholic he's an egoist, able to see in man nothing but his co-creator.

So what should the Church authority say? It has two alternative options: *one*, 'This attraction in itself is not good, and we have been wrong for centuries in thinking that it is. All those men and women who have had this orientation, who have flourished in the celibate life and enriched the Church in countless ways were, fundamentally, flawed, deviant'; *two*, to say, 'This attraction which has long been known to be good has a way to be acted upon that is chaste, as the heterosexual attraction acted upon in fidelity to one partner is chaste.'

If ever there were an answer to come from the *sensus fidelium*, this is a case for it. And in point of fact, that peculiar thing, theology, the perpetual mulling over in human discourse of the implications for the good life as modelled for us by the Word of God made flesh, is reaching the conclusion that the first of these two options is merely an *opinion*, not a *teaching* of the Church.

Is it not in this indirect way that moral positions in the Church are arrived at; that the most ancient institution in the world responds to the evolution of consciousness in society? There was a time when slavery seemed tolerable in the Church. No longer. The Church responds to society as a living institution, a very old and conservative one but, because alive, open to change.

Were Rome ever to abandon the notion of homosexuality as a deviance, in deference to the virtually unanimous medical opinion, she would find herself, for the first time, *ministering* to this disquieting minority of her children, and no longer abandoning them to the cruel moral universe of modernity except to wait for them in the confessional. Gay and lesbian Catholics would then encounter a much more severe approach, that of taking a homosexual attraction and befriending as seriously as a straight one. Commitment services of some kind, not to be confused with marriage, would appear not as a sign of decadence in the Church but as one of pastoral seriousness where such has never been shown before.

As things are, the gay or lesbian Catholic is between a rock and a soft place. The rock, which is anything but the rock of Peter, though it has established itself on that side owing to a scripturally ungrounded double identification: of the same-sex attraction with same-sex male anal intercourse seen as a parody of the marriage act; and of this form of inter-male intercourse with the 'sin of Sodom'. The overtones and undertones of 'sodomite' are formidable and have no place in a just moral estimate of the homosexual condition. At the beginning of *Brideshead Revisited*, the uncle advises his nephew going up to the university: 'Avoid Anglo-Catholics. They are sodomites with unpleasant accents.' Quotable sayings like this have done enormous damage to young men and women struggling with their sexual identity. The soft place is, of course, the gay subculture. We await the exercise of pastoral sensitivity on the part of the supreme authority in the Church, resting upon the real rock of Peter, to address this radical injustice to immortal souls.

Reflections on Taboo

The previous paper touched on the consequence, for the Church's official position, of the increasing acceptance of homosexuality in secular society. This paper explores this further. The Church is still in the grip of a cultural taboo, which at least in western society, has already fallen away. The magisterium's position looks increasingly exposed and untenable. As before an earthquake the ground is already shifting.

I wish I (we) knew more about taboos, for clearly the veto on homosexual practice is a taboo, and a very old, strong and nearly universal one. A taboo differs from a moral precept, whether the latter is accepted or not, in a way that involves a combination of 'don't do it' with 'don't talk about it!' This combination suggests that the subject tabooed is something perceived as a *threat* to the society that upholds it. An interesting thing about the 'don't mention it' part of the taboo is that it protects the one who infringes it. A sexual taboo makes it inappropriate to ask someone about their sexual behaviour and thus put them on the spot. 'Don't ask, don't tell' has recently been given semi-officially as the attitude of the armed forces.

Now if taboos are protecting a society against conduct that threatens it, there is surely a connection between the silence enjoined and the sense of threat. The word 'conspiracy' suggests itself. A society 'knows' what's bad for it, and lets this be known by its members. But how society is served by its taboos is a question that ranges from the obviously sensible (to us!), to the lore of a club. The classic instance is the incest taboo, which prevents inbreeding. One might set up a continuum from the useful to the *cosa nostra*, and ask where the taboo on homosexual behaviour comes on this continuum. As a society comes to feel less threatened by this behaviour, the taboo becomes more clubbish or snobbish. A further question is: 'Is a society wrong or frivolous or secularist in not feeling threatened by this behaviour?' I find it interesting that John Milbank,[1] who upholds an 'orthodox Christian' opinion on society and deplores a society that loses a religious moral sense, has recently cited the gay issue as one matter where he has 'learned' from the secularists, and that to find homosexuality evil is 'not quite real'. He is registering, surely, the unravelling of a taboo.

When one looks at the Bible – meaning the key texts, from Leviticus and the affair with Sodom in Genesis – it is clear that the kind of society that feels threatened by 'the man lying down as a woman' is what is now called patriarchal and widely viewed as something we are outgrowing. One would hardly expect to find in the average person today the feeling that the homosexuals are 'letting the side down' by not breeding. Is the absence of any such feeling a sign of decadence? Is a society, for which same-sex behaviour is tolerable, decadent? Is it a case of 'so much the worse for society'? If it sees nothing amiss in the two young men I saw recently waiting with their trolley in Tesco? John Milbank finds himself unable to think this way.

Now all these considerations are ignoring something of crucial importance, which may be brought out by comparing our taboo with the incest taboo. There is no class of persons, worldwide and world-old, that is incestuously prone, but there is such a class of persons that we now call 'homosexual'. So we have to try to put together the notion of 'society protecting itself' against this 'threat' and 'these persons' who will include the occasional cabinet minister, or military leader or head of a women's college. To uphold the taboo with the matter understood the way it is now becomes, as Milbank mildly puts it, 'not quite real'. The culture we live and survive in is one that acknowledges professional psychology as a necessary aid to living, and both the American and the British national associations of practitioners have struck homosexuality off the list of deviances, defined as disablers for healthy living.

To repeat, the taboo now upheld by religious authority is upheld against a class of persons, and any discrimination against a class of persons is abhorrent to Christianity. In this connection, it is very striking that both Catholic and Anglican episcopal statements in this matter start by saying, as emphatically as they possibly can, that

[1] John Milbank is an Anglican theologian who believes that, with the ending of 'modernity', theology has an opportunity to re-establish its place in culture and discourse. His position is sometimes called 'radical orthodoxy'.

homosexuals are not to be *discriminated* against. What is really being said is that if we go on as we have been till now, we shall be discriminating against these people, and so of course we mustn't!

It is the striking similarity between Catholic and Anglican official statements, each of them starting with a heavy anti-discrimination clause, that has given me the idea that what we are seeing today, both in the Catholic Church and in the Anglican Communion, is the behaviour of institutional religion faced with the collapse of the taboo. As the taboo erodes, the people it has been protecting by silence lose this protection, and are exposed and feel the draught. Hence the gay pride displays, which are becoming counter-productive and promoting an idea of sex that is obsessive. But overreaction is reaction overdoing it, and is not usefully opposed by counter-reaction!

Once the word 'discrimination' becomes the first thing authority talks about, the whole issue of same-sex relating becomes an issue about people who are liable to be discriminated against. So the people who were once protected by the taboo are exposed once the taboo starts wearing thin. And of course to say we must not discriminate against these people is to acknowledge that the taboo has gone and left them unprotected. What seems to be truly dreadful is, while leaving gay people unprotected by the taboo, to convert the taboo into an eternal moral imperative and use that to judge them. What are we to make, in this context, of the CDF's identification of Rome with the evangelical wing of the Anglican debate? The evangelicals are identifying with, for instance, Nigeria where the taboo is in full force and invites the death penalty. So what the CDF is doing is precisely what I have just described, converting the taboo into an eternal moral law and imposing this on the Church.

What a tricky and versatile thing language is, though! A friend of mine, an Anglican priest, remarked recently, concerning the recent Roman statement on homosexuality and the priesthood, that the document understands homosexuality to be a compulsion, like alcoholism. But it was only the word 'compulsion' that enabled me to clarify the matter and, thus clarified, to make a very in-your-face observation about the document. One should avoid turning a new insight in terminology into triumphant polemic!

The Last Place Where it Dare not Speak its Name

The elephant (pink) in the living-room
Could not be mentioned in the Holy Synod,
A silence like the silence of the tomb
Forbade this reference to the Fathers' innards.

They shut the window lest the gay parade
Rudely invade the sacrosanct proceedings.
Theology might think it had it made
Even convinced here of the Spirit's pleadings.

But it's too sensitive to bring it up
Although it is a matter for us teachers:
How very odd for this to be a cup
Not to be shared among our other features!

And does not this prove there is something wrong
That makes old ladies of the seeming strong?

An Ecclesial Problem '

The previous paper touched on the similarity of the problem in the Anglican and Catholic Churches in relation to their attitude to same-sex relations. But the Catholic Church will more easily find its way out of its impasse. For Catholic moral teaching is ultimately based on the concept of 'natural law' – what is good for 'human flourishing' is 'good'. Evangelical Anglican moral teaching appeals more to Scripture, which is open to interpretation and cultural bias.

The real question raised by the Anglican debate over homosexuality is different from what might appear. It is, surely: how is the moral permissibility or otherwise of unusual but increasingly accepted sexual actions to be grounded, whether to be affirmed or denied? Is it through the Bible? Surely not. A moral authority, albeit a Christian one committed to the Bible as the word of God, cannot give as the basis for forbidding something: 'The Bible forbids it, that's all!' The Natural Law tradition represents the belief, essential to Catholic Christianity, that the wrongs we do are wrong because they are opposed to human flourishing, so that it can be said clearly in what this anti-humanness consists. We cannot believe in a God who forbids certain human interactions for reasons of his own that we are not to know, other than as revealed.

The Catholic Church recognises this by grounding the veto on homosexual actions in their being destructive of human relations, not in their being 'against the Bible'. Now the Church has had good grounds for describing these actions as destructive of the value of community, in the strong and widespread institution of committed celibacy. In that context, these arrangements are destructive. We don't tuck up in pairs after Compline! What makes this unacceptable is celibate community life.

Notice that the *community*, as the value, was able to say 'No' to homosexual arrangements because it knew the goodness of the same-sex intimacy of which these actions were the damaging. I want to stress this, because it is, I suspect, the nub of the matter. What was forbidden was the spoiling of something good – which is exactly what 'doing wrong' means. But what is the 'something good' here, of which the breaking into full physical intimacy is the spoiling? It is the attraction which some people have to someone of the same sex when this attraction is experienced in a celibate community. How could the expression and fulfilment of this attraction be said to be 'not on'? Only in the celibate community context in which the thing happens! In other words, the celibate community, in having a human reason for forbidding people to be physically intimate, was in a position to affirm the goodness of the attraction itself. I may be wrong here, but my recollection is that the people who were saying (to the enquiring boy in a Catholic school for instance) that there's nothing wrong in feeling this way about another boy were the occasional sensitive Dominican or Jesuit or whatever, these men and women rather than laymen and women. The people who were affirming the okay-ness of being gay were the people who had a good reason for saying you shouldn't act on it, the reason being the celibate community whose integrity it threatened. People like Fr Bede Jarrett OP were, in the matter of overcoming the deadly virus of self-hatred in everyone and especially in homosexuals, pioneers.

The trouble was, when Church authority, confronted with homo-sexuality as a public fact, tried to export the okay-to-be-it-not-to-do-it to the general world. Then, no longer having the human value of *community* to urge against sexual intimacy, authority had to face head-on for the first time the contradiction of 'okay to be it, but never do it' by saying, for the first time too, 'Well, there is something wrong about "being it", it is a deviance.' I remember that when this definition of homosexuality as a 'deviance' was pronounced in 1986, my immediate reaction was: 'But this is going back on what I learned from Fr Bede Jarrett as a boy, in his CTS pamphlet, *Purity.*'

The Catholica is based not just on the Bible but on the Early Church Councils that show the biblical faith making sense of itself in the philosophic world of Athens and Rome. With this as its grounding, the Catholic Church, faced with a human problem such as same-sex coupling, goes not to 'Leviticus etc.' but to 'the natural law', a philo-sophically grounded moral self-understanding that can be intelligibly appealed to, and this leads to the further and truer question: is same-sex intimacy against the natural law? An overwhelming consensus of scientists seems to undermine the belief that it is, for natural law is derived by observation of human inclination universally and in all times. Thus the Church of Rome, unlike the Anglican Communion, has a basis that is going to find the belief that this universal orientation is against the natural law difficult, and we can see this process already at work in the very nuanced description of homosexuality in the New Catechism. It is admitted, for a start and for the first time, that we do not know whence comes this orientation, but that it is given not learned. The teaching that it is a disorder continues, but awkwardly. And besides this, the notion of a depraved original desire has been rejected by the Council of Trent against Luther.

So Catholic authority, following its traditional requirement to explain itself in terms of human flourishing and not to lean on 'the Bible', finds itself bound, *if* it is to continue to forbid sexual intimacy to gays, to rest this prohibition on the definition of homosexuality as a 'deviance', that is, a tendency that is against human flourishing, that, for instance, it cuts the couple off from others and from the demands of an unselfish life. But this is contested by homosexuals and by a large majority of scien-tists in this area. But a statement about human experience that is dis-verified by experience is thus reduced, in terms of moral theology, to the status of 'an opinion' as opposed to a statement of official teaching.

Now the point I am making is that Catholic teaching, by reason of its traditional appeal to 'human flourishing intelligibly described' as opposed to an external authority found in the Bible, finds itself com-pelled to demote the reason given for its prohibition to the status of a disputable opinion.

Thus it is the Catholic moral tradition committed to 'natural law' that has to retreat from the condemnation of homosexual intimacy: a paradoxical result, since the Catholic Church is notoriously intransigent where sex is concerned.

Thus you get the seemingly paradoxical result that it will be the Catholic Church, notoriously intolerant in the sexual area, that finds itself compelled by the way it has to think of morality as naturally shaped, not commanded, to allow the homosexual person to fulfil his or her way of being sexual, if only by the grudging admission that the grounds for its 'non-approval' (the official word now used by the Catechism) are only an *opinion*. The Anglican ecclesiology, at least its evangelical wing, on the other hand, with its reliance on 'the Bible' to ground moral prohibition, can never come to this crisis. For them 'the Bible' is always available for letting them off from thinking the thing right through (for one can always ask: 'Whose Bible, Akinola's or that of the Christian biblical scholar?').

So I have to modify my view of Anglicanism as the 'laboratory' of the Church where moral problems are worked through. They can never in the Anglican polity be worked through, since 'the Bible' is always available as a retreat. The Catholic 'lab' enjoys the possibility of working through at one remove from the actual pastoral situation. Instead of: 'Can that action be approved?' the question is: 'What is the reason for disapproval? Is it bedrock?' And the answer is that it is only an 'opinion', less and less verified by experience and science.

And, of course, in the Anglican reliance on the Bible as the ground for the prohibition of same-sex intimacy, it is the Bible that suffers, since it will serve the bias of those whose culture drives them to abominate what they can take the Bible as forbidding. The Bible becomes the banner of the biased, which, in the finest tradition of Anglican scholarship, is the very last thing that the Bible is.

CHAPTER 10

Friendship and Discipleship

This final chapter touches on other aspects of human relationship, notably friendship. It notices that Christ's invitation to us into friendship with him is, in fact, the 'call to discipleship' as it was for Peter. To be called into his friendship is to turn away from the violence and hatred of the world, and even from conventional 'religion', and towards the love and forgiveness of the risen Christ. To become a friend of Jesus is to take a big risk, as Jesus himself did. Yet his friendship transforms us completely – we can even use the word 'transubstantiation'.

So transformation of ourselves and our relationships is the dominant theme of this final gathering of essays and sermons.

Mending Quarrels: Making Friends

This first essay was written in 1997. Without referring specifically to 'focusing', it shows how being comfortable within ourselves enables us to be outward going and friendly towards others.

In a quarrel, each person is outside himself thinking about the other, in an ecstasy of disliking. We talk of someone very angry being 'beside himself'. Each person's thoughts are centred in the other, on how impossible he is. This negative mutual imitation-cum-fixation constitutes between people a kind of invisible glue. This glue is always there in a more or less benign state because we naturally imitate each other. (Aristotle sees our difference from other animals to consist in an enormously enhanced power of imitation. Not only do we do what we see others doing – as animals do – but we want what we see others wanting, sometimes at an unreachable depth of ourselves.) The glue is activated when two people quarrel – or fall in love (but that's another story).

Now Rule One is that resolution has to be, to start with, unilateral. You must be the first to change the pattern. You change the pattern by withdrawing your thoughts from the other back to yourself, your life, the things you enjoy. You de-obsess yourself so you can present yourself now comfortable with yourself to the other. The only way he can imitate you at home with yourself is to be at home with himself. This reverses the direction of imitation. It is the transubstantiation of the glue! The result is two people exposing themselves to each other, which is what friendship is. Being friendly is being who you are with someone else.

This mutual self-exposure is more than is normally happening between people, so a quarrel mended in this way is an advance on normal relations. It is a creative relating between people. Thus when Jesus says: 'Love your enemies!' he is giving the formula for changing the world by the insertion of an innovative element into otherwise routine relations that easily decline into mutual envy, into the glue.

Now the key moment in this change is the return to yourself from the obsession with someone else. But to make this return, you need to be at home with yourself. A medieval spiritual master compares someone not happy with himself to a man who has nothing to go home to but 'stinks and smoke and a chiding wife'!

Hence the need for centring techniques, for body-mindfulness. Christianity is the way of loving. Buddhism is the way of centring. They complement each other. Love without centring is do-good-ism. Centring without love tends to be self-indulgent.

But, to repeat, one of the two has got to start it. It won't start itself. When you do make a start, you may begin to find the other person attractive, in a new way, with the attractiveness of a person rather than a physical attractiveness. Love is a matter of being attracted to someone rather than by someone. 'You turn me on!' is not really what love is about.

The basic formula is: presenting yourself at home with yourself to someone else, thus putting him at ease with himself – reversing the common direction of mimesis. Being friendly is being who you are with someone else. A philosopher, concerned with verbal tidiness, will say that the term 'friend' is without meaning just used of one person without another. You can't be just friendly. As we know, this isn't true, and the philosophers are wrong. You can be just friendly. And indeed, unless you start being friendly, the quarrel will not end.

Being friendly, in a way philosophy can't make sense of, is not only the way to end a quarrel. It is also the way to start a friendship when there has been no quarrel. Hence the useful saying: 'If you want a friend, be one!'

Now one's capacity for friendship is enormously enhanced by meditation or contemplative praying. For in this exercise I become comfortable, not just with myself but with the huge mystery in which I live and breathe, which we are normally afraid of. If love begins to 'cast out fear' deep down in myself, I become a more potent centre of reversed mimesis, a transubstantiator of the glue. Hence the ancient saying: someone who has reached inner peace will be a source of peace for thousands.

I find I rather like using the word 'transubstantiation' here. The word was originally coined to define a change that is quite unlike any other change we can think of, namely the changing of bread and wine into the body and blood of Christ. What we do to the glue when we reverse mimesis is also a very odd kind of changing, very difficult to define, so the eucharistic model, by its uniqueness, draws attention to this. And the Eucharist is, after all, the primary agent of unity between people.

> Desire itself can be in other hands,
> Look with surprise upon an enemy
> Lifted above itself so that it stands
> Not sticks at one who has offended me.
>
> He is a pain, I do not change in this,
> At this plateau offence invites reaction:
> To stay here, though, is boring, bound to miss
> The chance of life beyond anger and faction.
>
> There is a higher level where I am
> Myself to you, invite you to be you
> And let us both out of a hopeless jam:
> The transubstantiation of the glue.
>
> This is the mystery of our desire:
> It fascinates, yet may be lifted higher.

From Religion to Faith

In this sermon the model of St Paul shows how Christ invites us from violence and hatred into his love and friendship. It could be an Ignatian exercise for the twenty-first century!

I am finding it possible to discover for myself Jesus as the man I kill and why. This is St Paul's discovery, of his own life made worth living by the assiduous keeping of God's Law, which came into crisis and involved him in the stoning of Stephen who represented some sort of dangerous alternative to 'the Law' coming out of a man recently executed. 'Saul was consenting to his death' by stoning; he was a willing participant in the mob's rejection of the new, organised by the priests of the old.

Surely I can find in myself a self-righteousness that needs to have others who are wrong, God my own way. I think this self-righteousness goes very deep. At bottom it tries to deal with the fear that my life may be meaningless, to be wiped out like the fruit fly. So, better my meaning than no meaning at all. I remember myself as a naval midshipman, a pious Catholic who could not go to communion with the slightest impurity unabsolved, but did not bother to mention in confession my part in a lynch-mob against an unpopular messmate. Being right with my God my way was more important to me than treating someone decently. And being right with God my way is how I deal with the fear that I might have no meaning in this cruel universe. Perhaps religion is the fight for meaning against death, and has to be transformed by faith, which addresses my deeper desire, which is for eternal life.

Now I can find that self-securing in myself, then and now, adapting itself to new circumstances but always with the same aim of self-securing; and then imagine Jesus as putting himself at the receiving end of my need to make the other wrong to keep me right, and letting me kill him, and then think of him as returning and not blaming me but inviting me to relax, at last, into him. This is an exercise you won't find in St Ignatius, but we're in the twenty-first century, with its privileged insight into violence, which means into ourselves as violent.

This is a spiritual thought-experiment, a DIY for this Lent. I used it in a painful situation, when I was being badly misunderstood by someone close to me and just couldn't pray myself out of it until I got that idea, to get in touch with my own self-righteousness against that person, and have it keep him wrong and have Jesus as my victim, and meet him risen from the dead perhaps for the first time. My first thought was: 'He is ingenious! He totally undermines me!' Then with prayer it soon ceased to be just intellectual, and sank in.

Scholars can go on and on exploring the mind of Paul, but we have a short cut through our own self-righteousness, bringing it into synch with Jesus on the cross and in his inviting risen life.

> Jesus I come to see you through the eyes
> Of Saul, thrown to the ground and blinded by
> Your light that takes religion by surprise
> Revealed as need to mean, but selfishly.
>
> I saw you so as, plumb-lining my past
> I saw my need for rightness, others wrong,
> As my defence against the icy blast,
> God on my terms, deaf to his lovers' song
>
> That now I hear in its eternal tones
> Sounded out of our victim unaccusing
> Leaving no evidence of buried bones
> My body soul with Spirit now infusing.
>
> This is my right, believing in your blood
> Turned light to lift me from outlasting mud.

A Relationship Transformed

'Have you ever admired someone whom you sometimes wanted to strangle?' Perhaps that is how Peter felt towards Jesus. Yet the risen Jesus transforms the relationship. This sermon is from 1994.

There is a modern American classic, a novel by John Knowles called *A Separate Peace*. The protagonist, whom I'll have to call John since I forgot his name, is visiting his old school. Though it is a dark November day, he goes straight down to the river – and there it is, looming in the gloomy mist – the tree. He stands by the tree for a long time, remembering...

He and Obi were inseparable, though they were quite unlike, he studious, Obi athletic, a thoroughgoing extrovert whose limitless vitality enthralled John, fed him you might say. Toward the end of term, John was getting nervous about exams, but he always let Obi pull him away from his work to get up to all sorts of pranks and dares. There was one in particular that they liked doing in the evening – the tree. It stood well back from the river, but one of its branches stretched all the way to the bank, and the game was to inch together along this branch, holding on to a higher one, until you were near enough to jump into the water far below. On this occasion, John was especially miffed at letting himself once again follow Obi when he was so behind on work. They worked their way along, and then, well before they reached the water, John suddenly jounced the branch, so that Obi lost his hold and fell to the ground, breaking both legs. His athletic life was finished.

Have you ever done anything like this – or wanted to even – so that afterwards you ask, aghast, how I could have done that? You feel terrible guilt, although you weren't really in control, and that is what is really troubling. Something made you do a bad thing to someone because they were beyond your control, as Obi was beyond John's. So you felt awful because you got out of control doing serious hurt to someone because he was out of your control! It's a thoroughly confusing state you are in.

One of the best questions I can ask myself, then, is: 'How do I identify with John? How do I feel about someone I admire, who seems to have it all and, somehow, to make me feel I don't have it all?' The reason why this is such a good question is that it is about the central relationship of what is still the great story, whatever they say or try to do: between Peter and Jesus. Let's look at that relationship.

After the big catch of fish, Peter says: 'Leave me alone, I'm just an ordinary average man!' When Jesus asks them, on a later occasion: 'Yes, I know what they are all saying, but who do you say that I am?', it is Peter who gets it right – and then immediately gets it wrong again when Jesus tells them about his coming ordeal, so that Jesus turns on him and calls him the Devil. All the ingredients are here, then, for a stormy relationship of the kind I'm talking about, between an ordinary and a quite out-of-the-ordinary person. And Peter doesn't know himself, he's baffled by his real feelings in this relationship. He says to Jesus: 'I'll follow you to suffering and death!' and Jesus says: 'No you won't! You'll deny you ever knew me – three times!' And when finally Peter is challenged, by a young girl, he says: 'Look, I do not know this guy – never set eyes on him!'

Now it wasn't only cowardice that made Peter react in this way. It was a confused rage against the man who had done this to him – pulled him away from his trade into something he never understood yet somehow wanted, and now here he was, alone, accused, and scared to death.

This is the relationship between John and Obi, intensified, universalised, having now for its theme the ultimate question of human destiny, the question about that man. In both cases, there's that deep, ill-understood desire to be rid of someone loved but too big for you.

But the gospel story goes on just where the story of John and Obi breaks off. Just as Peter is feeling a certain relief – grief, yes, but relief too, that the impossible dream has been buried – Jesus comes to him. Now how would Peter have expected Jesus to meet him, coming back from the dead: Jesus whom he'd denied and, worse, in some way that he did not understand, wished dead? Surely as awakening all this wretchedness in him.

In fact the coming-back of Jesus was the exact opposite. It was that unique thing, forgiveness coming from the slain victim of our violence. Jesus risen set Peter free from all his wretched confusion, to respond with love to his restored friend, and to rally the community, to 'confirm his brethren', as Jesus had said to him at the last supper. This is the difference between the return of the dead, our style, and the return from the dead, God style. Ghosts are ghastly. Jesus risen gives a party to those he is setting free, that we call Eucharist or Mass, that used to be called *convivium* or love-feast. Supposing, on that dark November day, by the fatal tree looming up in the mist, Obi had appeared and hugged his friend, with laughter. This would have to be in another dimension altogether, on the other side of death, in which a resurrected Obi would get behind that act of sudden anger to the love behind it. This is beyond the scope of a novel. But this is exactly what Jesus did for Peter, according to John's gospel. Peter had denied Jesus three times, so Jesus, risen from the dead, appeared to Peter by the lake and asked him three times: 'Do you love me?' He let Peter reverse, in love, what he'd said in confusion. And just to make sure he got the point, there was a brazier burning there to remind him of the brazier where he'd been warming his hands when he said: 'I don't know the man'.

The problem is to get inside this story, to feel it as the story of your life. Have you ever admired someone whom you sometimes wanted to strangle? Well, that's it, that's the dynamic, the DNA of the great story. Likelihood is, your friend was popular. And perhaps the crowd turned against him. And you were asked, at a riotous party, what you thought of him, and you heard yourself joining the crowd in what you said. And if that makes you search yourself and ask, 'Who am I, where do I stand?', that is the beginning of you as a person, that is Christ beginning to be you, and there's no end to that. It's the start of your emancipation from this God-awful society based on greed and fear. And it was Peter, the recovered coward, who proclaimed the resurrection with the words, 'Save yourselves from this perverse generation!'

There is an old saying: Money lost, little lost, honour lost, much lost, heart lost, all lost. The awful question is: 'How is the heart not lost? How is the heart saved?' To this question, the great story is the answer, if we can only get into it. And the incredible thing is, that Peter is still around – in Rome! Peter, representing all of us, still catching up with his original moment with Jesus risen awakening the lover in him, and making a mess of it, as any human is bound to do. The big story, the big 'out' from our muddle and misery, is there in the past, there in the present called Church. The task is to find it where alone it counts, in you, in me. Somewhere in you, somewhere in me, the fear of life that crucifies Jesus could receive him back from death, begin to change, and change this changeable world.

The Centrality of Discipleship to Salvation

The call to discipleship is a call to take a big risk, with our whole life, as Jesus did. This reflection was written in 2006.

The question: 'Why us, why me, why anything at all?' is a question seriously asked only by a person, only by someone. And it is asked for the whole of humanity.

The only answer that there can be, that is not just an answering echo like the 'oo-boom' heard by Mrs Moore in those caves in *A Passage to India*, is, as Dag Hammarskjöld put it: 'That existence is meaningful, and my life, in dedication, has a goal'.[1] The only thing heard is a call, a voice, a vocation.

[1] Dag Hammarskjöld (1905-1961), a Swedish diplomat, was UN Secretary General from 1953 until his death in 1961. He described himself as a Christian Mysticist, and his book *Markings* is frequently used as a source of spiritual inspiration. He was awarded the Nobel Peace Prize in 1961.

Anyone who says 'Yes' as Hammarskjöld did, if he or she is to act on this yes, is taking a risk. The notion of risk is bound into the notion of the question, the answer: 'Yes I have a purpose' and the further move toward action – find someone else who has a similar question, etc.

Now when we look at Jesus, coming where he does in the history of his people and humanity, the consciousness of the unknown as his Father, and of a mission received, the notion of risk appears again, this time full-blooded and historic. The mission, he comes growingly to see, is to bring about, in obedience to his Father, an order of humanity at variance with the power- and murder-driven order that is all there is in the world. It is the greatest risk that has ever been taken: the risk whose only possible outcome is his death at the world's hands.

Now this, the central risk for our ultimate divine destiny is required for anyone who will follow him. Discipleship is the risk that totally shapes a person's life.

We know the relentless process in which the disciple, at risk with friends, survival and common sense, is exposed, the mill in which life as he or she has known it is ground, the outcome of which is the resurrection encounter and Pentecostal empowerment.

It would be an egregious error to suppose that this dynamic only applies to the Church's first and founding epoch. It expands itself wherever and whenever a person is converted to the founding response to the call issuing in the crucifixion.

It is because 'joining the Church' is not joining a club but risking one's life within the original risk and its mysterious reward, that the focus of the profession of faith and of faith's eucharistic celebration is 'the death of the Lord until he come'. Not the risen Jesus except as of course present in the death, not the dogma with which the faith has protected itself from the ravages of muddle and sin but 'the death, the risk finally taken, shared by the disciple, and rewarded by the sober insobriety of the Spirit'.

It is worth repeating here an historic moment during a lecture by Donald McKinnon at Cambridge half a century ago.[2] Suddenly pausing, as he wandered away from the rostrum, he said:

[2] Donald McKinnon was a theologian who published little but was very influential on his contemporaries.

The whole question is, was there that which Jesus alone could do, in the way it had to be done, that was of such moment for humanity that the risk was justified, the cost well spent?

The Invitation to Discipleship
Another sermon preached in Advent 2001 to Downside School, on the same theme – Jesus as the 'other' who challenges us and invites us towards himself in love.

Most of us talk to ourselves, not out loud except when we're mad at someone or something. This has been called mental noise. We make a lot of mental noise, so we don't easily hear what other people are saying to us.

Now to hear what God is saying to us, we need to stop completely the mental noise. And this is easier than we think; all I have to do is realise that talking to myself makes two of me, me and myself, and this can't be true, so I can let this me-with-me collapse into just me, and that's where God is and has been all along. There are not two of me: love makes me one. It's a bit of a shock at first, but take a few deep breaths, and say, 'OK, I'm here, God. Your move!'

Monks down the ages have practised this way of paying unusual attention to what's going on all the time, to who's going on, the most intimate and unobtrusive friend. Even children are learning to do this with the Scriptures. God stops at nothing to get our attention.

Now let me walk us through today's gospel reading, letting it speak to me without the usual chatter. Truth is speaking to me, just me without the buzz, which is like interference in a bad radio receiver.

We're not making a gospel movie, which nearly always means a bad movie, people in long robes wandering around in a semi-daze uttering platitudes. I'm not going to pretend I'm a first-century Palestinian, about whom I know even less than I do about modern Palestinians, though it hurts to think of what they are being put through at this time. No, I'm going to be me now, speaking I hope for you as we put ourselves in the desert listening to this wild prophet. I've come to the desert to experience something like my real self, my only self, that's all cluttered up with who I'm made to think I am by the images of beautiful people smiling out of *Hello!* magazine or *FHM* or *GQ* and all the models of the good life that confuse me. Global capital keeps us chattering to ourselves about the yummy things it has on offer. And somewhere out in the windswept desert, there is me alone, not me with myself in the twosome that I am made into by the endless images for envy to feed on. I am alone, in the desert. I get the same message from the prophet that everyone else is getting: all the things you think you are, priests, chosen people, Downside people, count for nothing here where you are alone with the fact of your being. The priests get rough treatment. 'You brood of vipers!' he cries. Where ordinary people see pillars of society, the prophet may see snakes!

I let the prophet's rough words sink in, alone in my desert, our desert. But the prophet is not only stripping me down to my bare essentials. He is preparing me for something special, a stranger who is in your midst, and you don't know it. The prophet is not just stripping us down. He's creating expectation. Something's coming...

And then he is there, the stranger. You and I know perfectly well who this is, he's been around for two thousand years, and his image has worn thin. But now, in this carefully engineered desert moment, there is another possibility: that while the prophet is cutting me down to the person I am, no frills, the stranger is showing me to myself as the destined person I am in God's eyes. Jesus and John the Baptist come together in the story. But what I think we have to discover is how they come together for you and me when we try to access our deep self, our sense of our own story, our destiny. This is a whole way of reading the Scriptures, called *lectio divina*, which is now spreading far beyond its original monastic setting. It's all to do with learning to pay unusual attention, as you read the Scriptures, to your own inner life.

Now to return to the story. Strangest of all, the stranger is queuing up for baptism by the prophet. All four gospels report this, so it must have happened; they would much rather the stranger hadn't done this, hadn't been so unlike their notion of a powerful person.

After forty days and nights in his wilderness, the stranger will be back, calling occasional men and women into his company, making disciples. If I become a disciple, what will happen to me? Well, I'll surprise myself, for my mysterious inner being, so different from all my self-images, will get stronger. And then I know only too well what's going to happen. My old friends are going to start making fun of me for 'going with that lot'. Come back to us, be the guy we all know so well. Who hasn't experienced this clash of loyalties, between the person who is bringing out in you things you never knew were there, and the friends you get smashed with, who know you too well?

A person is a destiny. That's the best definition I know. The stranger of Palestine is my destiny. And at times, when he is becoming more and more unpopular, I'll wish I'd never known him. Look at Peter, the first pope, warming his hands by the brazier, trying to get lost in the crowd while the stranger, handcuffed and with a police guard, stands in the dock. When that wretched girl points to him and says, 'You're one of them!', he wishes he'd never known the man, and blurts out that he doesn't, and the stranger looks across from the dock, and that does him in, strips him down to the barest frightened essentials, so he'll be the first leader of the new people.

And this is who the stranger turns out to be: the true self in each of us, killed by us because we are afraid to be true to ourselves. And so I come to my last phase in this story, and he is there for us with death far behind him, alive as he never was before. And then the most extraordinary thing of all happens. To make contact with my true self, I had to be alone in the desert. Now that the stranger has come to me showing himself to me as the eternal in me, I am no longer alone among people. I am directed toward them in love. To be a believer is to have come to myself, so that I see in others not images for envy and distraction, but members of one body of Christ. For when Jesus rose from the dead, he rose into everybody, and into the whole universe, to be the cosmic Christ.

If you ask me how it is that Palestine, the place of the world's rebirth, has become the world's cockpit, where violence is plunging into an irreversible spiral, I don't know. All I do know is that Jesus Christ, 'yesterday and today and the same for ever', is who, in the loneliness of the world's night, I am and we are. In him I am not two but one, born eternally in the mind of God, conceived immaculate, as we celebrated yesterday. Here we all are, and there's the stranger, the pioneer, urging us to dive in at the deep end and learn to swim by so doing. In those first faltering strokes, we come to know him who is the water.

Our Real Fear

In taking away our deepest fear Jesus strengthens us for discipleship.

What would it feel like to have one's deepest fear miraculously taken away? The deepest, not the worst, not Room 101 with the rats, but the radical one? It would be bewildering, all the old landmarks gone, and being someone no more you.

The human animal is infinite in desire, with fear to match. Desire and the attendant fear to lose all is what throbs through the gospel story, the story of this group of men and women being pulled along by him to bring in what he called the Kingdom. For the story has a dark side that he refers to from time to time, and they avoid asking him about it – of him caught and savaged and killed and raised from the dead, whatever that might mean. You'd never have asked him to say more about that!

In today's gospel,[3] he asks about a perfectly sensible discussion they had been engaged in, about who was going to be who in the coming kingdom, but all he offers as model is a child, a non-person in that culture.

As the story comes to its dreaded climax, things suddenly become horribly clear: he's going to be caught and subjected to all the brutalities of the military, and Peter, their leader, says: 'Well I'll go with you, that's for sure, I'm ready to die with you!', to which Jesus' reply is far too well known for its deeper implications to show themselves. For the truth is that the leader is to have the full treatment, what is ultimately implied in being his disciple. And when the moment of confrontation comes with that cheeky girl, Peter, all the fingers pointed at him, suddenly sees what Jesus is in for and he too, and he publicly, and with an oath, dissociates himself from the man and thereby joins the crowd, joins all of us natural cowards.

Now the meeting with Jesus alive out of all that, with all that the last few days have done with his soul, is the most dramatic description we have, anywhere, of having our deepest fear awakened and removed by the man of desire, and being turned loose to change the world. I keep returning to that moment of all-recovery as an Ignatian meditation. Peter got the full treatment. That's how Jesus trained him to be the rock on which he was to build his Church.

We must all pray to have our share of the treatment as and when it is appropriate.

---

[3] See Matt. 9: 33-37.

And so to the End

In this final essay Sebastian suggests that – even before the crucial events of the crucifixion and resurrection – John's gospel tends to portray Jesus as the risen Jesus. Consequently Christianity, down the ages, has too easily over-looked Jesus' crucial teaching and action: overcome violence by meeting it with love. 'It has taken the Church two millennia to recognise that God put his Son in the world, as the man who took the greatest risk of history and was subject to a lynch-death, in order to give us an effective way beyond the myth of dominance, and from which we are set free into eternal life.'

In fact, the essay, originally entitled 'A Meditation for Holy Week', seems to converge on what all these papers have been striving towards. So I have also incorporated a final paragraph, a form of testimony, with which Sebastian wished to conclude the whole collection.

As we approach Holy Week, the Church hands over to John, his gospel that one scholar has called the maverick gospel. John is inventing the historical Jesus in the strong light of Jesus risen and Spirit-giving. And by way of a compendious introduction to the drama, John's Jesus says: 'I lay down my life of myself, no one takes it from me, I lay it down and take it up again, in obedience to my Father.'

How are those amazing words about his death-to-be addressed to me, to you, to those curious 'Greeks' who 'wanted to see Jesus'? Well, they tell the deepest truth about his passion, knowable only in the light of Easter: that the atrocious death was something he was 'doing', a pioneer action that disarms in love all our violence, and creates a new people of God, the 'peaceable kingdom'.

We see Jesus on his cross, victim of all our violence, and we know from him risen that this is God undermining violence with vulnerable love, so let us be vulnerable like Jesus, follow his dangerous teachings in the Sermon on the Mount, because God is behind us. Being non-violent in a violent world, we're on the winning side, as Abbot Chapman says about being a Christian.

But this doesn't work if we forget what John is doing, inventing Jesus while remembering, for instance, the Emmaus journey. John's Jesus talks like someone risen from the dead before he undergoes his frightful ordeal in which he invites us to join him in prayer, to 'watch one hour with me'. He is prematurely oracular, with his 'I am' all over the place. Those words about laying down his life and taking it up again in obedience to his Father, if read 'straight', applied to him before the passion, make him the sole protagonist. The lonely agonist of Gethsemani becomes the protagonist of the drama. And lo, come the Thursday, he is at supper as the first Christian liturgist, celebrating his death with a ritual, and I've never heard or preached a sermon that did not fall into this trap. It's a simple short circuit: *directly connecting the man to be crucified* with the result, leaving out the awful in-between where his bunch of scared and scattered followers and you and I are.

Why does this 'short circuit' happen? I've just said why! It stops him doing his wonderful thing in us that disturbs us. And also, it deprives us, and those we teach, of the model that humanity has wanted from its beginning, the gentle divine model in the midst of violence, who says: 'Learn of me for I am meek and humble of heart, and be light of the crushing burden you put on yourself by joining in the power game.'

With this short circuit in place, the risen Jesus – instead of revealing the crucified as the model the world has always cried out for, non-violence as the power and wisdom of God in our violent world – has created a new, 'non-moral' area for the Christian mind.

So the far-reaching call on *us* to risk all, to meet violence with love, which changes our community relations, no longer has in it the power and Spirit of the risen one. And surely all the divisions in Christianity stem from this original cutting off of the risen, triumphant Christ from the unaccusing victim of our violence. About the risen Christ as the God-Man and a new start, you can dispute. About him who says 'Learn of me and be free of the burden you put on yourselves' there is no disputing, except between courage and cowardice.

We must learn to contemplate the figure on the cross as drawing us and all things to himself as the exemplar of life beyond the enslave-ment of having to vie with each other for the upper hand. The man on the cross, the 'fool on the hill' picked up in one of the lyrics of the Beatles, speaks to the very deepest thing in us, the desire to be in love not war. 'If I am lifted up, I will draw all things to myself.'

It has taken the Church two millennia to recognise that God put his Son in the world, subject to a lynch-death, to give us an effective way beyond the 'myth of dominance' (which is a modern name for Paul's 'reign of death'), from which we are set free into eternal life by the man who took, under God his Father, the greatest risk of history.

Moreover, what Jesus risen proved to his disciples and to all of us was the truth of what he had always said *about God*. He is *our* loving Father. He whom we have sought to placate by countless slaughtered lambs and by the human sacrifice for which these were the substitute, he the enigmatic, untrustworthy Almighty one (primary causality if one chooses to philosophise), is the tender loving one who cares for *us* down to the last hair of the head. Theology has been so concerned to have the resurrection prove the divinity *of Jesus*, with God *his* Father in the mystery of the Trinity, that it has lost sight of what Jesus died to establish: the tender *universal* Fatherhood of the God that men fear and try endlessly to appease. In the Sermon on the Mount Jesus preached of God as *'your Father'* who 'sees in secret what is in the heart', and for whom not one sparrow falls unrecognised. This most wildly extravagantly spoken-for God was proclaimed by a man who knew what he was talking about, because this God was his own Father.

The Fatherhood of God radiates out from the risen Jesus, in the risen Jesus to all universes, to settle once for all the whole business of sacrifices of animals and humans. Jesus lived by, lived for and died for, *this* tender fatherhood as opposed to the enigmatic liable-to-get-angry God of the Scriptures.

Selected Verse

Boy at a Burial

The funeral was typical
Of Downside at its best,
While solemn, yet affectional,
The latter, though, unstressed.

Something I never shall forget
Was how one of the boys
Surpliced, liturgical cadet,
Suddenly lost his poise.

As he came up abreast the grave
He looked, and lost his eyes
And all his confidence misgave
Faced with a new surprise.

I'm sure he never saw before
The oblong, deep-dug hole
That is already waiting for
Each one, bereft of soul.

Is that where I am headed, then,
And not for a career
And all the other works of men
Of which alone I hear?

Worse than a guilty secret in
A troubled family

This unattended javelin
Comes at him from the sky.

He stared and stared and nearly fell
The way his eyes were cast,
So suddenly compelled to dwell
On where he'd be at last.

The poet with his ready word
Misses this silent shock.
'Alas, poor Yorick!' is a fraud,
Denial for the Cock.

There is no word to catch this shaft
That poleaxes the heart:
The hole was there before we laughed,
Remembered to be smart.

Nor can he read in any face
Among the standing crowd
The comfort that in other ways
Tunes out a world too loud.

This one you have to face alone
Is what the faces say
But silently, for none will own
The ending of our day.

But I shall not forget that gaze
At the red earth exposed
As the raw ending of our days
Wherein we are enclosed.

12 November '93

An Old Monk Remembers his Mother

'From him we never hear of family'
Was said of me in my monastic home
Which was indeed the first there was for me
My interest now wedding me to Rome.

And yet I wrote my mother every week
Until she died, and shortly afterwards
I had that breakdown, falling from a peak
Of ecstasy monastic whose rewards

Dried up on me, and still I never knew
What had gone wrong, except that once
I dreamed her young, but that was not she who
Was keeping me emotionally dunce.

There is another time: long dead, she spoke
Inaudibly and freed me from my yoke.

To My Mother

Soft with this baby, with me growing stern
And never fun as you are growing now
As I begin in a shared death to learn
To take the furrows from a worried brow.

Now breasts of consolation absolute
In the high song his banner over me
Who breaks in gratefulness cannot be mute
And cries 'relief!' at knowing I am free.

Thank you for blank approaches ecstasy
As a moth bumps against the warning lamp
And I against the pain of being me
The children's elephant to stamp and stamp

And cry for you in memory of the night
Invaded by the God knows panic fright.

Monastic Vilanelle

I saw beyond what I am trained to see
When I was left to a long single bed
And what I made of this still baffles me.

I am a monk and so I live with me
And only dream of other lives instead
Yet saw beyond what I was trained to see.

Forbidden fruit and a forbidden he
My only image of the others wed
And what I made of this still baffles me.

Memory sinks a plumb line in the sea
I come from and will sink into for dead
Yet saw beyond what I am trained to see.

Another bafflement Gethsemani
Made murder into breaking of the bread
And what I make of this must baffle me.

Destabilizing monasticity
Is for the heart alone not for the head
That saw beyond what it is trained to see
And what I make of this still baffles me.

The Performer

I was brought up largely as a performer,
Made a fool of myself too easily
And when my body spoke, it was a stormer
For what it said was: I want dignity.

Just now I'm feeling in my infrastructure
Coming-apart of vital elements
And have to let it be with no conjecture
Only to say yes, wholly you make sense

Of a kind not accustomed, all of now
Assembled like the bones of Israel,
The why of me declining to the how
You now are whisking my soul out of hell

Where lie the pompous in eternity
Until the end when all of us shall see.

To Phoebe Working with Autistic Gabriel

Now how I love you people of the flow
Who bring alive those called dysfunctional

Who only speak within until they know
Another in their rhythm, the sweet fall

Into our loving that the normal miss
Whose inwardness aseptic and quite boring
Prepares them for a sexy goodnight kiss
A loving that knows nothing of adoring.

When Jesus said the last would be the first
He spoke of the dark world you bring to light
While we the normal stay the God-accursed
Legitimate the world's continued fight.

Phoebe this is of you and Gabriel
Whom without effort you bring out of hell.

Isabel – Peter

We have forgotten how to stay in love
But you, my dears, have breathed a clearer air
About the Garden where the heart will move
All seasons into one confirming prayer.

Change has bewildered us, while you have changed
Only into fresh moods of the firm heart
That contemplates our time as high hills ranged
That you have travelled with a lover's art.

Now that the dark has come, all this is seen
Too clearly for possession in the world
That only knows what is and what has been,
Is to the future as a foetus curled.

You two with stronger eyes, that faith has schooled,
Look forward with us to where love is pooled.

For Tina Beattie, Woman Challenging the Church

Those who had seen the failure and the Lord
Are subjects of a dangerous memory
Triggered, on hearing of the holy word,
By something that we others do not see

As we sail gaily on our rhetoric
And wonder why we bore the listener
Who only knows that he or she is sick
Of the old stuff, the endless as-it-were,

So thank you Tina as you now disturb
The confident male language of the church
Driving your new car up onto the curb
The pavement of our confident research.

Under the words that conjure up the *numen*
Some hearers see a man stripped down to woman.

In a Troubled Time for the Church

To feel the warmth of a consuming fire
Softens the heart of me to neighbour love
As the fulfilment of our first desire
Requiring no commandment from above.

The church's present looking desperate
Awakes the heart to feel a future God
And a new sense of what it is to wait
Dissociating this from the soul's plod.

To wait upon a lover who delays
Is the soul's ecstasy, dark sleepless night
As a new energy puzzles and prays
With a new certainty of coming light.

I knew this as there breathed across a psalm
A future against which we do not arm.

For the Conclave

I crucify my body till I hear
From it that I am crucifying Christ
I then become and put an end to fear
In such a freedom as cannot be priced.

I spell this out, but stay under the spell
That hangs over the church in this dull time

And know only from him that all is well
Who does his own thing with us in our crime.

Remember how it must have been at first
With Jesus risen and their only God
In seeming competition till there burst
The Spirit making airborne men who plod.

Would that first Trinity explode in us
And rid his church of all the useless fuss!

The Church Proclaims the Body Free of Death

The church proclaims the body free of death
Manifest in the man we killed in fear
Whose power is exercised from underneath:
Love though is of the body now and here,

We know this in his breaking of the bread
Makes festal his acceptance of our hate,
The body now no longer with the dead
But universal, losing its dead weight

What of the church, though, that still lives in fear
Of body she proclaims as glorious:
With sex as plumbing she will never hear
The living word that she proclaims to us,

With fear and love our only opposites
Hot is the seat today where Peter sits.

The church proclaims the body free of death
Manifest in the man we killed in fear
That terrorizes us from underneath
While he sits us above, his now and here,

But the church dreads the body she proclaims:
Beguiled by sex she sees only as thrall
And cannot feel the glory that she names
Through priests she bids ignore the body's call

Through sex the simulacrum of desire
Which is our love in embryo, while she
Materializes its consuming fire
To lose the body wherein we are free,

With love and fear our only opposites
Hot is the seat today where Peter sits.

Vilanelle

There's someone who has always coped with me,
And draws me and this is the way I pray,
It changes me and leaves me always free.

Every so often I say: 'Now I see'
And come more clearly into a good way
With someone who has always coped with me.

The teasing interchange of I and we
Encircles an elusively today
That changes me and leaves me always free.

Islands upon a salt estranging sea
Become the city where the people play
For someone who has always coped with me.

My other as myself is now my key
That one alone can turn in his own way
Who changes me and leaves me always free.

The celebration of Gethsemani
Where love absorbs all in us that says 'Nay'
Discloses one who's always coped with me
And changes me to leave me always free.

Break-out

Now feels like me the knot you are untying
In water moving where my hawser lies
And loosens, murmurs 'me I'm crucifying'
From which you rise in me to my surprise.

You said 'they do not know what they are doing'
And this is me in an unnoticed habit
The very atmosphere, itself not showing
In which I live, at heart the scared rabbit.

Gently ease into this my taking-out
On me not to be a nuisance to the other.
The truth about me that the stones will shout
From my own heart of stone turned to a brother.

But as I let this happen, be aware
This habit may be practised in my prayer.

The preacher said, will yourself hammering
The nails into his members one by one.
He did not say, though, that I am the thing
I punish in me as my duty done.

And so he reinforced what Jesus ends,
Self-hatred as the root of all our ills,
We see the crucified as that which bends
The will of God who wants the blood that spills.

How could we keep alive the awed hush
With God the victim, our self-hate the stronger
Than God as love: the spirit had to rush
On timid men, God patient no longer.

The violence concealed in self-defence
Is felt at bottom sitting on the fence!

Our God includes us who punish ourselves
And cannot wriggle loose into the love
That rushes us while solo thinking delves
And the immovable begins to move.

The awed hush at human sacrifice
Perpetuates itself in our askesis
That never notices the hidden vice
Within desire that moves into mimesis.

And when the church came under Constantine
Calvary too became the sacrifice
That God allowed and hid in bread and wine
To hide the victim who was to suffice.

Self-hatred we hold on to for dear life
Prefer to live safe-shadowed by the knife.

Gethsemani

Accepted once, the body could not take it,
It took an angel him to hold together
There was no way humanity could fake it
Accustomed only to our changing weather.

That was the only time an angel showed
Toward his end, his start with them infested:
They did not understand what was toward,
Here even the angelic mind was bested

With one entrusted with the sweat of blood,
Instructed simply to encourage all
That in a man is wired for the good
Whatever counter-horror may appal.

Dare I bring my own poor self-punishment
To see itself mirrored in this event.

Jesus you mind my punishing myself
Instead of getting on with your design
For me and others we put on the shelf
Neglectful of your ritual table sign.

How these two vectors of my life now touch:
Self-punishment and you up on the cross
With God the punished, not the Father judge
Who leaves the faithful always at a loss.

The Father angry and my self-infliction
Are glued together till they come apart

The father feeling with the crucifixion
And my routine admits the Spirit's art.

A Jesus suffering the Father's rage
My self-infliction Spirit would assuage.

Make it New

The only physicality he has
Is to be eatable and drinkable
So that a meal is what we know him as,
This is his sacrifice, its place the table.

This he foretells in John's austere sixth chapter
In terms repugnant to his audience
But for his faithful, there for the soul's rapture
Mysteriously given to new sense.

How is it, then, that the recovery
Of Mass as meal has made it trivial
If not because we simply cannot see
To love each other with a shared meal?

It is humanity we must relearn:
This is his resurrection and our turn.

The Taste of the Eucharist

Jesus I love your sacrifice in me
Touching desire to be another's joy
With you in both of us together free
With love that nothing ever will destroy.

There is this taste of you in Eucharist
Who have, you tell us, overcome the world
That presses in me when my breath is missed
And I into first nothingness am hurled

I woke this morning and was short of breath
Which became life and I could disappear
Into our unimaginable death
You entered for us carrying our fear.

Sweet point of contact, your death with my own
Desire to end for others life alone.

Remember!

Jesus you deed of God and God indeed
Sacred Heart statue with a difference
Perceptible implanting of a seed
Sacred Humanity in a felt sense,

God happened, there was you with all the kitsch
That touched and meant me hardly noticing
Something inside that registered a switch
Telling desire there was no need to cling.

Both your Teresas, Catholic affluence
Displacement of the sacred by the holy
To warn me about sitting on the fence
Ecclesiastical in roly-poly.

How you make me and others met attractive
Is simple, it's your Holy Spirit active.

Recollection

The feeling one has never really loved
As now one understands true love to be
May be the sign of something that has moved
In the great mass of sludge that I call me.

Keep it and will it, this grasp of a gold
Of spirit in a heart now seen to store
Inside the will that knows only to scold
The wild adventure that we call adore.

And you, dear friend, I think you have it too
The unknown power to invent a Christ
Whose cross we so inaptly call the true
Missing the love in it that has sufficed.

Breathe easily this newfound poverty
A touch of Catherine's 'pacific sea'.

(Catherine of Siena starts her *Meditations* by having God say: 'I invite
you to come into the pacific sea!')

I am wanted

Thank you for telling me that I am wanted
Who, self-unsure, keep wanting to belong
And that unknowingly my heart has panted
For you – how do I know I am not wrong?

You show what some are showing me already
Assist the inner breakdown of my old
Habits for keeping me upon a steady
Course with my caution as a curb to bold.

On course? The old assurance in my prayer
Confirms in its own way and not in mine,
It has to do with care and do not care
And waits upon an unattended sign.

The 'all is well' of our complacency
Differs from yours incomprehensibly.

You told me I was wanted when the world
Told me I wasn't and this ravished me
So that this foetus of me came uncurled
Awake original hilarity.

You said: be wanted and go out to one
And learn in embryo that I am love
And have you in the Body of my Son
And learn that in my Trinity you move.

'To be someone for someone' – this I taught
For years – we teach what we want for ourselves:
I knew this a contagion I had caught
From you for me and for the heart that delves.

To be for you alone is just to be
For others, it is, simply, to be free.

A Gay Man Speaks

I had to learn that I was different
And hated this, it meant no place for me,
But now I learn that what I thought was bent
Is quite a fashionable way to be.

So I'm a beachball tossed from man to man
And this is worse than how it was at first
And more remote from what I truly can,
Irrelevantly blessed what once was cursed.

I pray and want to hear, 'No, you are not
Different for me who know you as you are'
From Jesus Christ the one of God begot:
The church, though, holds in place my early bar

Which must give way for Jesus to come through
And let me be to God and myself true.

The Enduring

Aridity, the Missa Normativa,
Is all the culture of our day deserves
Needing our contemplation as a lever
Over the humps and the precarious curves

Of meanings now but barely understood
And pasted on to what we now are doing
Enough to know the absolutely good
Whetting the appetite for deeper clueing.

And all the time, what cannot be disguised
Is Jesus's ritual meal before a death
That all the world so knew and solely prized
Good Friday when the world once caught its breath.

If this spare diet loses its appeal
We need a shock a deeper self to feel.

The Practice of Focusing

This paper, on the practical aspects of focusing, was written for the Downside Community in August 1999, following a workshop that Sebastian attended.

We tend to ignore our feelings, except when they are hurt. Then we over-react. As a result, we never get to know them. It is in fact very difficult to know just what you feel, to be able to name it, apart from the most generic words such as angry, sad, frightened, happy, frustrated. Nor is this state of affairs helped by a cliché of spiritual writing that 'feelings don't matter'.

This neglect of our feelings shows itself in the style of a community. Observers of our community discussions have made this sort of comment. People seem to connect through their heads. All sorts of intelligent ideas come up, but they don't seem to come straight from the speaker. They don't carry his feelings – these are sifted out, and the opinion is only in the head. Diagrammatically, you've got bodies together, but what they say goes up to the head and only thence outwards to each other. It is as though our bodies merely provided location and mobility for talking heads. The monastic habit, with its genderlessness, facilitates this verbal ballet.

This said, it seems to follow that we must let go of this reserve and express our feelings openly in 'a free and frank exchange of views'. Wrong! What is really amiss with our way of living is that we do not acknowledge our feelings to ourselves. As long as we are like this interiorly, we naturally feel reluctant to share our feelings. *Nemo dat quod non habet.* No one shares what he does not own. Much more significant than our confinement to the head is its cause, the non-acceptance of our *feelings*.

The Discovery

It was this difficulty in saying just how one feels that lay at the root of one of the most important discoveries ever made in the field of psychology. About twenty years ago, an American psychoanalyst, Eugene Gendlin, wondered why only a few people benefit from psychoanalysis, why, as someone put it to me, the statistics are abysmal. He persuaded his colleagues to let him have tapes of their treatment sessions. Very soon he noticed that occasionally the client, asked to say what he felt, dithered, and it was these conversations that got somewhere so that the client seemed to be moving toward self-discovery. It was when the client was *too* ready to name his feelings, in language acceptable to the therapist, that the relationship became dead-ended so that you had a triangular situation of therapist, client, and the client as objectified by therapist and client and in fact non-existent, a hole into which countless hours and dollars would be poured.

Gendlin then devised a method whereby a person can come to name his or her feeling about a situation or a problem. The method is called 'focusing'. Two American Jesuits learned the method from Gendlin, and have been teaching it jointly in workshops all over the world. With a colleague, I attended one of these earlier this year, and it is the unusually fruitful effect of this, on our two very different characters, that makes me want to recommend the method. Anyone who gets interested and is prepared to do a little very rewarding homework will begin to discover 'a whole new continent' as Peter Campbell (one of the two priests just mentioned) calls it. We can begin to own our feelings. And feelings unowned own us.

The Method

It is difficult to recommend the work of focusing without giving some idea of what it consists in, so here is a very brief description. I take some time out, take a few deep breaths, and ask myself is there anything just now that is getting between me and feeling contented and relaxed, any anxiety or worry? If there is more than one thing, I make a choice. I move this tiresome thing into centre stage, away from the sidelines whence it nags me obliquely. Worries have this interesting knack: they don't face me, because I don't want to face them. They nag from a half-attended-to position. They don't present themselves as themselves, but as getting in the way of something else. They interfere, like the interference in a bad radio reception. (Note the metaphor of 'focusing' in its similarity to 'tuning-in'.) So I grasp my worry, and let go of everything else in my mind. This action is a befriending of the anxiety. It takes me out of the mind into the body. And the question becomes: 'What is it I am feeling at this moment?'

It is at this stage that there may come to me, as it were out of the blue, a word or a phrase or a picture. Is this it?, I then ask. I try to match the new word or image with the thing that's bugging me. Is it like this? If it is, this is unmistakable. There is a sigh of relief. It is most important to be grateful for this untoward light on the situation.

The Fruits

Now as a result of this process, I find that my relationship with the worrying situation changes. There is not a solution, but there is resolution. Real, understood-at-first-hand feeling, once it is allowed to 'speak its name', will show me that I am part of the problem I am encountering. Here is an example. Gendlin was doing a talk-show on television, to which people could phone in. One caller said: 'I am a journalist. My husband has just retired, and he just sits all day in front of the box with a six-pack, it's driving us all crazy. What can I do about this?' Gendlin got her into a relaxed state and then, after a pause, asked her: 'Does any word come to you?' To her surprise, the word was 'snooty'! Body wisdom had focused on her contemptuous attitude, which of course was keeping the man this way.

Thus, to allow my real, immediate feeling to 'speak its name' is to 'come alive' just a little. It is to become more connected with others. The crucial spiritual significance of immediate feeling has been recognised by our contemplative tradition at its liveliest, represented by de Caussade and Abbot Chapman. Chapman says repeatedly in his letters, 'Everything you feel is God's will for you' (a teaching, incidentally, praised by Alan Watts, one of the better modern gurus). He is extending the reach of God's will in the event to the inner world of feeling, the event felt. But when you bring your basic feeling into focus and hear its name in a way that releases tension and elicits a sigh of relief, then God's will becomes not only 'to be accepted' but 'to be desired', for it is recognised as good for me. This is a spiritual advance comparable, I think, to that made by Ignatius when he spotted the difference between the good feeling after reading saints' lives and the morose feeling left by reading 'romances', a distinction that gave him a very humanistic understanding of Paul's 'discernment of spirits', an understanding that he developed in the Spiritual Exercises.

'Discernment of spirits' becomes 'discernment of feelings'.

So what comes into focus is my immediate, spontaneous feeling response to everything that happens, everything that people do and say. This first pre-reflexive response to the event, which is the event in me, is God's present moment, his will for me at this moment. And when it gives its name, this is God's will for me with a human face. And this wonderful humanising of the Spirit as a result of focusing works for the climactic gospel injunction: 'If anyone will come after me, let him deny himself, take up his cross and follow me.' What does it mean to deny myself, or rather, what has it come to mean? Superficially, giving up things I like. More deeply, some sort of a mystical meaning picked up from spiritual books and retreats. But why not see the 'self' to be denied as 'me in the head' (interpreting my feelings in reference to my fears), out of which I resolutely move when I embrace the messy incompleteness of the present moment, which is my cross, my 'sacrament of the present moment'. This is to follow Christ who pioneers this new and terrible freedom in the decisive agony of Gethsemani, becoming the willing scapegoat of a humanity lost in the immemorial darkness of its violence. With focusing, a track is opened, out of the head into the body, and this provides a psychology for understanding the words of Jesus. Without such a psychology, the notion of self-denial is a devout mystification. And, to anticipate, 'into the body' means into the Body of Christ whose sacrifice in head and members the Mass is. An authentic, truly valid celebration should always cause in us the pain of being unloving, dragging our feet as the disciples did on the road to Jerusalem, duly acknowledged in a penitential rite.

Children as young as five are being taught not to get caught in their feelings but, as one little girl put it in class, to 'be quiet with what I just feel, even when it's scary'. Surely this is taking up the cross, the process unencumbered with adult baggage.

Deep Implications

We read that Jacob wrestled all night with an angel, to whom he said: 'I will not let you go until you give me your name.' We touch here an idea that had enormous power in the world of the Bible. Adam's naming of the animals is not a charming *Just So* story, but the first covenant of humanity with the God of nature. Now the naming of feeling today is tapping the same power that the ancients found in the name. But it is tapping it in a way that allows feeling to become power, *virtus*, virtue. As someone put it recently: 'When I lose control, suddenly I have access to what controls me.' This is the meaning of 'self-control', and why Paul can list it among the fruits of the Holy Spirit. And this is a meaning of self-control that is nearly inaccessible to a culture like ours for which to control is to 'break in' and dominate. It is only in the self-naming of feeling that the true meaning of self-control can appear. It is simply the self in control as opposed to the self under alien control, which is our lot as unfocused feelers.

Now the more we understand this transformation, from the self controlled to the self controlling, the clearer it becomes, I think, that we are in touch with the mystery of transformation itself. An exciting moment was reached in the conversations of Fathers McMahon and Campbell with Gendlin, when one of them asked: 'If we follow your method, are the results assured?' The reply came – to these two dog-collared visitors! – 'No, it's what you guys call grace.' Hearing this, they knew they had struck oil. The notion of a 'point of intersection of the timeless with time' as a meeting between the utter mystery that is over all and the averagely screwed-up psyche presages a revolution in psychology.

This revolution is, in short, the coming of the body into its own: from providing location and mobility for talking heads, to being the seat of wisdom. John Robinson says a tantalising thing in his seminal Pauline study, *The Body*, to the effect that when Paul says we are the Body of Christ he is speaking 'not corporately but corporally'. This statement is opaque to our rationalistic culture that can only see 'the Church as body' as a corporate metaphor. As each of us begins to discover, in his own body articulate, his involvement in other bodies (the discovery of the woman who got 'snooty!'), Paul's language begins to make a new and exciting sense, especially when he says: 'As in one body there are many members (so far this could be a corporate metaphor) so it is with Christ' – the body crucified and risen and mystical and eucharist, Scripture and liturgy come alive in the midst of our dreary sensible world. For me, at least, focusing is the key. I just begin to glimpse what John could mean when he says: 'We know that we have passed from death to life, because we love the brethren.'

General Reflections

The phrase that keeps coming to me in writing of focusing is 'middle ground'. Feeling in focus exposes and occupies a middle ground between the awful mystery in which all life has to be lived and the movements of the heart. This is disturbingly innovative, the two areas being jealously guarded by the defenders of orthodoxy and of humanism respectively. Monastic history is a battleground between spirituality from the top down and spirituality from the bottom up.

Closely connected, if not identical, with this midpoint, is the midpoint, also disclosed by focusing, between self and other. Feeling acknowledged, named, and owned, is spontaneously addressed to the improvement of our interhuman situation. The body comes to itself in the Body.

Thus, feeling in focus is the midpoint, vertically, between higher and lower, and horizontally, between self and other. Don't all our problems boil down in the end to reconciling the 'high' with the 'low' and reconciling the 'here' with the 'there'. This dimensional language makes sense, because we are bodies in space.

There is, it seems, a scientifically observable dimension to focusing. In her introduction to Gendlin's book by that name, Marilyn Ferguson writes: 'The brain's alpha and theta rhythm activity shifted just before the focusers signaled a felt shift. The patterns of subsequent electro-encephalographic activity suggested "reorganisation at a higher level of integration"...' It appears that the phenomenon of the felt shift (the name Gendlin gives to the moment when focusing 'works') may actually reflect whole-brain knowing. This would account for the sigh of relief that signals the coming of the word or image. This evidence of science, in a culture for which science is the only thing people really believe in, is of great moment.

In *The Intelligence of Feeling*, Robert W. Witkin says that it is vital for the young today to be able 'to name the source of their discomfort'. This is a comment on the horrible things that happen today, like the slaughter of students by students at Littleton, Denver.

In conclusion, sanity today can no longer be taken for granted. It requires homework. Focusing seems to be precisely this homework.

Haiku for Focusing

I ask how dare he
and then I ask how fare I
find my self loving

In the deep rhythm
I move of the universe
where problems are not

The god of the dead
vanishes before Jesus
deathless before us

When I forgive you
I expose to you my space
to enter or kill

Jesus is the air
spoken on the living breath
death yielding its sting

Priests have to control
experiences they lack
that's called religion

Sex is divided
between doers and teachers
because all are mad

My rage at the church
implodes into affection
and I feel better

Our last century
goes with scores of centuries
into the full void

I come together
long before I came apart
in the universe

Beginning of time
cannot have itself happened
God is a big tease

God solves no problem
solved problems keep their pieces
apart without God.

Absence as presence
is what I enter to pray
become my body

Beware of cheating
cleverness with mystery
is not difficult

Check with the body
where is the woman in me
fought with all my life

Tummy can tell me
that I am back to square one
wanting the young flesh

Body needs sickness
whence it can reassemble
into better shape

Sweep them all away
rising words of resentment
filling up mind space

The snake inside me
used spite to define people
and keep them off me

The church has to speak
to desire and urge it on
otherwise to fear

Do not be afraid
but let the resurrection
empty mental space

My indignation
takes up all my mental space
without dignity

To find your good place
is to find plenty of room
for all the people

Desire becomes love
in the victim crucified
alive in his death

Now I ask myself
as who do I come to mass
but lost tender me

A dream of morning
in a parade of gay pride
a Vatican float

Breath is amplitude
music of the universe
all as is of now

Before the big bang
a quite natural question
god cannot answer

Stay in my wriggle
as I enter prayer space
I am glad of it

What is the good news
if it does not touch desire
free in mental space?

BIBLIOGRAPHY

Recommended Reading

Alison, James, *On Being Liked*, London, Darton, Longman and Todd, 2003.

Beattie, Tina, *God's Mother, Eve's Advocate*, London, Continuum, 1999.

Chapman, John, *Spiritual Letters*, London, Sheed and Ward, 1935.

Fitzpatrick, P., *On Breaking of Bread*, Cambridge, Cambridge University Press, 2006.

Gendlin, Eugene T., *Focusing*, New York, Bantam, 1981.

Helminiak, D. A., *What the Bible Really Says about Homosexuality*, Alamo Square Distributors, 1975.

Kirwan, Michael, *Discovering Girard*, London, Darton, Longman and Todd, 2004.

McMahon, Edwin, *Beyond the Myth of Dominance: An Alternative to a Violent Society*, Kansas City, MO, Sheed and Ward, 1993.

Tolle, Eckhart, *The Power of Now, A Guide to Spiritual Enlightenment*, Vancouver, Namaste Publishing, 1997.

Weiser Cornell, Ann, *The Power of Focusing*, Oakland, New Harbinger Publications, 1996.

Other Books

Abelard, P., *Héloise and Abelard*, Tr: Betty Radice, London, Harmondsworth Penguin, 1974.

Allen, John L., *Cardinal Ratzinger: The Vatican's Enforcer of the Faith*, New York, Continuum, 2000.

Anonymous, *A Woman in Berlin*, London, Virago Press, 2005.

Barth, Karl, *Church Dogmatics*, New York, Scribner, 1936.

Becker, Ernest, *The Denial of Death*, The Free Press, 1973.

Benedict XVI, *Deus Caritas Est*, 2006.

Bonhoeffer, Dietrich, *Ethics*, Tr: N. Horton Smith, London, SCM Press, 1936.

Byatt, A. S., *The Virgin in the Garden*, London, Chatto and Windus, 1978.

Catherine of Siena, *Meditations*.

CDF (Congregation for the Doctrine of the Faith), *Letter to the Bishops of the Catholic Church on the Pastoral Care of Homosexual Persons*, Vatican, 1986.

Cozzens, Donald, *Faith that Dares to Speak*, Collegeville, Liturgical Press, 2000.

Forster, E. M., *A Passage to India*, London, Edward Arnold, 1924.

Garcia Marquez, Gabriel, *One Hundred Years of Solitude*.

Guzie, Tad, *Jesus and the Eucharist*, Paulist Press, 1970.

Hammarskjöld, Dag, *Markings*, New York, Knopf, 1965.

Henson, John, *Good as New*, O Books, 2003.

Hugo, Victor, *The Hunchback of Notre Dame.*

Jarrett, Bede, OP, *Purity*, London, Catholic Truth Society.

John Paul II, *Man and Woman He Created Them: A Theology of the Body*, Tr: Michael Waldstein, Pauline Books and Media, 2006.

Jordan, Mark, *The Invention of Sodomy in Christian Theology*, Chicago, University of Chicago Press, 1997.

Kant, Immanuel, *Critique of Pure Reason*, Tr: P. Guyer and A. W. Wood, Cambridge, Cambridge Univeristy Press, 1998.

Kavanagh, William, *Torture and Eucharist*, Oxford, Blackwells.

Kertzer, David, *Popes Against the Jews; the Vatican's role in the rise of modern anti-semitism*, New York, Knopf, 2001.

Kirsch, Arthur, *Auden and Christianity*, New Haven, Yale University Press.

Komonchak, Joseph A., *New Horizons in Theology*, Catholic Theology Society Annual Volume 50, 2004.

Knowles, John, *A Separate Peace*, London, Secker and Warburg, 1959.

Lonergan, Bernard, *Method in Theology*, Toronto, University of Toronto Press, 1973.

Lonergan, Bernard, *Insight: A Study of Human Understanding*, London, Darton, Longman and Todd, 1958.

Meier, John P., *A Marginal Jew: Rethinking the Historical Jesus*, London, Doubleday, 1991.

Orwell, George, *1984*, London, Secker and Warburg, 1949.

Oughourlia, Jean-Michel, *The Puppet of Desire: Psychology of Hysteria, Possession and Hypnosis*, Stanford University Press.

Pelikan, Jaroslav, *Mary Through the Centuries, her place in the history of culture*, New Haven, Yale University Press, 1996.

Pixner, Bargil, *With Jesus Through Galilee: According to the Fifth Gospel*, Corazin Rosh Pina.

Radcliffe, Timothy, *What is the Point of Being a Christian?*, London, Continuum, 2005.

Robinson, John, *The Body, a study in Pauline theology*, London, SCM Press, 1952.

Tolkien, J. R. R., *The Lord of the Rings.*

Trible, Phillis, *God and the Rhetoric of Sexuality*, Fortress Press, 1978.

Waugh, Evelyn, *Brideshead Revisited, the sacred and profane memories of Captain Charles Ryder.*

Wilson, A. N., *Jesus*, London, Sinclair-Stevenson, 1992.

Witkin, Robert W., *The Intelligence of Feeling*, Heinemann Editions.

A Course in Miracles, Foundation for Inner Peace, 1976.

Gaudium et Spes, Documents of Vatican II.

Poems Mentioned in the Text

Auden, W. H., *A Summer Night.*
Blake, William, *Garden of Love.*
Causley, Charles, *From a Normandy Crucifix of 1632.*
Donne, John, *Batter my Heart.*
Eliot, T. S., *The Family Reunion; The Waste Land.*
Herbert, George, *Love.*
Hopkins, Gerard Manley, *The Wreck of the Deutschland.*

INDEX